D1460132

24. NOV 03

Leeds Metropolitan University
17 0117251 9

Writers whose work reflects the experience of empire betray the anxieties and contradictions at the heart of the imperial enterprise. Zohreh T. Sullivan's new reading of Rudyard Kipling's writings about India expands our sense of colonial discourse by recovering the cultural context and recurring tropes in his early journalism and fiction, in *Kim*, and in his late autobiography. She charts the fragmentation of Kipling's position as child, as colonizer, and as "poet of empire," finding in his representation of childhood's loss the site of repressed desires and fears that resurface in later work. In using Kipling's troubled intimacy with empire as the link between history and narrative, Sullivan sees in Kipling's ambivalence his negotiation between the desire for union with his golden, "best-beloved" India and the historic imperatives of separation from it.

NARRATIVES OF EMPIRE

NARRATIVES OF EMPIRE

The fictions of Rudyard Kipling

ZOHREH T. SULLIVAN

Department of English, University of Illinois at Urbana-Champaign

CAMBRIDGE
UNIVERSITY PRESS

Published by the Press Syndicate of the University of Cambridge
The Pitt Building, Trumpington Street, Cambridge CB2 1RP
40 West 20th Street, New York, NY 10011-4211, USA
10 Stamford Road, Oakleigh, Victoria 3166, Australia

© Cambridge University Press 1993

First published 1993

Printed in Great Britain at the University Press, Cambridge

A catalogue record for this book is available from the British Library

Library of Congress cataloguing in publication data

Sullivan, Zohreh T.
Narratives of empire: the fictions of Rudyard Kipling / Zohreh T.
Sullivan
p.   cm.
Includes bibliographical references and index.
ISBN 0 521 43425 4 (hardback)
1. Kipling, Rudyard. 1865–1936 – Criticism and interpretation.
2. India in literature.   3. Imperialism in literature.   4. Colonies in literature.   I. Title.
PR4858.I48S85   1993
828'.809-dc20   92-17956 CIP

ISBN 0 521 43425 4 hardback ✓

LEEDS METROPOLITAN
UNIVERSITY LIBRARY

1701172519
BSIC ✓
309738   9.11.95
10.1.96
823.8 KIP B

For
Taimur and Kamran
&
for my families in
Tehran – Karachi – Lawrenceville
Champaign – Urbana

Contents

Acknowledgments

Although I chanced to live and study for many years in places haunted by Rudyard Kipling in India and Pakistan, I paid no attention to Kipling – or to the Lahore Art School, or to Kim's gun, or to the offices of the *Civil and Military Gazette* – the sites we saw from our tongas during the years I attended Kinnaird College in Lahore. It wasn't until the 1970s when I began to read *The Just So Stories* to my sons Taimur and Kamran that I first discovered the rich and ambiguous delight of tales that prepared me for the turns and counterturns of Kipling's adult fiction.

It is a pleasure to list my debts to a few of the many colleagues and friends who have been part of my daily nourishment and also my finest readers. Among these I must highlight James Hurt who did funny, critical, and always generous readings of several versions of the book; Robert Dale Parker whose meticulous eye illuminated even the gaps; Richard Powers whose insights raised new questions about the worlds designed by the children we traumatize; Keya Ganguly and Mary Loeffelholz whose rigorous readings of an early chapter opened up new theoretical possibilities. Other friends for whose comments I am grateful are Ali Behdad and Robert Nelson. I must also thank the anonymous readers for Cambridge University Press for their helpful suggestions, and the editor, Kevin Taylor, for his patience and encouragement. Sara Suleri's *The Rhetoric of English India* (University of Chicago Press, 1991) came out after I sent my manuscript to press, which is the only reason that I have not made use of its brilliant contribution to our understanding of colonial discourse. Thomas Pinney's much awaited two volume edition of *The Letters of Rudyard Kipling* (University of Iowa Press, 1990) also arrived just after I completed a final editing, and though I have made use of some of his punctuations, I stayed with my original references to the Kipling Papers.

For permission to quote from the Kipling Papers at the University of Sussex, I thank the National Trust. For the use of the Kipling Papers, I thank the librarians at the University of Sussex, and for quotations from the manuscript of "The Brushwood Boy," I am grateful to the Pierpont Morgan Library in New York. A version of chapter 2 originally appeared in *Prose Studies* (1989) as "Memory and the Colonial Self in Kipling's Autobiography." And a version of a section in chapter 4 was published in *Modern Fiction Studies* (1984) as "Kipling the Nightwalker." I am grateful to both journals for their permissions to reprint. An adapted segment of chapter 1 is appearing in my essay 'Kipling and India' in *English Literature and the Wider World Volume IV* 1876–1918: *The Ends of the Earth* (Ed. Simon Gatrell. The Ashfield Press, 1992). All of the work on this manuscript was done during sabbaticals and release time from teaching for which I thank the English Department and the Research Board of the University of Illinois at Urbana-Champaign.

Abbreviations

A&R	*Actions and Reactions*
CMG	*Civil and Military Gazette*
DW	*The Day's Work*
JB	*The Jungle Book*
K	*Kim*
KP	*The Kipling Papers*
LH	*Life's Handicap*
LM	*From Sea to Sea; Letters of Marque*
MI	*Many Inventions*
MK	*The Man Who Would Be King and Other Stories*
PTH	*Plain Tales from the Hills*
SJB	*The Second Jungle Book*
SM	*Something of Myself*
SS	*From Sea to Sea; The City of Dreadful Night*
SS1	*Short Stories: vol.1: A Sahib's War and Other Stories*
ST	*Soldiers Three; The Story of the Gadbys; In Black and White*
Verse	*Rudyard Kipling's Verse: Definitive Edition*

Kipling's India

Rudyard Kipling's art, like the story of imperialism, was a family affair. Marked by unnamed and unacknowledged longing, desire and fear, his texts became the body on which to inscribe the contradictory politics of everyday life in British India. His fiction negotiates an uneasy series of truces between the resistance of the self to the authority of empire, and between the antithetical longings for empire, England and India to be his source of origin, his "very-own" home. Reading Kipling demands a recognition of his alternation between unstable opposites – home/England/empire and home/India/jungle – with himself eternally divided in unreconcilable longings for both. Reconciliation could, however, be found in metaphor. By projecting metaphors of the inner circle of family, home and club onto the outer circle of nation and empire, Kipling could blur difference by domesticating encounters with the alien kind. And alternately, he blurs the distinction between the dominators and the dominated by including priests from Chubara, carvers from Ala Yar, Jiwun Singh the carpenter and Gobind the one-eyed storyteller within the intimate category of "mine own people" ("preface" to *Life's Handicap*) – a turn by which he can appropriate the colonized into the domain of his "own" imaginary family.

The epigraph to *Life's Handicap* – "I met a hundred men on the road to Delhi and they were all my brothers" – may be read as an overture to all Kipling's fiction, which is haunted by a variety of familial configurations from the intimacy of the opium den, to that of the Punjab Club, to the multicolored bondings on the Grand Trunk Road, to Mowgli's magical family in the jungle. The splittings in these family configurations are also the ambivalences of colonial discourse: Kim and Mowgli are both divided between their desire to be loved and their need to control and be feared ("all the Jungle was his friend, and just a little afraid of him" *SJB* 130). Yet Mowgli will

leave the jungle sobbing for the loss of his only family and only home
in which he is the acknowledged master. When he leaves the jungle,
however, Mowgli enters the service of the British government as a
forest-guard. So too will Kim leave his much loved Lahore street life
for the British Secret Service. This swerve from India as site of desire
to India as site of power and control is Kipling's particular
reterritorializing of desire into power because desire is coded within
a colonial system that sanctifies control and domination. Kim will
therefore be split between the desire to identify with and to correct
the errors of his native peers.

   The contradictory pattern of desire – to be loved and to control –
underlying the familial trope of a world in which mother England
would be caretaker to lesser children of imperial Gods was produced
by the political machinery of empire. But it also fed into a personal
fantasy that charged the longings of a Rudyard who at the age of six
felt he had been expelled from the Edenic bliss of his first home in
India. In rewriting that original scene of expulsion and separation
from familial enclosure, Kipling's writings about India are also
produced by the larger historical strains of late nineteenth-century
empire as it reacted with increasing authoritarianism to post-Mutiny
(1857) fears of their own expulsion from the land they called their
"jewel in the Crown." Nineteenth-century English Imperialists,
increasingly threatened by separatism after the loss of the American
colonies, were accustomed to discussing relations with empire in
familial terms: "It is pretty much with colonies as with children; we
protect and nourish them in infancy; we direct them in youth, and
leave them to their own guidance in manhood; and the best conduct
to be observed is to part with them on friendly terms."[1] The familial
metaphor, common to colonial discourse, superimposes the domestic
and familiar upon unknown territories and imposes linguistic order
on an uncontrollable relationship. By so doing, it appears to deny
difference as it delivers the subject from the anxieties of political
complexity. The return of the socially repressed in the form of Mutiny
or Revolution is subsequently a source of uncanny shock that disturbs
colonial hierarchy psychically and provokes irrational responses of
terror and brutality even in that humane creator of Little Nell and
Household Words: in a letter to Miss Cotts, Charles Dickens, whose
second son Walter was in India in 1857, justifies blasting Indians out
of cannons and proclaims that, were he commander-in-chief in India,
"I should do my utmost to exterminate the Race upon whom the

stain of the late cruelties rested" (Moore-Gilbert 1986: 76), certain of course that the "savages of Cawnpore and Delhi" were, as ungrateful rebellious children, the culprits.

The metaphor of empire as "family" was part of a colonial construct of British imperialism in India that saw Queen Victoria as "ma-baap" (mother/father), the native as untrained child, and the empire as drawing room – a refined and civilized space where appropriate rules of conduct would ensure permanent occupancy. On June 22, 1897, Queen Victoria was driven (in state) for three hours through the streets of London in celebration of her Diamond Jubilee. On that day, the *Times* published an ode by Sir Lewis Morris from which the following extract will suggest the all-pervasiveness of the metaphor:

> Mother of freemen! over all the Earth
> Thy Empire-children come to birth
> Vast continents are thine, or sprung from thee
> Brave island-fortress of the storm-vexed sea.
>
> (in Beloff 1970: 21)

The metaphor was used by both Imperialists and Separatists. England as "mother country" would, when the time was right, ideally wean the child-colony from permanent dependency by educating it into the responsibilities of membership in the larger British empire. The stress to which the trope was subjected can be seen in later references to this construct, most famously perhaps in the quarrel between Ronny and Mrs. Moore in Forster's *A Passage to India*. Ronny's declaration that "India isn't a drawing room" (p. 50), followed by his recognition that the balance of power represented by that earlier metaphor has changed ("India likes gods") violates his mother's liberal hope that the domestic virtues of kindness and courtesy might create a passage of hearts and thereby make "the British Empire a different institution" (p. 51).

This book is about how Kipling reproduces and complicates the ideological structures that determined imperial patterns of thought; it is also about strategies of indeterminacy and ambivalence that mark Kipling's narratives about India, his inability to secure some absolute ground either for the cause of empire or for his "best-beloved" India. The simplest way of reading Kipling's position is to argue that, because his primary identification was with the land of his childhood, his narratives betray the ambivalence of his position as colonizer. Angus Wilson, for instance, recounts an anecdote about the child Kipling walking hand in hand with a native peasant, calling to his mother in Hindi, "Goodbye, this is my brother" (1979: 4). Wilson perceives this as a paradigmatic moment that conveys Kipling's persistent sense of India as a Garden of Eden before the Fall and of "the Indian peasantry ... his first love, his beloved children for the rest of his life" (p. 4). Kipling's Indian fiction is filled with moments in which the familial trope is rewritten in terms of empire, for India was after all the land of Kipling's birth, his golden childhood, and his first, lost family. And it is precisely that source of identification that becomes the troubled site of ambivalence and contradiction in Kipling's discourse because India and empire are also the sources for his personal loss and oppression.

Yet this relatively simple biographical reading of the psychic economy of colonial discourse needs to be embedded in the historical matrix that produced the contradictions in colonial discourse. For Edward Said, colonial discourse constructs representations of the Orient as negations of the West which is its audience. Homi Bhabha, however, problematizes Said's opposition between the representation and the real by reminding us that colonial discourse, though "stricken" by instability and indeterminacy, mimics the official ideals of the imperial mission and becomes a means to power and knowledge (1984). Colonial authority and the colonial subject are both constructed out of deeply fragmented moments of hybridity where the self articulates the Other out of similarity and difference, "repetition and displacement" (Bhabha 1984). The contradictions he exposes in the words of Macaulay, for instance, ("Be the father and the oppressor of the people; be just and unjust, moderate and rapacious" [1985a: 74]) are also those that can be seen in Kipling's ideal administrators from Strickland and Colonel Creighton to Kim. The point of my own method is not to suggest an absolute or true "India" that is somehow belied by Kipling's imaginary or Orientalized India, but rather to understand through Kipling's playfully and profoundly ambivalent narratives the larger imperial episteme or field of knowledge and to understand a way of knowing a world whose strategies of configuring race, gender and power in binary terms are still with us.

The strained familial model through which Kipling chose to contain his disturbed relationship with India is at once a metaphoric solution that attempts to transcend the social and political, and it is also a claustrophobic hell; it is at once a scaffolding in a land where rules are few and a desperate prop to disintegrating faith. In addition to the pitiless family dramas in "Little Tobrah" (where a brother explains pushing his sister into a well with the chilling argument that it is better to die than to starve), in "The Story of Mohammad Din," or "Without Benefit of Clergy," all the relationships in *The Jungle Books* and the lyrical father-son relationship between Kim and his lama are problematically familial because of the hierarchy of explicit power and racial superiority that are imposed onto "family" structures. In "The Phantom Rickshaw," the narrator's understanding of his relation to the colony is described in terms of guest (the English) and host (India). Cherished for her "great Knowability," India becomes an extension of "home," an infinitely flexible private space where Englishmen may travel without paying hotel bills, and where, "if you belong to the Inner Circle ... all houses are open to you" (p. 26). The symbolic boundaries that circumscribe individual, familial and communal identity (Kipling's inner circles) are emphasized, often pathologically, in proportion to Kipling's anxieties about self loss as he loses a sense of the geographical or structural boundaries defining his own community and himself. Who, after all, are "Mine own People" – the subtitle of *Life's Handicap*?

I introduce the trope of family because, in reading Kipling's work as a way of entry into aspects of colonial discourse, I want to be both formal and psychoanalytic, to connect power and desire, to see the political in the familial – "There is no outer sign without an inner sign" (Volosinov 1973: 39) – , and to politicize the subjective by drawing attention to how the colonizer and the colonial subject are marked by the ambivalence of fantasy and defense, sameness and difference. Kipling's lack in his childhood "House of Desolation" is reinscribed in the psychic and physical geography of colonial protagonists in perpetual pursuit of lost objects of desires, of surrogate homes and impossible solutions to problems that lead to mutilation, madness and death. That colonial inscription is split, as Homi Bhabha tells us, between the consciously authoritarian and authorial site of mastery and its articulation in the discourse of fantasy, displacement and uncertainty (1985*b*: 150).

If the analysis of the relation between culture and literature requires our attention to the construction of individual need and social possibility, Kipling's unacknowledged need, tempered by the ironic recognition of its impossibility and danger, was for empire to provide him with what he lacked in childhood – the impossibly eternal extended family. Because he yearned for the solidarity of the integrated community, his earliest work proceeds to analyze that "community"; and the result, far from a monolithic idealization of that group, can be seen in the alternately lyrical, savage and ambivalent *Plain Tales from the Hills, The Man Who Would Be King and Other Stories*, and *Life's Handicap*. These early stories are among the most important articulations of colonial fantasy, desire and fear. My reading of his Indian stories departs from earlier criticism of Kipling that reads his early work (to use Louis Cornell's terms) as "apprentice work" or false starts for his later more mature fiction. And my approach separates me from those (Tompkins and the critics of the 1960s and 1970s) who thematized his fiction in terms of his humanist values, his accurate representation of Anglo-Indian life, and his artistry. I am more interested in Kipling's narrative strategies that position him within colonial history, that reveal the constitution of the colonial subject, and that reproduce the structures of Kipling's own subjective interpellations as master and child, as Englishman and native, and as the quintessentially divided imperial subject.

If the tropes of family and home seem central to Victorian imperialism, it is, as some historians have reminded us, not because it was an age of faith but because it was an age obsessed with the disintegration of faith and of the old structures of religion. The old structures, however, were not discarded; rather, the age found suitable surrogates for them in such secular systems as work, home, imperialism and nationalism – and each was a construction designed to ward off its undesirable Other. If work was defense against neurosis, home was the fortress to be guarded against the work-a-day world. India provided the chance for the Englishman to play at "the Great Game," to play authoritarian parent, and to rewrite the failed family romance once again with England playing the role of a mythical Prospero, the stern father who, having failed in maintaining power at home, now tries to do better the second time around by controlling a Caliban's kingdom.

The first half of the nineteenth-century agenda in India was characterized publicly in terms of sentiment, mission, reform and Orientalism, ideals subsequently institutionalized in the Asian Society, the Royal Geographic Society, and the Royal Colonial Institute; yet imperialism was also privately understood to be a necessary material enterprise to handle burgeoning unemployment, surplus population and excess production. Lenin quotes, of all people, Cecil Rhodes for the evidence he draws on in *Imperialism*: "I was in the East End of London yesterday and attended a meeting of the unemployed. I listened to the wild speeches, which were just a cry for 'bread,' 'bread,' 'bread,' and on my way home I pondered over the scene and I became more than ever convinced of the importance of imperialism... My cherished idea is a solution for the social problem, i.e. in order to save the 40,000,000 inhabitants of the United Kingdom from a bloody war, we colonial statesmen must acquire new lands to settle the surplus population, to provide new markets for the goods produced by them in factories and mines..." (1939: 79). Inspired by economic need and defeated by political reality, British imperialism in the second half of the century was marked by what Hutchins calls the reactionary ideology of permanence: "The certainty of a permanent empire... seemed to increase in proportion to its fragility, and to serve for many people as a defense and retreat from reason" (1967: xii). In an age of "muscular Christianity," the late Victorians who came to rule India brought, as part of their mythological baggage, the cult of games, exercise and youthful celibacy, the belief that the world could be run by schoolboys who had learned the rules of world government on the playing fields of Eton. But far from replacing work with play, Daniel Bivona argues for the ideological function of the blurring of distinction between the two in imperial literature. In Disraeli's novels, for instance, Bivona sees "an early manifestation of a phenomenon which was, in a roundabout way, to press empire as an imaginative adventure into the service of 'domestic' social needs: empire is also a privileged realm of play, a play denied an outlet in the English workplace" (1990: 36).

History, as Hannah Arendt and others contend, needs myths and legends in order to contain what otherwise could not bear examination. Historians, popular writers and statesmen – those who help to create and formulate the stuff of legend, ideology and mythology – are also those who shape group identity and shore up the idealizing fantasies of a community, thereby arming the culture against external reality (see Wurgaft 1983: x-xii). Kipling provided legends and myths that were types of colonial mimicry both reenforcing *and* deflating British fears of the educated Indian, their adulation of the Pathan, and their faith in English schoolboy codes of manliness, sportsmanship and honor ("The Head of the District," "His Chance in Life," "On the City Wall," "To Be Filed for Reference," "The Phantom Rickshaw," "The Dream of Duncan Parrenness"). Kipling's place in the history of English ideas lies in his shifting and unstable relation to collective representations of Anglo-Indian imperial territory, to social contracts and to group psychology. His use of the small detail to unsettle the larger story, his willingness to open a territory to fictional question, the opposing temptation to close circles, and his alternation between the yearning for the centered, unified and familial (the ultimate Sussex) versus the movement outward towards the larger decentered wolf pack that included all Others – these are some of the marks of Kipling's fiction.

Kipling's stories problematize the breaking point of boundaries, of the lonely nightmare of the private self in India; but, in addition to that knowledge, there is an awareness of other multiplicities that strain against it and resist its control from within (see Deleuze 1987: 249). In spite of the constraints of formal boundaries and rigid frame narrators who fear transgression, Kipling's fiction transgresses borders: with Mowgli he enters the world of animals, with his "best-beloved" the world of eternal children, with the ghost of Mrs. Wessington and with the dead children whose laughter fills the landscapes of the story "'They'" he enters the metaphysical. Kipling's packs and multiplicities transform and cross over some of the rigid binary constructions of nineteenth-century racist and gendered thought, entering in the process fluid and luminous borderline spaces. But it is precisely in those borderline sites that Kipling's anxieties over definition and structures become more exaggerated. His hedged and tightly framed narratives, then, expose, contain, limit, and defend themselves against the fearful yet seductive stories of Indian life, and in their ambivalence towards the embedded tales suggest some of the cracks in the ideological structures that sustained the dreams of empire.

Kipling's India helped construct a mythology of imperialism by reflecting both the real and the imaginary relationship between the British and their Indian subjects. What the community at home and in India generally chose to see in their enterprise was not what Kipling saw: they chose to see history and the work of imperialism in the relatively static and glorified terms that Thomas Macaulay and Conrad's first narrator in *Heart of Darkness* saw it – jewels flashing in the night of time. But Kipling, like some of his contemporary sociologists, implied a disturbing analogy between the inner and outer circles, between private breakdown and public facade, between the private truths known by the colonizers about themselves and cracks in the larger system. (Noel Annan, for instance, sees Kipling's place in the history of English ideas as analogous to those of Durkheim, Weber and Pareto – the European sociologists who revolutionized the study of society.) But unlike Durkheim, Kipling could provide no single model of thought (such as mechanical or organic communal solidarity), only a proliferation of fictions, anxieties, and ambivalent modes of discourse.

Robert Buchanan's famous attack on Kipling, "The Voice of the Hooligan," was characteristic of the complaint that instead of representing "the true spirit of our civilization" Kipling represents "the vulgarity, the brutality, the savagery" of "what the mob is thinking" (in Gilbert 1965: 20–32).[2] Buchanan wanted to see the empire idealized and given speech as a single and monolithic structure and the multitudinous mob silenced. His position is characteristic of European racism, which, as Sandra Kemp tells us, wished to ignore process and history; but, she adds, "ambivalent or multiple perspectives undermine their assertion of a colonialist will to power and knowledge" (Kemp 1988: 6). Kemp's recent reading of Kipling illuminates Foucault's and Said's earlier work on the problems of representing Others: knowledge of others reflects the power of the knowing colonizer who represents natives because they cannot represent themselves. The "Oriental," therefore, is never allowed the position of subject. Rather, the Westerner who mediates our knowledge of the East either stereotypes the native, or in the case of T. E. Lawrence, becomes "an unmediated expert power – the power to be, for a brief time, the Orient" (Said 1979: 243). My work counters Kipling's reputation as bard of empire whose voice represents unproblematically and transparently the discourse of imperialism by reading his fiction as energized, at least partially, by lines of flight towards and away from the competing forces of imperial representation and domination. I use Deleuze and Guattari's phrase with a difference: Kafka's line of flight was a way out – right, left, underground, or in any direction. Kipling's flight is sandbagged from the start. Yet we hear, in spite of his self-imposed narrative fencing and framing, the slippery, interrogative voices of evasion and resistance. Kafka's Gregor, trapped in the Oedipal family, will find (though he will fail and die in the process) his line of flight in

becoming-insect. Fleete in "The Mark of the Beast" will meta-
morphose into a wolf – a process that the narrator uses to underscore
the limitations of colonial knowledge and the power of the native to
take vengeance on English insolence. This is a line of flight, not for
Fleete who is unconscious of the process, but rather for the narrator
to speak his moment of resistance to imperial arrogance and
ignorance. Fleete has disgraced himself in his drunken desecration of
an idol; Strickland and the narrator disgrace themselves as Englishmen in effecting his return into human form by torturing and abusing
a native leper. The story itself has been marked by the beast because
no matter what the narrator says to define his position as colonizer,
his power and knowledge have been permanently changed. The last
line of the story therefore ironizes, deflates and subverts the position
he and Strickland have fought so hard to sustain: he concludes that
no one can believe such an unpleasant story because "it is well known
to every right-minded man that the gods of the heathen are stone and
brass, and any attempt to deal with them otherwise is justly
condemned" (*LH* 191).

Although he was popularly represented as the voice of authority
who provided the English with codes for surviving India, Kipling's
work in the 1880s and 1890s also created alternative fictions of empire
that demythologized while it venerated the work of the English in
other lands. His verse, journalism and fiction generally form part of
a larger colonial discourse, one which Edward Said and other critics
see as built on Manichean binaries in which the Eastern "Other" is
the silent object incapable of representing itself (Said 1979). While
acknowledging the importance of Said's work, I prefer to read
Kipling's narratives differently, focusing, with Bhabha, on the
ambivalence of desire in the forms of narcissistic and aggressive
identification, in sites of fixity and fantasy (Bhabha 1986: 164). But
I also see it as a more dynamic, slippery and sometimes oppositional
discourse which, while mimicking the varied voices of its uneasy and
half-denied ideology, yet questions official structures and raises the
possibility of repressed and alternative rereadings of official imperial
mythology.

Still, at least one of the many "languages" and voices of Kipling
preserved and petrified the "legend of empire" as the eternally
responsible parent who could be relied on to provide permanent
support for the rest of the world. Although Kipling established what
Arendt calls the "foundation legend" of empire, the anxieties of his

writing suggest his awareness of the contradictions between the imperial values celebrated in his tales for children and the politics constructed by such men as Cecil Rhodes or Lord Curzon (Arendt 1973: 209). The construction of an idealized paternal imperialism that would protect childlike Indians may have compensated in part for the absence of protectors when Rudyard the child most needed them, for the violence of his own childhood deprivation of "reliable" parents, for his subjection to six years of abuse in the English place of childhood exile he called "The House of Desolation," and for the necessary repression of his "underground self" – the Indian child who was his Mowgli self. The contradictions in Kipling's art, therefore, reflect those at the heart of the imperial enterprise *and* those in a particular family that provided the ideology responsible for producing the literature of desire and fear – the desire for the forbidden countered by the fear of punishment, fear of the "dark places of the earth" combined with the desire to master and control them, the need to master combined with the desire to rebel against authority.

Kipling's fiction then gives voice to the full fragmentation of the colonizer's many subject positions and ambivalences. It operates within the framework of an imperial culture, yet constantly shifts position in relation to that dominant ideology; it ironizes the transcendent "knower" or narrator; it alternately exoticizes and pathologizes India; it desires the native woman whose body disintegrates shortly after it seduces and maims the colonizer who dares to transgress its boundaries; it occasionally appears to give power to native narrators (in *Life's Handicap* and *In Black and White*), yet selects and appropriates only those voices that serve the imperial purpose; he allows natives to survive while the colonizer goes mad and alternately, the colonizer to survive while the native disintegrates. A man who praised Allah for giving him "two sides to my head," Kipling at his most lyrical (*Kim*) celebrates diversity by using a discourse apparently marked by unified, singleminded stances towards empire that are then undermined by other decentering and "centrifugal" forces. Kim's numinous celebration of his journey on the multicolored, musical and jewelled Grand Trunk Road, "broad, smiling river of life," for instance, is made possible by his chosen, temporary identity as Indian and beloved "chela" (disciple) to his lama; but that position is later reversed by his confirmed identity as an Englishman whose "fettered soul" will see only a "great, grey, formless India." These contradictory images of shifting identities that construct different Indias are repeated in a series of other historically inscribed contradictions, chief among which are Kim's desire to be loved by India as "little friend of all the World" and to be its master-sahib-imperialist.

Even an apparently simple allegory of empire like "Naboth" demonstrates the instability of apparently stable structures in Kipling's world as well as the paranoia and legitimized violence endemic to colonial discourse. The story narrates the gradual appropriation of an Englishman's garden (in India) by a poor street vendor towards whom he had made a thoughtlessly charitable gesture. A nightmare of the lone English narrator victimized by but ultimately triumphant over ungrateful, insolent natives (a version of "The Strange Ride of Morrowbie Jukes"), it ends with the following lines:

Naboth is gone now, and his hut is ploughed into its native mud with sweetmeats instead of salt for a sign that the place is accursed. I have built a summer house to overlook the end of the garden, and it is as a fort on my frontier whence I guard my Empire.

I know exactly how Ahab felt. He has been shamefully misrepresented in the scriptures. (*LH* 289)

It is this final unsettling allusion to Ahab that is so characteristic of Kipling's slippery mode, of the contradiction between the logic of his narrative sequence and its repressed secret which the narrative has been at pains to repress. The story in Kings 21 tells of the annoyance of Ahab, king of Samaria, at discovering that Naboth the Jezreelite had a vineyard in Jezreel beside Ahab's palace. When Naboth refuses to accede to the king's demand to sell his land, Ahab sulks until his wife Jezabel has Naboth stoned to death. Ahab, the biblical colonialist, then takes possession of his coveted vineyard. The biblical allusion destabilizes the monologic imperialist narrative voice and raises questions repressed by the apparent allegory. Whereas Kipling's narrator dispels the reader's pity for the Indian and instead sees the Englishman as victim to native ingratitude, the biblical story reverses the hierarchy of Kipling's story, compelling readers to question their early response to the problems of ownership, territoriality and colonialism, to question the narrator's self-awareness, and to realize that the last sentence sets in motion an alternative story about representation and misrepresentation. The biblical Naboth's story, like that of the native Indian's, is a silent unrepresented story.

As product of a longing for "mine own people," Kipling's fiction swerves between the desire for a union between the rulers and the ruled and the imperatives of the imposed historic separation between the two. The longing for union is split between desire and dread: the idealized bond is realized in the native family structures that nurture Kim and Mowgli and in Kipling's acknowledgment through the cryptic defense of the subtitle (to *Life's Handicap*) and proverb that the native population encountered on the road to Delhi are all "my brothers" and "Mine Own People." But the dark underside to this idealized (though proprietary) union is the terrifying bond seen in images of engulfment – opium dens ("The Gate of the Hundred Sorrows"), brothels ("The City of Dreadful Night"), nightmare cities of the dead ("The Strange Ride of Morrowbie Jukes"), and, by extension, miscegenation ("To be Filed for Reference," "Beyond the Pale," "Without Benefit of Clergy").

That conflict between desire and dread reveals itself in Kipling's use of metaphor and metonymy. The metaphoric mode in Kipling blurs boundary distinctions by balancing forward movements towards discovery with backward movements controlled by fears and dreams that threaten disintegration. It risks the assertion of similarity between the self and Other, between the narrative voice and the blind face that cries and cannot wipe its eyes ("La Nuit Blanche"), and between the Englishman whose insomnia drives "the night into my head" and the Indians in the cities of "dreadful night." The metonymic and ironic tropes in Kipling reenforce distance, contiguity, and denial of connection with the Other. The all-knowing Kipling narrator of the early frame tales uses irony as his official voice and as defense against the terror of breakdown into an India of the mind. Kipling's Indian tales are pervaded by this dialogic battle between voices and tropes that threaten to undermine each other – the adventurer's desire for action, for example, countered by an opposite movement toward an ordered stasis. In *Kim*, for instance, the boy's apparent pursuit of adventure and freedom from familial and national obligations, signified by his initial choice of lama as father and by his journey on the Grand Trunk Road into ever-wondrous images of India, is a forward movement that is contradicted by what we soon perceive to be the trajectory of his life – the rediscovery of emblems of empire, of the Red Bull on a Green Field, of lost fathers, and of an inexplicably happy collection of parental figures whom he reterritorializes at play in the fields of a fantasy India.

These contradictory movements in Kipling's fiction match the conflicted attitudes of the colonizer towards the Other and towards competing ideas of imperialism. The vision of the united procession on the Grand Trunk Road in *Kim* can be read as an imaginary construct of a visionary prefallen India; or it can be historicized in terms of a golden age (which some historians might read as pre-1857) before mutual distrust and suspicion led the British to adopt increasingly harsh authoritarian stances towards natives; or to a time before the British felt justified in reneging on the 1858 proclamation promising that entry-level jobs in the government would be based on merit. (Kiernan says that "statues of Queen Victoria were to multiply faster than jobs for Indians in the higher civil and military grades" [1969: 51]). Quite contrary to Kipling's Grand Trunk Road vision of a multicolored empire marching towards the ultimate family reunion, the British began to adopt increasingly repressive police methods to contain revolution and relied on an India divided against itself as the structure necessary to sustain their presence. Yet Kipling's vision of colonial relationships is an important intervention in the construction of a mythology of empire that became part of national memory.

Although Kipling's own return to India in 1882 coincided with the growing agitation in Bengal that led in 1885 to the National Congress Movement (founded by Allan Octavian Hume), most of his fiction appears to ignore native and British desires for independence. The anxieties in Kipling's earlier short stories, however, can and need to be contextualized in terms of such desires and the subsequent fear of loss. As the vernacular press in India was growing increasingly vocal in its opposition to British Rule, as the voices of jingoism grew more intense in England, and as educated Indians began agitating for more power in government, the seventeen-year-old Kipling was beginning his seven hard years in India as a cub reporter for the *Civil and Military Gazette* in Lahore and for the *Pioneer* in Allahabad trying to shore gravel against the tides of political change – against the Ilbert Bill and Gladstone – by writing essays demonstrating the inability of Indians to govern themselves. The country was for him too large, too diverse to be governed by anything other than a united empire. But although his articles were fearful of inefficiency and destruction if Indians governed themselves, the bulk of his fiction during these years was about the inefficiency and self-destructiveness of Englishmen. Madness, alcoholism, self-doubt, and suicide haunt the characters who live in the plains and hills of his early volumes of stories.

Kipling's greatest defense against the horror of self-loss and disintegration lay in his discovery of a narrative stance at once distant, ironic, hedged and wishing it could be monologic – a voice that reminds us of his characteristic fictional narrator's voice so persistently contradicted by the polyphonic voices of the embedded tale, and by the diverse voices of native India. That single-minded and easily caricatured voice belongs to the daytime Kipling who staunchly defends imperial values and institutions. But what distinguishes Kipling's work is the presence of other voices, dissonant and self-contradictory, that war with the official voice and signify Kipling's ambivalences towards the dominant preoccupation of his early and middle fiction – how to parent India. Kipling's fiction of the 1880s and 1890s looks forward towards resolving the problem of how to survive the potential political and personal loss of India ("The Bridge-Builders"), and backward to a primal loss ("Baa, Baa, Black Sheep," "The Strange Ride of Morrowbie Jukes") that reacts to such a possibility with hysterical defensiveness, paranoia and denial.

The paradigmatic figure of these contradictory movements in Kipling's fiction is sight and sightedness. The most striking such moment in his poetry is in "La Nuit Blanche":

> Then a Face came, blind and weeping,
> And It couldn't wipe its eyes,
> And It muttered I was keeping
> Back the moonlight from the skies.   (*Verse* 28–9)

That face will, of course, return to haunt the insomniac to death in "At the End of the Passage." Kipling's stories are full of images of perception – ghostly, half-eaten, mutilated faces ("In the Same Boat"), blind men (*The Light that Failed*), blind women ("'They,'" "The Wish House"), nonhuman creatures whose ghastly eyes are "sightless – white, in sockets as white as scraped bone, and blind" ("A Matter of Fact"), and the twin figures of Kim, who *sees* in brilliant colors a painterly India, and his lama, who refuses to see and who denies the significance of sight. But sight is as terrifying as blindness, and variations on the problems of too much perception resonate through his poetry and fiction: the fear of vision and revelation that results in the destruction of the first microscope ("The

Eye of Allah") in a thirteenth-century monastery, the literalizing of
the metaphoric fear that "truth blinds the perceiver" ("A Matter of
Fact"), and the suggestion that those granted special sight are also
damned to madness and early death ("The Phantom Rickshaw"
and others). The fear of seeing the self as Other occurs in stories of
doubles ("The Dream of Duncan Parrenness") and most starkly in
his poem "The Mother's Son":

> I have a dream – a dreadful dream –
> A dream that is never done,
> I watch a man go out of his mind,
> And he is My Mother's Son...   (*Verse* 784)

The connection between insanity and blindness is yet another
borderline site of contestation in Kipling. If the modern episteme of
identity and unified selfhood is to be found (as Foucault contends)
through knowledge, then travel, experience and the sight of Others
add to the sum of collective knowledge. But if we are constituted by
others seeing us, if the gaze brings us into being, if sight is the means
to circumscribe our boundaries and mark "difference," then
Kipling's use of sight can be seen in terms of its shifting power from
self to Others. As the child in Edenic India in *Something of Myself* he
was the center who controlled the power of sight; but his geographic
removal to England at six and the loss of his parents led to the
appropriation of that power by strangers in the House of Desolation.
These figures reversed the process by turning him into the object of
the powerful gaze of Others, by reconstituting him, as it were, into an
object of mockery, abuse and powerlessness; and his first experience
with hysterical blindness appropriately comes at a time when his
Southsea guardians leave him alone for a few days, when he no longer
is subject to the defining powers of their gaze, when his sense of self is
annihilated by the absence of authoritarian tormentors.

But Kipling's project in life was to overcome such destruction. The
absence and lack suggested by blindness he therefore met by the
opposing urge to see all – even the forbidden city streets of nighttime
Lahore – and to confront the fear of immobility by obsessive traveling
in both fiction and life as if traveling would reempower his nightmare
loss of self that was also the loss of sight. In his fiction, Kipling became
the divided framer of tales in which a survivor sees the forbidden and
tells of the dismemberment, madness, or death of another who
ventured where frame narrators fear to tread. Kipling's ironic and

metonymic layering of narrators and stories refracts the connections between himself, his narrator, and the embedded tale, thereby repressing the metaphoric figures associated with loss of self by displacing them into a contained and embedded tale. His stories, in other words, commit acts that appropriate and therefore appear to transgress the official by centering what imperial society had marginalized – the dirt, the smells and the tastes of India, the British failure, the suicide, the syphilitic soldier, the rebel, the Indian child, the Indian woman, the dying, and the dead.

Elaborate tropes, the coyness of public school "in" languages, and the armored style of military language conceal internalized disorders that seem inexplicable. Mysterious suicides are explained only by "had a touch of the sun, I fancy" ("At the End of the Passage"), or syphilitic fits interpreted by doctors as "Locomotus attacks us" ("Love-o'-Women"), or madness diagnosed as "hydrophobia" ("The Mark of the Beast"). The fear in most of these stories is of internal rather than external "powers of darkness." The epigraph to "The Phantom Rickshaw" returns as a hymn sung by one of the men in "At the End of the Passage":

> If in the night I sleepless lie,
> My soul with sacred thoughts supply;
> May no ill dreams disturb my rest,
> ....
> Or powers of darkness me molest!   (*LH* 146)

Both ill dreams and the powers of darkness drive Englishmen into early graves. But the men in "At the End of the Passage" envy the suicide and prefer his death to their endless assault by isolation, heat, sleeplessness, stress, overwork, and monotony. Hummil, the man who has reached the end of his passage, dies of fear, haunted and hunted in his sleep by "a blind face that cries and can't wipe its eyes, a blind face that chases him down corridors." Kipling represents Hummil's disorder as fear of regression: "He had slept back into terrified childhood ... he was flung from the fear of a strong man to the fright of a child as his nerves gathered sense or were dulled" (*LH* 151). Hummil's servant believes that his master has descended into "the Dark Places, and there has been caught," which is another way for a native voice to reenforce the Englishman's fear of psychotic breakdown, regression into the terrors of an infantile past and into "the echoing desolation" of India as a projection of the anxieties of that past. The fear of boundary loss, of "slipping backwards" into childhood, darkness, alcoholism, passion, quicksand, or an abyss is hardly countered by the assurances of the frame narrator who appears as evidence of survival. Such professional survivors (like the speaker of the poem "If") speak with such cynicism of the cost of survival that the point of survival is lost. When McGoggin, the civilian expert in "The Conversion of Aurelian McGoggin," suffers a stroke followed by aphasia, the doctor warns: "there are a good many things you can't understand; and, by the time you have put in my length of service, you'll know exactly how much a man dare call his own in this world" (*PTH* 85). McGoggin goes to the hills, we are told, "in fear and trembling" unsatisfied by "the legitimate explanation" which is of course the colonial lie that sustains the machinery of empire.

The problem of survival in colonial India, therefore, realizes itself in psychic and relatively ahistorical chains that cross specifically social and historical chains of meaning. Kipling maps his human failures – the blind and the mutilated – by certain recurring tropes charged with the fear of slipping backwards into a past that might once again be lost. Chief among these are nightmare images of wounds or scars in the geographic landscape that are metonymically related to corresponding bodily mutilations. The gaping hole of the village of the dead who did not die, for instance, traps the unwary Morrowbie Jukes, who finds himself at the mercy of a native with a scar for which he has, sometime in the past, been responsible. The native, in turn, has caused a huge hole in the back of another dead Englishman discovered by Jukes in yet another cavity in the hole. The one-eyed priest in "Bubbling Well Road," who carries "burnt between his brows" the scar of the torturer, guards an eerie, haunted well that is "a black gap in the ground" (*LH* 266). The gaps in the ground and in the priest's face are metonyms that, by definition, are not only endless, but also "constantly confused, traversed by other chains... a crossroads, a vertigo" (Lyotard 1985: 30), that serve also as historic metonyms of the black hole – the ultimate Marabar Cave – where the Englishman in India might fear to meet his living death. These powerful early stories, marked by colonial and racial fears, undercut the illusions of common inheritance and "grandeur of race" that served imperial power, not as historical facts, but as "the only reliable link in a boundless space" (Arendt 1973: 182). And the well into which Little Tobrah pushes his starving sister is one of many silent spaces in India that speaks not only of its own loss, but also of the endlessly postponed and displaced negation that signifies Kipling's search for the forever evasive and absent "cause" that is forever a lack. Little Tobrah's case is "not reported because nobody cared by so much as a hempen rope for the life or death of Little Tobrah" (*LH* 256). Yet the story is built on contradiction: the unreported story will be reported by reporter Kipling who completes a lack by fictionalizing a tale at once structured on incompletion and metonymy. This tale of the murder of one hungry and abandoned child by another similarly victimized child is one of many narratives charged with loss and desire; but also, as Sandra Kemp reminds us, the child is part of Kipling's hidden narrative, "always an important repository of suggestiveness" and part of "an anarchic subjective realm where the self is no longer shielded from terror by adult frames of identity" (Kemp 1988: 18).

The ambivalence of Kipling's subject position appears in his earliest journalism in his construction of the English traveler and in the repeated fear of loss countered by the waggish presence of colonial authority. In the *Letters of Marque* (1887), his frame is split between the traveling Englishman whom he admires because it is himself renamed "the King of Loafers," the "grimy scallawag with a six days' beard and an unholy knowledge of native States" (*LM* 188) who "knows" India differently from those other Englishmen he calls "the Globe Trotters," men who are experts on hotels and food (*LM* 188), who greet each new sight with banalities, who "never get farther than the 'much pleased' state under any circumstance" (*LM* 40). He mocks the Globe Trotter's pretensions at "knowing" the places he travels and criticizes him for his lack of reverence (*LM* 6): "'I don't say that I've done it all; but you may say that I've seen a good deal.' Then he explained that he had been 'much pleased' at Agra; 'much pleased' at Delhi; and, last profanation, 'very much pleased' at the Taj. Indeed, he seemed to be going through life just then 'much pleased' at everything. With rare and sparkling originality he remarked that India was a 'big place,' and that there were many things to buy" (*LM* 7).

Kipling's perceptions too are split between those mediated by the texts of European masters and his more immediate sensual impressions. The view in Jeypore is "as unobstructed as that of the Champs Elysees" (*LM* 13). The entry to Chitor is read twice – through the "facts" in the local Baedeker, and then again differently, for we are

told that the Baedeker "leaves out of all account the Genius of the
Place" (*LM* 89). And Dore, Zola, Ruskin, the Book of Ezekiel, and
Viollet-le-Duc are used to reread or preread Indian scenes: "If, as
Viollet-le-Duc tells us to believe, a building reflects the character of
its inhabitants, it must be impossible for one reared in an Eastern
palace to think straightly or speak freely or – but here the annals of
Rajputana contradict the theory – to act openly. The cramped and
darkened rooms, the narrow smooth-walled passes with recesses
where a man might wait for his enemy unseen, the maze of ascending
and descending stairs leading nowhither ... all these things breathe of
plot and counter-plot, league and intrigue" (*LM* 20). Yet he adds "if
a man desired beauty, there was enough and to spare in the palace"
(*LM* 21). One of the places he most admires ("Ruskin could describe
the scene admirably"[*LM* 35]) is the Museum at Jeypore run by an
English Curator: "Let those who doubt the thoroughness of a
Museum under one man's control, built, filled, and endowed with
royal generosity – an institution perfectly independent of the Government of India – go and exhaustively visit Dr. Hendley's charge at
Jeypore" (*LM* 35).

Daring to look further than museums, Kipling's travels make him
look into several "hearts" of India, even "the heart that had ceased
to beat" (*LM* 22). What he experiences in these bodily sites,
particularly in Chitor, lies beyond the scope of official discourse.
"One cannot 'do' Chitor with a guidebook" (*LM* 90), he writes as
he mocks the quaint description of the town by an English missionary.
Instead, Kipling describes a journey into a libidinous space where a
"strange, uncanny wind" springs from nowhere, where trees wrench
slabs clear off walls, and where "marauding trees" and "crazy stone
stairways," the calm face of an enthroned God holding the Wheel of
the Law and the "appalling lavishness of decoration, all worked
toward the instillment of fear and aversion" (*LM* 92) and frame his
entry into the Tower of Victory. His dizzying entry traps him into an
ambivalent space: "The tower, in the arrangement of the stairways,
is like the interior of a Chinese carved ivory puzzle-ball. The idea
given is that, even while you are ascending, you are wrapping
yourself deeper and deeper in the tangle of a mighty maze" (*LM* 92).
From the Tower he descends into a "terrible" watery space the Gau-
Mukh (the cow's mouth) which, once again, he names as "uncanny"
and which then reappears as the center of darkness in *The Naulahka*.
Objectifying himself into the third person narrator, "The English-

man" feels he has "done a great wrong in trespassing into the very heart and soul of all Chitor" (*LM* 95); he has literally slipped into a sexualized landscape of absence split between a tower and a gaping watery hole that contains "the loathsome Emblem of Creation" (*LM* 94), with flowers and rice around it. The terror he feels at seeing the phallus (the lingam) underwater enclosed by incense, vegetation, and "oozing," "trickling," and "slimy walls" makes Kipling feel he has been led "two thousand years away from his own century ... into a trap" and into the fear that he "would fall off the polished stones into the stinking tank, or that the Gau-Mukh would continue to pour water until the tank rose up and swamped him, or that some of the stone slabs would fall forward and crush him flat" (*LM* 95). Sweating with what he terms "childish fear," he decides "it was absurd ... Yet there was something uncanny about it all" (*LM* 96). Although this piece was written about twenty years before Freud's essay on "The Uncanny" (1919), it is remarkable for its precise anticipation of the term: what the Englishman sees in the phallus dismembered and enclosed by water is the return of the repressed fear of absence, castration, and self-loss. That fear is replayed in Kipling's dream story "The Brushwood Boy," where the boy dreams of a house containing a fearful Sick Thing, an It, whose head threatens to fall off, and in "The Man Who Would be King," where Dravot's decapitated head and Carnehan's crucified body and stigmata are signs not only of their journey into a forbidden Indian darkness, but also of the penalty for crossing a sexual boundary.

Kipling's "Englishman" travels through an India in which the authoritative measure of knowledge is Western. Jodhpur is therefore described as the Land of Houyhnhnms, whose Maharajah wears an English ulster, speaks English and sees to it that the Crown Prince studies English with one of the English officials of the State; and the condition of the horses, we are told, "was English – quite English" (*LM* 128). These letters of travel are written by an Englishman whose "unholy knowledge" of the land, so he claims, is richer than that provided by "quaint" missionaries and dull Baedekers and ignorant native guides. He is empowered by his familiarity with the Gods and the Princes, with temples and palaces, with gossip about Kings and Rajahs, and with the histories of cities, men and animals. Yet, after all his journeys, India remains in these reports the heart of an alien darkness.

Writing in a world charged with the desire for possession and ownership ("Expansion is everything," said his friend Cecil Rhodes, "these stars... these vast worlds... I would annex the planets if I could" [Arendt 1973: 124]), Kipling turns the central event of his Indian stories into acts of transgressing an inner circle, a family, or a world that is contained, questioned, and sometimes repressed. The violation of territorial, sexual, and moral boundaries sometimes occurs in stories where the act is sanctified by religiosity ("The Man Who Would Be King") or sentimentalized by making the transgressor a child (*The Jungle Books* and *Kim*), or distanced into dream ("The Brushwood Boy"), or ironized by a frame narrator whose language and stance attempt to neutralize its impact ("Beyond the Pale," "Naboth," "The Phantom Rickshaw," "The Mark of the Beast").

Kipling's most powerful early Indian stories, versions of his longed-for imaginary union, tell of Englishmen who attempt to violate divisions between the colonizer and colonized by learning too much about nighttime India, by consorting with native women and thereby succumbing to the seduction of drugs, alcohol and the Other. Such surrender might lead to madness and death – or to writing the ultimate book about India. "To be Filed for Reference" is the last story in *Plain Tales from the Hills*, the last word (at least in 1888) on the colonizer's transgression into native India. Here the Oxford scholar McIntosh Jellaludin is evidence of the cost of transgression; now perpetually drunk and "past redemption," cared for by his native "wife," he calls the narrator to him as he dies. The book that is his life's work, "my only baby" (*PTH* 241), which he wishes to bequeath to the narrator, is called "the Book of Mother Maturin"; and while the narrator begs to be dissociated from its authorship ("remember ... that McIntosh Jellaludin and not I myself wrote the book of Mother Maturin" [*PTH* 241]) we know that Kipling's most ambitious project in India was to be an epic novel called *Mother Maturin* about a Eurasian woman "not one bit nice or proper" that dealt with "the unutterable horrors of lower class Eurasian and native life as they exist outside reports" (Page 1984: 158). It is this slippage in Kipling's Indian fiction between himself and the Other, himself in disguise as the Other, himself in love with the Other, yet not the Other but instead a cold, armored, and distant narrator that makes his fiction so characteristic of his metonymic mode of narrative – one that can never quite locate its center, or name its unnamable desire.

That which is named as fearsome, undesirable, or objectionable in one part of his work, for instance, often returns (and this is a central characteristic of the metonymic mode) to haunt another part of his fiction as ambivalent object of desire. The series of articles, for instance, that Kipling wrote about Calcutta (*The City of Dreadful Night*, 1888) charts an infernal spiral descent from the surface "whited sepulchre" (*SS* 196) to the Calcutta Stink ("the essence of long-neglected abominations" [*SS* 224]), down through labyrinthine layers of brothels, "from love by natural sequence to death" (*SS* 243); the infernal descent reserves the worst layer for the last – the sight of European women, once wives of British soldiers, now working as prostitutes. The section ends with the reporter's urge to climb the spire of a church and shout: "O true believers! Decency is a fraud and a sham. There is nothing clean or pure or wholesome under the stars, and we are all going to perdition together. Amen!" (*SS* 238).

Here and in the story of the same name, Kipling expresses the wish to climb a spire, to ascend to a position of superiority, defense and distance from which ("like Zola") to frame a view. In the earlier "City of Dreadful Night" (1885) story about a sleepless night in Lahore, he does what he wishes to do in the later piece – climb the top of a minaret and then look down on the city: the characteristic stance of the narrator who finds ways to distance himself from immersion in the destructive element. In each version of the tale, the heart of darkness is death – the Eurasian prostitute is the death of illusion, and the all-night walk through Lahore begins and ends in death. The opening paragraph of the story is a familiar vision of India – "a disused Mahomedan burial-ground, where the jawless skulls and rough-butted shank-bones, heartlessly exposed by the July rains, glimmered like mother o' pearl on the rain-channelled soil" (*LH* 270). The narrator who has begun by complaining that the dense wet heat "prevented all hope of sleep" ends the story and the journey through yet another night of insomnia by seeing a double, a nightmare image of yet another victim of that heat – the corpse of a woman of whom someone says: "She died at midnight from the heat" (*LH* 276).

Desire and fear in Kipling's split discourses about India yearn towards and reject the heart of their darkness that lies in the labyrinthine alleys of nighttime Lahore. Kipling's stories of India struggle between nighttime desire for knowledge and the opposing daytime need for surface stability – for the familial enclaves of the inner circle, the club, the home, and the empire. His negotiation of those desires in his early fiction produces tensions between the privileged, dominant and dispassionate position of the frame narrator and the more inflected positions contained within the embedded and enigmatic tales. Those embedded tales often release voices that oppose the official voice of imperial hegemony. It is Lispeth the hill girl the reader supports and not her English lover or the English missionaries who try to educate her into civilization. Sometimes that dominant voice is compromised by irony, sometimes by an elegiac compassion for crazy adventurers who would be kings and who go beyond the pale into forbidden India; but the stance and voice are always slippery and evasive even when such men meet with mutilation, decapitation, or crucifixion. The survivors, often those who are supported by fantasy families, are always in danger of losing those families: Mowgli the "Frog," amphibious child of jungle and city, of humans and animals, can live precariously as Lord of the Jungle and be not of the Jungle; Kim the orphan, loved by a host of multicolored parental surrogates, can be "little Friend to all the world" and master; and Adam, son of Policeman Strickland, can earn the "double wisdom" necessary to survive imperial India with humanity and dignity. Other Englishmen are allowed to survive India because they are granted the privilege by ancient Hindu gods who, in reversal of the colonial hierarchy, are represented as the real controllers of "the day's work" when they allow bridge builders to realize the rewards of their labor.

But all these certainties are threatened by the persistence of Kipling's original trope of uncontrollable loss and terror at unknowable India: in spite of the Englishman's hard work, Naboth will invade the garden when the Englishman least expects it; the Indian gods will cause floods to undermine the work of empire; Morrowbie Jukes will lose his head, start shooting howling dogs at midnight and fall into the city of the dead from which there is no escape; Fleete will turn into a werewolf; the ghost of Mrs. Wessington will return to haunt Pansay to death; and unnamed boys will blow their brains out for no namable reason. Kipling's writings about India, produced during the post-Mutiny realizations of potential failure and loss of yet another colony, implicate the reader in some of the recurring controversies about the human and psychic cost of power, and of maintaining the Indian empire.

This book, then, is a reading of Kipling's writings about India as narrative interventions between past anxieties of the self and present crises of empire. These fictions are necessarily political because they are part of the defining discourse of colonialism and of the contradictions embedded within it. They also reinscribe cultural hegemony and the cultural schizophrenia that constructed the division between the Englishman as demi-God and as human failure, as colonizer and semi-native. I focus on Kipling's early fiction on India. But the ordering of my chapters moves from his late autobiography to the early fiction because it assumes that the autobiographical impulse which charges Kipling's discourse with its particular ambivalence is an impulse that precedes and reflects his armored posture to the outside world. I therefore frame the early fiction in the shadow of his posthumously published and unfinished autobiography: the second chapter, "Something of himself," reads Kipling's last published work as a final fiction that attempts to integrate the fragments of his life – one in which he becomes the frame narrator looking back at the pieces he is willing to recall, and in the process constructing a hedged and dualistic discourse so characteristic of his early fiction.

Kipling's early framed stories are of course marked by unconscious ideological contradictions together with his own (resistant) collusion with the narrator's official authority. But what makes his early narrators so interesting and problematic is the ambivalence of their position in relation to the stories they choose to retell. The third chapter, "The problem of otherness: a hundred sorrows," examines in the first four stories the young Rudyard wrote after he arrived in India the construction of the colonial subject and the ambivalence of his desires at the moment of entry into the imperial social order. These are nightmare journeys into a pathologized India that is "a gate of a hundred sorrows," a "village of the dead," where Englishmen are swallowed by climate, landscape, intrigue, madness and death. The fourth chapter, "The worst muckers," examines some of the stories in his first three volumes: *Plain Tales from the Hills*, *The Phantom Rickshaw*, and *Life's Handicap*, stories whose narrators enclose and contain disturbing tales of failed efforts at political power and at constituting a unified subject fit for the work of empire. The chapter is framed by an early sketch whose conflation of blurred gender lines and imperial misrule unconsciously call for the reconstitution of gender roles and sharper boundaries, thereby anticipating other forms of paranoia and masculinist anxiety common to colonial discourse. The fifth chapter, "The bridge builders," focuses mainly on two major stories of the 1890s from *The Day's Work* in which Kipling, now away from India, tries to restore and rebuild possibilities of empire. These are stories that naturalize and idealize the inevitability of English rule by giving (to turn Barthes' phrase) historic intention a mythological justification (1972: 9–11; 141–2). As the title story "The Bridge-Builders" suggests, Kipling finds ways to bridge the gaps and limits of a crumbling ideology that provided unsafe scaffolding for the dreams of empire. The last chapter, on *Kim*, considers how Kipling fictionalizes and further attempts to mediate the contradictions of imperial fantasy – the possibility that the English boy born and bred in India can be both master and beloved child to the natives, equally loved by India and by England. Here (and elsewhere) what Kipling leaves unsaid is a key to the problems with his intervention into imperial ideology. It also explores the metaphysical dualisms that underlie Kipling's problems in representing the Other. In spite of its yearnings for all that the lama represents, the rhetoric and the logic of the novel finally draw Kim away from the margins and return him to the centers of imperial surveillance and power as a spy. And the lama, as the ultimately idealized Other who exemplifies uncorrupted goodness, innocence and nature, must finally be stereotyped, feminized and mystified as the eternally deferred and static object of colonial desire.

CHAPTER 2

Something of himself

The imaginary India of Kipling's childhood was a space of Edenic unity where he felt magically beyond all divisions of race, religion and caste, where the Indian child could be his imagined brother, and where his self could be enclosed within concentric circles of loving solicitude. This of course was before he knew of the "dark land" that was England, of its darker rooms "full of cold," and of the empire whose mission he would embrace as if its power could heal the fissure of separation from his earliest objects of desire. Kipling's ambiguous position between his lost Eden and the larger colonial structure was the subject of his life's fictions. The last fiction of his life was his unfinished autobiography *Something of Myself for my Friends Known and Unknown* (1937) written during the last five months of his life. I use this work as an opening into Kipling's early fiction because we see in it some of the defenses that resonate through his life and art – the skepticism, the effort at self-protection, and the construction of synthetic world views as antidotes to the anxieties of division. Determined to control and yet passive in its acceptance of destiny and design, his method of narration reminds the reader of his tales as does his strategy of silence about certain deeply felt anxieties revealed more fully in his fiction. Even so, the book sheds light on Kipling's lifelong habits of dualistic discourse. The polarized structure of his autobiography resembles that of his early fiction, which, in turn, reflects the structure of his personal and political identity. The "autobiographical occasion"[1] for this book, written at seventy and published posthumously, a year after his death, is that of the old man looking back and refiguring the whole of his life. The impulse to frame, to impose margins and to establish authority on the landscape of his life suggests a dual need to limit, to domesticate, and to colonize as it were, in order to explore the territory of one's past. The narrative form Kipling chooses is one familiar in his fiction: it is an embedded

27

story told by the elderly narrator who selects and organizes memories, images and events in roughly chronological order, implying his authorial control over the past and his invulnerability to its effects on his emotional, intellectual and social identity.

Like *Kim*, the *Jungle Books*, and several of Kipling's short stories, this work too is a *bildungsroman* in which the protagonist learns the art of survival by acquiring certain forms of psychological distance from both internal and external threats. Consequently his autobiographical strategy is not the Wordsworthian or Dickensian one of reliving the past (Spengemann 1980: 125ff) but rather a more distant, defensive strategy of looking at the past from an eerie perspective beyond the grave. In the last sentence of the book, for instance, most unusual for an autobiography, he writes of himself as if he were already dead, as if the author's relationship to his life were to a finished, completed object.

Left and right of the table were two big globes, on one of which a great airman had once outlined in white paint those air-routes to the East and Australia which were well in use before my death. (*SM* 248)

Kipling's distanced, fixed and unmovable stance contrasts with the troublesome malleability of his vulnerable subject and reenforces his lifelong need to split the performing, working, writing self from the more passive, inarticulate, suffering self that would then be translated and saved into language. The oscillation between passivity and control, and between metaphoric and ironic discourse that we see also in his stories is apparent in the narrator's assumption of authority over the embedded tale of his often victimized protagonist and in the opposing images of identity through which Kipling defines his sense of his life.

Kipling's fundamental ambivalence towards his own identity is revealed through his career-long choice of dualistic forms – the dream story with its split between waking and dreaming, the frame tale with its split between outer and inner story, and, in this case, autobiography with its characteristic splitting between the younger victim and the older commentator. At the core of Kipling's dualistic narratives is an alternation between mastery and its lack, control and its absence – an ambivalence acknowledged implicitly in Kipling's view of himself as artist split between controlled craftsmanship and daemonic possession. His implied resolution of this contradiction – to woo the visitations of the daemon but to shape and control it by conscious craftsmanship – is typical of his various resolutions of other social contradictions. Craft must rule inspiration as England must rule India and as, in his favorite metaphor for art, the great three-masted ship must rule the waves.

Although Kipling's autobiography, like so many others, starts chronologically with his first memories and his sense of origins announced in curiously elliptical terms with a date, an epigraph and a frame, it commits immediately an act of self-censorship. The dates 1865–1878 (birth to age twelve) involve the formative period of his life – his first six idyllic years in India followed by six traumatic years in the "House of Desolation" (his foster home in Southsea, England, where he and his sister were left by his parents who returned to India). But the epigraph only draws attention to the first six: "Give me the first six years of a child's life and you can have the rest." The "rest" of those childhood years is repressed and denied not only in the epigraph, but by and large in the autobiography itself. It is only his fiction – "Baa, Baa, Black Sheep," and the opening of *The Light that Failed* – that allows for the return of the repressed, the anguish of maternal abandonment and loss of self. This double pattern of official and censored story versus the repressed and denied plot appears repeatedly in Kipling's fiction and shapes the telling of his life story.

A series of brisk chapter titles ("The Interregnum," "The Committee of Ways and Means," "South Africa") builds up to the last completed chapter, "Working Tools" – one that allows the artist to display the instruments of his mastery, the tools of his craft, which contain and order the daemonic Other who energizes the civilizing worker. The metaphoric language Kipling uses in the last chapter to summarize his life suggests both the public and private dimensions of the psychology of colonization: the need for boundary control over a potentially anarchic Other, even though the Other is in this case only the self: "I have told what my early surroundings were, and how richly they furnished me with material. Also, how rigorously newspaper spaces limited my canvases and, for the reader's sake, prescribed what within these limits must be some sort of beginning, middle, and end" (*SM* 222). The metaphor of "limit" contained in these lines is what James Olney would call a "metaphor of self" – a construct that governs his personal perspective in his fiction and autobiography – but it is also a metaphor of culture: a construct that governs the conscious and unconscious politics of imperialism. It is a version of his other favorite metaphor of the breaking of the colt as the necessary path to adulthood; and Kipling finds a way to excuse oppression, discipline and bullying because it is "brutal as the necessary wrench on the curb, that fetches up a too-flippant colt" (*SM* 40). That "wrench" runs through *Puck of Pook's Hill* and *Rewards and Fairies* in the image of iron – most vividly in "Cold Iron," where the fairy child falls into the limitations of humanity only when he fastens a slave ring of iron around his own neck.

Kipling's discourse is threaded with strategies of defense, of attempts at definition and redefinition within increasingly constricting limits and boundaries between what is allowed inside and what is excluded outside. The dual plot of Kipling's life and art at its most vital involves a dialectic between the accurate, the official and the prescribed as against the dreamlike, the repressed and the outlawed. That duality, though in part a deeply sedimented product of his own childhood experience, is also a source of Kipling's ethical system and a reflection of systems of education and child rearing in colonial culture. The spatial configuration of limits, boundaries, and the division of inside and outside might have its unconscious private source in his traumatic abandonment in England at the age of six, but it is also a mirror of a culture that insisted on drawing lines of separation between England and India, the West and the East, and on harnessing and breaking whatever was youthful, imaginative or "beyond the pale" in the service of empire. The form this dialectic takes in his autobiography is the conflict between certain colonial metaphors of difference – between the self seen as limit setter, club member and Imperialist, on the one hand, and the self as explorer, active creator, gipsy nightwalker, and dreamer on the other.

This chapter will draw attention to Kipling's metaphors of limitation, his needs for order and structure, and his fictional penchant for framing that contain and compress dreamlike moments of explosive memory. Distance from the past organizes, misremembers and orientalizes childhood's India – memories that culminate in literal blindness. It then surveys some of the more creative consequences of such containment in the return of the repressed – the invasion of the margins into the official centers of Kipling's life.

FRAMING AND GAMING

The frame is introduced (in the first sentence) in terms of a game and the recurring conceit of a deck of cards (pp. 3, 74, 85):

Looking back from this my seventieth year, it seems to me that every card in my working life has been dealt me in such a manner that I had but to play it as it came. Therefore, ascribing all good fortune to Allah the Dispenser of Events, I begin: – (*SM* 3)

The narrator looks at his own past as something delivered from above by chance, as something alienated from his authentic self. He defines himself as an intermediary between "authority" or the dispenser of the cards above, and the private self to whom the cards are dealt below. That split between the dealer and the receiver of cards reflects the recurring duality between the controlling and victimized sense of self conveyed by the autobiographer but also (as Bhabha might say) a contradiction in Western knowledge of the self split between its construction as master and as victim of its empire.

The stance Kipling announces towards himself at the start carries the sign of the author – a distance, an obliqueness, and a passivity that reveals itself in memories that are either impressionistic, poetic and dreamlike or factual, terse and mechanical; and in sentences whose energy is defused through the use of heavily embedded matrix constructions laden with passive or qualified verbs. The grammatical structure of the opening sentence, for instance, qualifies and removes responsibility from the speaker: "seems to me," "has been dealt," "I had but to play it as it came." It is therefore appropriate that the controlling images in these first two sentences – the deck of cards and "Allah the Dispenser of Events" – are both invested with power so that the writer can claim a certain dependence on external authority. The hybridized writer of stories overpopulated with the voices of the Other also enters here in the voice of the speaker who "ascribes all good fortune to Allah" – one who occupies a gray zone between irony and faith characteristic of so much colonial discourse.

Kipling interprets his childhood self in terms of defenses he learned at an early age, and the habit of framing or embedding was among the earliest: "I have learned since from children who play much alone that this rule of 'beginning again in a pretend game' is not uncommon. The magic, you see, lies in the ring or fence that you take refuge in" (*SM* 12). Safety, for Kipling, always lies within a circle, a frame, a game, a club, a room, a house, or an empire: abused and tortured by mother and son in the Southsea "House of Desolation," the child Rudyard learned to fence himself in imaginatively and physically with language, in repeated hypnotic images of active power ("'nine white wolves' coming 'over the wold'" and "certain savages who 'thought the name of England was something that could not burn'") and with wordless games that helped him to endure solitary confinement in "a mildewy basement room." The game he most fully recalls is one inspired by his reading of what has since been read by many as the archetypal Imperialist text, *Robinson Crusoe*:

My apparatus was a cocoanut shell strung on a red cord, a tin trunk, and a piece of packing-case which kept off any other world. Thus fenced about, everything inside the fence was quite real. (*SM* 11–12)

The habit of framing that has its roots in childhood necessity is part of the child's early lesson in duality and the art of splitting (or distancing) himself from painful experience. Angus Wilson and John McClure both draw attention to the social and political dimensions of this childhood game of "fencing in" as a paradigm of his later need to circumscribe and construct his circles of refuge and safety from a hostile world. Kipling's first experience of an alien and hostile world at Southsea is followed by four years at United Services College, a small public school that subjected the child to common forms of bullying and other humiliations. His rationalization of the pain, isolation, and internal splitting necessary for survival of this experience involves a characteristic defensiveness reminiscent of his attitudes towards later anxieties about colonial politics: "Nor was my life an unsuitable preparation for my future, in that it demanded constant wariness, the habit of observation, and attendance on moods and tempers; the noting of discrepancies between speech and action; a certain reserve of demeanour; and automatic suspicion of sudden favours" (*SM* 17). The "preparation" is for a specifically imperialistic vision of a life which expects repeated immersion into hostile and threatening territories. The function of English public school education, as Hannah Arendt and, most recently, John McClure and Joseph Bristow have taught us, was to train young boys in the art of self-defense, suspicion, and power in order to prepare them for the brutality and deprivation of colonial life.

Kipling's childhood awareness of the discrepancy between speech and action led him to suspect speech as abstract and therefore partially false and to so value action in the form of work and individual experience that C. S. Lewis was prompted to call him the second prophet (after Carlyle) of work in the English language. The irony that this early suspicion of language would result in creating such a prolific poet and writer is but one of the many contradictions of Kipling's personality.

The most reliable system of defense Kipling acquires during his early years is that of language, and his earliest memory associates its acquisition with the father. His ambivalence towards language can perhaps be traced to that earliest memory. What he values most in language is its ability to reduce, to transcend, to control and to transform mere reality – in short, its ability to order chaos. His earliest recollections about language are of its charms of consolation and salvation. Later he will find in language an instrument of power. Among his early memories of Indian childhood is one of terror neutralized by the magic of language: while walking to his father's School of Art, the child passes what he describes as "the edge of a huge ravine a foot deep, where a winged monster as big as myself attacked me, and I fled and wept" (*SM* 5–6). But he is completely consoled once his father draws him a picture of the tragedy with the following rhyme beneath:

> There was a small boy in Bombay
> Who once from a hen ran away.
> When they said: "You're a baby,"
> He replied: "Well, I may be:
> But I don't like these hens of Bombay."   (*SM* 6)

The simple empiricism of the father's rhyme opposes the perceived abyss of the child's anxiety and compels a split between wordless terror and the mechanical rhythms soon to become his apparatus of defense. Weeping in flight from threatening Others will be repressed and later Orientalized in Indian stories and poems. But the rhythms and the simple, accessible and consoling sentiments of this early limerick will grow into the jingling rhymes of such memorable adult poems as "If" in which the test of manhood is the ability to transcend and survive the horror of life as a pit of unending trial and torment, deceit and loss.

Once the young Kipling is abandoned in the House of Desolation, language in the form of books becomes a defense against his tormentors (who deny him, in one of their varied punishments, the pleasure of reading) and a lifesaving connection that links him to his lost parents. Rescued by his mother at the age of twelve he is delighted to find that she writes verses, that his father wrote "other things," and that "books and pictures were among the most important affairs in the world" (*SM* 22). In the child's unconscious mind, the comfort of language serves, not only as defense, but as partial compensation for the loss of a primal family. Writing subsequently will become the means by which he tries to control the chaos of experience and defend himself against any further varieties of self-loss.

If in childhood he learns defensive wariness as emotional protection, in school he learns to value the ways in which others transform detachment into art, and to admire the ways in which his instructors and friends use language as armament. His favorite instructor, his English and Classics master, has the "gift of schoolmaster's 'sarcasm' which must have been a relief to him and was certainly a treasure-trove to me... Under him I came to feel that words could be used as weapons" (*SM* 36). The art of writing as he learns it from his headmaster is précis-writing, which "meant severe compression of dry-as-dust material, no essential fact to be omitted" (*SM* 41). Writing becomes a tool, an instrument, a machine to control, compress and digest what is most indigestible in his environment: "Here Crom Price's training in *précis*-work helped me get swiftly at what meat there might be in the disorderly messes" (*SM* 54). His admiration for one of his closest friends is based on his impersonality, his "invincible detachment," and his command over situations through distance and language:

I think it was his infernal impersonality that swayed us all in our wars and peace. He saw not only us but himself from the outside, and in later life, as we met in India and elsewhere, the gift persisted. At long last, when with an equipment of doubtful Ford cars and a collection of most-mixed troops, he put up a monumental bluff against the Bolsheviks somewhere in Armenia (it is written in his *Adventures of Dunsterforce*) and was nearly as possible destroyed, he wrote to the authorities responsible. (*SM* 30–2)

What this recollection reveals is the analogy Kipling draws between verbal, emotional and military defense. It also reminds us of the attractiveness of seeing "from the outside" which is not only a mark of the frame tale and its detached narrator, but a sign of Kipling's recurring terror of being on the inside – engulfed and vulnerable to the darkness of enclosure.

Uncontrollable emotions, groundless fears and nameless anxieties – as with political Others – can be contained and colonized. He learns in his adolescent years to enclose and to frame his hatreds as if that might control them: "I bought a fat, American cloth-bound note-book, and set to work on an Inferno, into which I put, under appropriate torture, all my friends and most of the masters" (*SM* 38). The idiosyncratic terseness occasionally detected in Kipling's style may, in this context, be read ideologically as an extension of his fascination with mechanical defense, a deliberate blindness or resistance to human, social and linguistic flexibility. That resistance reveals itself at times in mechanical fictional characters who "like soldiers on parade ... wear a fixed set of idiosyncrasies like a uniform" (Dixon Scott, quoted in Wilson 1978: 124); it is also apparent in his description of language that uses the vocabulary of imperialism and warfare to colonize with precision the chaos of imprecise words. Kipling's language shares with other colonial literature what David Spurr has called "discourse as an arsenal, with weapons of varying degrees of sophistication ... employed either in a progressive escalation against the objects of anxiety, or all at once" (Spurr 1985: 45).

Kipling's ambivalence towards language is grounded in the gap between the imaginary unified childlike safety that needed no words and the fractured adult world of society's inexplicable threats that required the acquisition of a vocabulary of defense. He recalls his reconciliations with his four-square coterie (his family) made up of himself, his sister and his parents in idealized metaphors of an unbroken, totally satisfying, almost oceanic, Imaginary unity violated only by separation and Others: "I do not remember the smallest friction in any detail of our lives. We delighted more in each other's society than in that of strangers; and when my sister came out, a little later, our cup was filled to the brim ... " (*SM* 46). "My Father with his sage Yorkshire outlook and wisdom; my Mother, all Celt and three-parts fire – both so entirely comprehending that except in trivial matters we had hardly need of words. I think I can with truth say that those two made for me the only public for whom then I had any regard whatever till their deaths, in my forty-fifth year" (*SM* 97). This illusion of safety and power within the small group feeds his alternate need to protect himself mentally and emotionally from Others and allows him to negotiate formal and social spaces between object and subject, and between the self and Other.

Kipling's habit of framing and of using language as defense against fear creates a singularly circular and delayed approach to certain representatively lurid and gruesome memories. In the apparently cheerful context of passages describing his return to England and his proud initiation to British clubs, he gives a curiously deadpan account of a man cutting his own throat. Although disturbances in Kipling's memory are consciously willed into oblivion, they are in fact repressed and marginalized for disguised recovery in fiction.

When the fog thinned, I looked out and saw a man standing opposite the pub where the barmaid lived. Of a sudden his breast turned dull red like a robin's, and he crumpled, having cut his throat … A pot-boy with a bucket of steaming water sluiced the blood off into the gutter, and what little crowd had collected went its way. (*SM* 94–5)

This sequence of observations – a moment of violence followed by cleansing and ironic closure – is characteristic of Kipling's defensive vision. The visual cleansing of the concluding line is partly a metonymic counterpart to Kipling's selectively detached and anti-septic social perception, and partly a way of defusing the emotional impact of the occasion. The epistemological bind into which he weaves himself is evident in his concluding comments on this incident – a curious criticism of the pious British householder who bores his way back from theatres " through all this sifting, shouting brotheldom … eyes-front and fixed, as though not seeing" (*SM* 95). Clearly the British householder and Kipling have been taught the same arts of indirection, schoolboy cynicism and ironic defensiveness which leads to adult evasion of painful social and emotional realities. The dramatic recollection itself is doubly framed, first within narrative recollections of the twin securities of club and family, and then within the dreamlike matrix of the entire chapter:

in the autumn of '89, I stepped into a sort of waking dream when I took, as a matter of course, the fantastic cards that Fate was pleased to deal me. (*SM* 85)
…
that period was all as I have said, a dream, in which it seemed that I could push down walls, walk through ramparts and stride across rivers … (*SM* 94)

This fragmentation of memory into dream experience and concrete happenings, into distancing impressionism and focused realism, into the safety of club and family and the exaggerated dangers of the outside world, reenforces Kipling's splitting of his identity into active participant and passive observer, the wise, controlling autobio-graphical narrator and the innocent autobiographical protagonist. If his earliest recollection of language has involved the split between the father's poem and the boy's wordless abyss, the acquisition of language for the boy-writer-autobiographer is a form of entry into fatherhood and internalizing into his own identity those early splittings between the word and the wordless; the paradox of becoming one's own father is analogous to being one's own autobiographer – an act that necessitates writing after one's own death.

MEMORY AS ORIENTALIZER

Just as Kipling managed the vicissitudes of his past by containing and releasing them in the language of defense and in the distance of frames, so his deepest anxieties are displaced onto dream, fiction and India. This displacement is an "Orientalizing" act: ideological dualisms map on to splittings in the child's development; both the unconscious and the colonized landscape of India become (to use Said's description of the Orient) "less a place than a *topos*, a set of references, a congerie of characteristics" (1979: 177) whose origins, because infantile and unclear, suggest a space that needs restructuring and domination. That displacement keeps working/daytime life and England clean, and Orientalizes dirt and chaos onto India: "Now, this is the road that the White Men tread / When they go to clean a land – " ("A Song of the White Men"). If the metaphors that shape and give meaning to Kipling's life and art are to be traced to his memory of earliest childhood – and the form of the narrative appears to privilege that time over later years – then his memory of that time must contain the filters through which the mind organizes its disturbances. Although those first six years appear to have been idyllic years in a warm secure haven of "light and colour and golden and purple fruit," of stories, songs, music and art, India nonetheless is remembered not in terms of wholeness but of division. Only the first paragraph of the memoir is free from the deliberate imposition of opposites that will in later years accumulate ideological values. The second paragraph begins to construct a pattern of perception that underlies his memoir, a sinister underside to his Eden that he imposes in retrospect, disguised so that the pattern beneath the representation is exposed as in a palimpsest or dream. Early childhood walks by the sea in the shadow of palm-groves are reread by the aged writer in terms of safety and threat: "When the wind blew the great huts would tumble, and we fled – my ayah and my sister in her perambulator – to the safety of the open. I have always felt the menacing darkness of tropical eventides, as I have loved the voices of night winds through palm … "(*SM* 4). Even his "little house on the

Bombay esplanade" is not free from the menace of memory as he now chooses to insert what he then did not know, that next to their house were "the Towers of Silence" where the Parsees exposed their dead "to the waiting vultures on the rim of the towers, who scuffle and spread wings when they see the bearers of the Dead below" (*SM* 4). He recalls his mother's distress at finding a dead child's hand in their garden and her anxious secrecy and warning that he not ask questions about it, followed by his own determined curiosity: "I wanted to see that child's hand" (*SM* 4).

Death – the Towers of Silence, the death of a child, dismemberment and mutilation – haunts both by its presence and by its loud absence. The seventy-year old man recalling his blissful childhood and yet recording images of death is obliquely grafting onto his own childhood the silent and otherwise unmentioned deaths in his life which will metonymically be associated with India. In a way the child Rudyard died when he was exiled at the age of six from his Indian Eden ("those days of strong light" [*SM* 6]) to England ("a dark land, and a darker room full of cold" [*SM* 6]). That first death was followed by many more painful ones – the death of the kind captain who was his only refuge during the years at Southsea, the later deaths of unsuspecting Englishmen in India, the devastating loss of his friend Wolcott Balestier, and most painfully, the deaths of his children – Josephine, his "best-beloved," and his son John. The dead child's hand in the shadow of the Towers of Silence speaks not only for all the fragmentation and loss about which Kipling is most silent, but reemerges in other poignant images of hands in Kipling's fiction: the shocking vision of Bisesa's stumps where her hands used to be – her punishment for violating a law – in "Beyond the Pale" (1888); the touch of the dead child's fingers followed by its kiss on the narrator's palm in "'They'" – the "fragment of a mute code devised very long ago" that reveals simultaneously to the narrator and the reader that the hidden child is the protagonist's own dead daughter; and the crucified hands of Peachey Carnehan in "The Man Who Would Be King." As a frozen moment in time, the tableau of the child's hand in the garden also comments on the silence of men and gods who distantly watch the slaughter of innocents.

Most telling in this context of displacement or psychological Orientalism is a memory that Kipling transposes onto India so that his earliest recollections of death are connected not with England but with India. He tells us of a night when mother comes home from one of her many "Big Dinners" to tell him that "'the big Lord Sahib' had been killed ... This was Lord Mayo, assassinated by a native" (*SM* 5). Angus Wilson, however, tells us that Lord Mayo was killed while Rudyard was in England with his mother during the birth of a second child (1979:16). The autobiographical displacement of the killing Orientalizes the violence and prepares the reader for the dislocation that occurs in Kipling's life as he reverses the hierarchical oppositions of his childhood when dark and desolate England stood in the cold margins of a loving and warm Mother India.

The place that was the source of his fear of the unknown (which he displaced onto India), of the contradictions that energized his art, and of his later allegiance to order, control, hierarchy and empire, was the House of Desolation which Kipling was to call "Hell in all its terrors" (*SM* 8). The traumas in this house forever isolated him from security and from England; yet at the same time bonded him to what had been most repellent to him then – authority and discipline. The metaphors that emerge out of this period of deprivation and despair are not only those of terrifying enclosures which get displaced into the many pits, ravines and death traps of his early stories ("The Strange Ride of Morrowbie Jukes," "At the Pit's Mouth," "The Man Who Would be King," "Little Tobrah"), but also that ultimate of all enclosures, blindness. Unable to understand the "calculated torture" to which he is subjected daily, the boy finds his nightmare world intensified first by encroaching blindness and then by a "sort of nervous breakdown" in which he imagines "shadows and things that were not there" (*SM* 19). Blindness here and in his fiction serves as a complex and overdetermined symbol with contradictory meanings. On its regressive level it represents the horrors of absence, helplessness and vulnerability and the loss of mastery and control over the infantile self, or the subject in need of colonization. And it haunts him ever after in the dream image of the blind child that cries and cannot wipe its eyes ("La Nuit Blanche" 1886, "At the End of the Passage" 1891). On its adult level (most clearly seen in *The Light that Failed*) it reflects a larger myopia, a denial of reality, and a fear of the irrational. The breakdowns of sight and mind are displaced in his fiction onto the threat of India. In *Kim* senses are split between the English and the Indian, with the lama as a stereotypical example of the Oriental whose inadequate senses require the protection of the English who are given control of sight. The curator gives the lama a gift of glasses, and Kim serves as the lama's eyes.

Hysterical blindness in real life and symbolic blindness in art have their formal counterpart in Kipling's obsessions with boundaries and frames: both are means to evade and transcend a particularly painful objective reality. As with insanity, blindness in his fiction and autobiography serves as an extension of "splitting the ego in the process of defense" (Freud 1964: 23), a way to avoid confrontation with problems of identity and its uncertainty, of power and its dispossession. The child Kipling had literally been marginalized and dispossessed of all he once owned by those in whom he placed the greatest trust – his parents. The defenses the boy learns during these years are designed to combat vulnerability to such human and cosmic uncertainty. Those who fail to learn the lessons of necessary blindness, who actually *see* into the heart of colonialist darkness go mad, commit suicide, or simply die as in "At the End of the Passage," "To be Filed for Reference," or "Thrown Away." Those who remain content with partial vision and see from the margins of frames become ironically detached narrators who have long since learned the lessons of survival, distance and reticence. Yet Kipling distrusts Englishmen who stride brashly through chaos, and knows that what is perceptible to sight is often a fraction of that which lies beneath the surface in the dark ("I do not know what proportion of an iceberg is below water-line... " *SM* 149). The ambivalence of Kipling's preoccupation with perception is most marked in his last chapter, "Working-Tools," where he half-heartedly admits to powers of extrasensory perception, a confession he immediately retracts: "But there is no need to drag in the 'clairvoyance,' or the rest of the modern jargon. I have seen too much evil and sorrow and wreck of good minds on the road to Endor to take one step along that perilous track" (*SM* 232). He recalls a dream that later reenacted itself in waking life, but does not pursue the larger question of "how, and why, had I been shown an unreleased roll of my life-film" (*SM* 233).

THE INVASION OF THE MARGINS

If, in early childhood, dark England stands in the margins of bright India, in adolescence, the reverse becomes true, and this initial displacement, added to the earlier mechanisms of splitting, repression and the return of the repressed, creates his particular version of the ambivalent colonial personality. Kipling's fear of the unconscious and of the repressed is analogous to those unexpected moments of threatening unpredictability in his memoirs when the things he has denied or marginalized return from the repressed to haunt him. As a child, his fragile and youthful sense of self as whole and invulnerable is threatened by images and stories of violence and death. His acquired and exaggerated sense of unified identity is assaulted throughout youth and adulthood by internal and external fears, which, though displaced and repressed, return to him in dreams, in the inevitability of certain patterns of repeated events, and most inventively in fiction.

Kipling's acquired apparatus of defense is subjected to repeated assaults from what appear to be scenes from the past, even as his body is invaded by his Indian past: "my health cracked again ... when all my Indian microbes joined hands and sang for a month in the darkness of Villiers Street" (*SM* 101). His journeys of apparent adventure outward spiral around an intense core of nostalgia for a center and a "real home"(*SM* 112). The original passage away from childhood's India and the return at sixteen is followed by a furious and compulsive need to travel by ship from land to land – repeated journeys from India to England, Japan, America, Canada, South Africa, New Zealand and Australia – as if each journey were a new beginning and would, through repetition and framing, conquer the fear of his first and devastating journey into exile.

Travel serves a dual function for Kipling: it is a means to define the self against Others, a way to see, experience and constitute a new sense of self. But it is also a way to empower the self against the past. And each new country exiles him in some way that repeats the first expulsion from his childhood Eden: he leaves Japan after the abrupt and humiliating end to his honeymoon when the banks suddenly declare bankruptcy. He hopes for a while that America (Vermont in particular) will be his permanent home. But his alternate swings of love for American ideals of work and creative freedom and of rage at American lawlessness and politics suggest that it had indeed become another charged and metaphoric home in more ways than one. Although it is still an unbroken colt, it has not yet learned to build defenses against the moral barbarians within and without. America, like South Africa, replicates familiar splittings, denials and divisions, replays some of the worst aspects of colonialism in the guise of moral rectitude: "Every nation, like every individual, walks in a vain show – else it could not live with itself – but I never got over the wonder of a people who, having extirpated the aboriginals of their continent more completely than any modern race had ever done, honestly believed that they were a godly little New England community, setting examples to brutal mankind" (*SM* 133). But a comment like this also suggests Kipling's awareness of the social construction of that imagined community that is the self and its nation, of the proximity of the civilized and the savage within, and of the analogy between ontogeny and phylogeny.

No matter how hard Kipling tries to establish himself in the center of accepted colonial life in India, nightmare is only a dream away. In spite of his family, his club, his success at newspaper work, and his acceptance (though he was under age) into the Freemason's "Lodge," nighttime sleep was a torturous impossibility: "Often the night got into my head as it had done in the boarding-house in the Brompton Road, and I would wander till dawn in all manner of odd places – liquor-shops, gambling and opium-dens ... in and about the narrow gullies under the Mosque of Wazir Khan for the sheer sake of looking" (*SM* 59). His memories about his return to India at the age of sixteen not only intensify the splittings in his already divided life, but announce separations and boundaries between the center and the margins. The margins are his night world and the Indian world of death, disease and chaos, but "as regarding ourselves at home, if there were any dying to be done, we four were together. The rest was in the day's work, with love to sweeten all things" (*SM* 47).

Kipling's insistence on home with its creativity, order and rationality as the desired center necessarily marginalizes all things "Other" as native, fearsome and uncontrollable. But, as his fiction and autobiography suggest, those less valued and repressed experiences, parenthetically enclosed in half-phrases, or as mechanical parts of long lists, return repeatedly to energize, invade and inspire both memory and fiction. So too with the polarized world he describes in India. Although he tells us that "This was the setting in which my world revolved. Its centre for me – a member at seventeen – was the Punjab Club" (*SM* 48), the previous paragraph has told us something far more vivid about the setting that this paragraph appears designed to repress. Beneath the witty descriptions of meals, alcoholic proofreaders, and other curious types of men he meets at the club, lies the nightmare of his marginalized world. The preceding paragraph has told us that the present is like a ghostly palimpsest over the past:

LEEDS METROPOLITAN
UNIVERSITY
LIBRARY

The dead of all times were about us – in the vast forgotten Moslem cemeteries round the Station, where one's horse's hoof of a morning might break through to the corpse below; skulls and bones tumbled out of our mud garden walls, and were turned up among the flowers by the Rains; and at every point were tombs of the dead. Our chief picnic rendezvous and some of our public offices had been memorials to desired dead women; and Fort Lahore where Runjit Singh's wives lay, was a mausoleum of ghosts. (*SM* 48)

A surrealist's image of perpetually collapsing landscape against which the Englishman's civilized garden walls, flowers, picnics and forts can offer no resistance, this colonialist double vision also informs those terrifying early stories, "The Strange Ride of Morrowbie Jukes" (1885) and "The City of Dreadful Night" (1885). It is therefore no wonder that such a paragraph must be immediately followed and censored by what Kipling loudly declares to be the true center around which his world revolves – the Punjab Club.

Kipling's masterplot (to use Peter Brooks' term) in this autobiography involves both the undesirable and the desirable ways of coping with returns of the repressed fear of loss and exile. Both involve repetition though only the second involves what Brooks after Freud calls a "binding" of anxieties that need to be mastered (1984: 101). The "undesirable" is evident in the nervous rigidity with which he skirts painful choices, beliefs and events, and his occasional retreat behind a facile conservatism. The "desirable" is of course those aspects of memory that lead to creativity. And these are many and always delightfully surprising.

Creativity for Kipling came in work, especially the building of houses, and in writing, which was always pleasure. His obsession with his original lost home is apparent in repeated journeys to "the only real home I had yet known" (*SM* 112) wherever that might be. His wanderings around the globe always take him to the homes of others that he idealizes, calls "Paradise" (*SM* 179), and whose descriptions include strong colors and scents that remind the reader of Kipling's earliest memories of Edenic India. Because he felt a perpetual exile, he persistently searched to find or to build the ideal shelter, "a house of their own – a real House in which to settle down for keeps" (*SM* 191). And chapter 7 is appropriately titled "The Very-Own House." He and his wife move from Bliss Cottage in Vermont where they were "extraordinarily and self-centeredly content" (*SM* 119) to a house they build on a ten-acre field that they call the "Naulakha" (misspelled, so Pinney [1990] tells us, in the novel and the first edition

of the autobiography as "naulahka.") But after another journey, they
decide that Naulakha, "desirable as it was, meant only 'a house' and
not 'The House' of our dreams" (*SM* 142) whereupon they leave for
England and buy a large, bright house in Torquay. In spite of its
apparent suitability, the house in Torquay inflicts upon them the
bleakest depression, which Kipling attributes to "the Feng-Shui –
the Spirit of the house itself – that darkened the sunshine and fell
upon us every time we entered, checking the very words on our
lips" (*SM* 143). They subsequently flee its "Spirit of deep, deep
Despondency." After several other houses in between, they finally
settle at Bateman's, the ultimate house at whose first glimpse they
cry: "That's her! The Only She! Make an honest woman of her –
quick!" (*SM* 193). The house in his autobiography is an ambivalent
maternal shelter that protects and isolates, and that contains,
threatens, expels, and saves. The image surfaces in many of his
stories, most memorably in "'They,'" "The Brushwood Boy," and
"The House Surgeon."

Kipling's attitudes towards writing are marked by a characteristic
rhetoric of opposition, and by the construction of a self split between
control and its lack. On the one hand he sees it as a craft created by
training in précis-work, careful editing, and diligent but mechanical
experimenting "in the weights, colours, perfumes, and attributes of
words in relation to other words" (*SM* 78). On the other he sees
writing as an irrational activity governed by a Daemon. The very
title of his last chapter (8), "Working-Tools," appears to disguise his
focus on the importance of his personal "Daemon," and the
unconscious inspiration beneath the mechanical authority of the
craft. Before confessing its revelatory importance in his writing life, he
approaches the subject from a tangent:

Let us now consider the Personal Daemon of Aristotle and others, of whom
it has been truthfully written, though not published: –

> This is the doom of the Makers – their Daemon lives in their pen.
> If he be absent or sleeping, they are even as other men.
> But if he be utterly present, and they swerve not from his behest,
> The word that he gives shall continue, whether in earnest or jest.

(*SM* 225)

The chapter characteristically oscillates between dream and
reality, the actuality of psychic experiences immediately undercut by
Kipling's own disbelief; it also acknowledges the return of submerged

moments and images from the past that find their way into his fiction, though, of course, he does that occasionally throughout the auto-biography. On one of his many sea journeys (recalled in chapter 5), for instance, his steamer "came almost atop of a whale, who submerged just in time to clear us, and looked up into my face with an unforgettable little eye the size of a bullock's" (*SM* 138). When illustrating the *Just So Stories*, he remembers and strives after that eye (*SM* 138). In Auckland (New Zealand), he hears a petty officer telling of a woman who "never scrupled to help a lame duck or put her foot on a scorpion" (*SM* 109), and "those words gave me the key to the face and voice at Auckland, and a tale called 'Mrs. Bathurst' slid into my mind, smoothly and orderly as floating timber on a bank-high river" (*SM* 109). He admits the absence of conscious mastery in the creation of his best tales, but his very awareness of that suggests the presence of an unconscious momentum that leads to the ultimate pleasure of creativity ("Mercifully, the mere act of writing was, and always has been, a physical pleasure to me" [*SM* 223]). He tells us that early ideas of writing tracts on the education of the young "for reasons honestly beyond my control, turned themselves into a series of tales called *Stalky & Co*" (*SM* 144); that at the Paris Exhibition in 1878 (when he was twelve years old) he saw and never forgot a picture of the death of Manon Lescaut and theorizes "that a germ lay dormant till my change of life to London ... woke it up, and that *The Light That Failed* was a sort of inverted, metagrobilised phan-tasmagoria based on Manon" (*SM* 244); that *Kim* simply came to him and grew "like the Djinn released from the brass bottle" (*SM* 149). That Djinn is of course a version of his personal Daemon who speaks to him, directs his hand towards certain solutions, and tells him when to stop a tale. His Daemon is with him in his finest works, in the *Jungle Books*, *Kim*, and both Puck books "and good care I took to walk delicately, lest he should withdraw" (*SM* 227). And in this same last chapter "Working-Tools," he warns: "*Note here*. When your Daemon is in charge, do not try to think consciously. Drift, wait, and obey" (*SM* 227).

This split between conscious and unconscious control of his art extends into the metaphor he uses to describe his ultimate and unrealized work of art – that of a three-decker ship on an ocean:

I dreamed for many years of building a veritable three-decker out of chosen and long-stored timber-teak, green-heart, and ten-year-old oak knees – each curve melting deliciously into the next that the sea might nowhere meet resistance or weakness; the whole suggesting motion even when, her great sails for the moment furled, she lay in some needed haven – a vessel ballasted on ingots of pure research and knowledge, roomy, fitted with delicate cabinet-work below-decks, painted, carved, gilt and wreathed the length of her, from her blazing stern-galleries outlined by bronzy palm-trunks, to her rampant figure-head – an East India man worthy to lie alongside *The Cloister and the Hearth*. (*SM* 245)

The image of a carefully structured and furnished ship to describe the ideal fiction recalls his privileged use of other orderly structures (like empire) that control, protect, and contain disorderly structures (like India) that ironically sustain it. In the relationship he imagined between ship and sea, specifically in the hope that "the sea might nowhere meet resistance or weakness," we can see his awareness that conscious mechanisms of art rely on unconscious structures. Too much resistance to the sea would represent Kipling at his weakest, so absorbed in his craft that his art becomes mechanical. Kipling's art, like all art, lies in the interplay between sea and ship, between the unconscious and the form that functions sometimes as defense against and sometimes as an expression of that unconscious.

Examined further, the image of the ship lends itself to under-standing the metaphoric construction of self and culture in Kipling. Like other obsessively recurring images (houses and sight) in his narrative, the ship is an overdetermined symbol because it involves a conflict between two opposing functions (Ricoeur 1970: 496). On the level of regression, and in the context of his autobiography, the image is yet another return of the repressed infancy in which the ship was the instrument of his loss, his fall, and his years of exile and wandering in search of some original lost home. That nonrational, painful level of the symbol, concealed and denied because of its matrix of fear and anguish, is opposed by the adult and rationalized status of the symbol, by his recognition of the ship as symbol of order, control, art and civilization, and as a construct that masters the sea. The dialectics that control the formation of this metaphor are analogous to those that control Kipling's attitudes towards power and op-pression. That which is to be most feared will be associated with the "imaginary" and the infantile, will therefore be repressed, and will return to haunt his memory and his fiction.

In fiction Kipling displaced onto India what he feared in his dreams, and displaced onto his dreams what he most feared in India. In his autobiography, the darkness early associated with England is later reassociated with a skull-infested deathly India that in turn is a projection of colonialist ideology and of a self-conscious, deeply divided mind terrified of its own interiors. If India becomes for Kipling a recurring image of the alien Other that needs (like language and the unconscious) to be controlled, ordered, ruled and colonized, that need is in part a displacement of an even less acknowledged inner need for definition, boundaries, control and order. Kipling's humanity is defined and energized by this ongoing tension between the wish to order and limit, to manage his catastrophes by remembering them through distanced and detached voices, and the reality of the other Kipling who cannot manage or defuse pain and anxiety. The problems of defining and editing his own unconscious, of wishing for permanence while practicing colonial adventure, are somewhat analogous to the tensions expressed by the dreamers of empire who also wished for a hegemony beyond the grasp of the realities of the self-contained nation-state.

In its need to build a mythology of self, writing becomes for Kipling a sort of empire building – a process of expansion and reterritorialization. And if we consider the relationship of auto-biography to self-control as analogous to that of colonialism to world politics, Kipling's fiction will further reflect the complexity of positions framed by the private and the political, by the illusion of an indefinitely expanding empire and by the real boundaries necessary to the political functioning of the nation-state.

In "Working-Tools," Kipling suggests that his sister's mental breakdown was the result of tampering with spiritualism and with the occult: "There is a type of mind that dives in after what it calls 'psychical experiences'... " (*SM* 232), but that "road to Endor" is one from which wisdom restrains Kipling. The unwillingness to "dive in" reminds us not only of Kipling's controlling metaphor of restrained limitation, but of the cultural implications of that geographical and spatial metaphor – of dark hidden centers that are at once intolerable, irrational and destructive. The analogy between the secret and dangerous darkness within the mind and the geographic and threatening darkness of the uncolonized world is part of the underlying philosophical structure that sanctioned the conquest of the earth. Thus, for Kipling as for colonial ideology, journeys into psychic interiors or into alien cultural or political interiors suggest the desperation of his need to control the un-controllable, and to confront in writing the troubling contradictions and necessary failures of efforts to govern the self and its empires.

CHAPTER 3

The problem of otherness: a hundred sorrows

When Kipling returned to India in October 1882, he was not yet seventeen years old. Allan Octavian Hume (then fifty-three) had just begun a temporary retirement at Simla, Lord Ripon was the Viceroy appointed by the Liberal Prime Minister Gladstone, and the Ilbert Bill (1883), which allowed native judges to preside over European subjects, had not yet scandalized Anglo-India. A year later, when the *Civil and Military Gazette*'s editorial seemed to support the Ilbert Bill, the members of the Punjab Club hissed at the bewildered young Rudyard as he entered the club dining halls (Birkenhead 1978: 79; Wilson 1979: 107). Kipling, however, was not then nor was he later a public supporter of "liberal" reforms in India. Alternately exhilarated and frustrated, divided between allegiances to home, work, and nighttime Lahore, Kipling spent the next seven years as reporter and writer first for the *Civil and Military Gazette* in Lahore and later for the *Pioneer* in Allahabad. He used the fortress of his family, cherished and idealized as his "Foursquare," as a retreat from the turbulent outside world where "parboiled," fevered and sleepless he worked over sweat-drenched typewriters. But his nightly insomnia also produced fertile wanderings through the alleys of Lahore that in turn provoked his earliest stories told by narrators who had access to both Indian worlds.

His nighttown narrators appropriated stories of the Other, and sometimes the voice of the Other – a strategy that necessarily reminds us of the larger appropriations of European imperialism – but with a difference. Kipling's narrator sometimes enters into a dialogue with the native and the native storyteller and thus attempts to bridge the gap between the colonizer and the colonized through language and the collapse of radical difference into common materiality. The problem of the Other in Kipling is therefore not a simple alterity outside the self because, as Lacan teaches us, the Other is the first

48

object of his desire (*Ecrits*, p. 264 quoted in Weber 1991: 129). Like all other European knowledge of human society and the construction of history itself, Kipling's dominant stance is often from the vantage point of a Western eye that stereotypes, categorizes, and universalizes absolute knowledge about the Orient and its Orientals. But he also sees the West from the vantage point of the internalized Other, the underground Indian child who is always and unavoidably within him.

Thomas Pinney's introduction to his fine collection of Kipling's early newspaper sketches draws attention to two different ways Kipling had of looking at India. He calls the first "the Official View, essentially paternalistic and administrative and not different from what one might suppose any responsible and mildly progressive Indian civil servant to have held" (1986: 18); the other view, "more personal and humane," surveys "the Indian scene delighting in its variety and copiousness, and responding to the individuality of its people" (p. 22). What strikes me in the sketches is their lack of an anxiety that seems to have been saved for his fiction. It was Noel Annan who first (I think) zeroed into what marked Kipling's early volumes of stories – the picture "of a society which politically, nervously, physically, and spiritually quivered on the edge of a precipice" (in Rutherford 1964: 102). That precipice was in part the result of the contradictory packaging of post-Mutiny reassessment of the real, rather than imagined, relationship between the government and the people of India.[1] In part, if we wish to use Lacan's terms, anxiety is a means to approach a lack, a continual and "perpetual loss." Or, anxiety may be related to the lack that is entrapment or "confinement" "(*Angst*, from *Enge*: narrow), to 'lack,' if you will, but above all, to a lack of *breath*. Anxiety is perhaps what one feels when the world reveals itself to be caught up in the space between two frames: a doubled frame, or one that is split, who can tell?" (Weber 1991: 167).

It is often the anxiety of the marginal, repressed voice and the unsaid in Kipling's newspaper sketches and stories that energizes them; and what he leaves unsaid concerns the turbulent politics of the 1880s. By 1883 Hume had once again begun agitating for native rights and for a parliamentary government. To achieve this he wrote letters to every graduate of Calcutta University asking for "fifty volunteers to begin a movement for the regeneration of their country: 'There are aliens like myself,' he wrote, 'who love India and her

children... but the real work must be done by the people of the
country themselves'" (Moorhouse 1983: 198; Majumdar 1965:
529). 1884 was the year that Lord Ripon acknowledged to Lord
Kimberly (the Secretary of State for India) that the most important
problem in British India was the emergence of a new class of Western
educated Indians (Martin 1969: 1,15ff). It was the failure of the
Ilbert Bill that provoked educated Indians into acknowledging the
inadequacy of kind intention to secure results in spite of the
intercession of such caring and committed English officials as Allan
Octavian Hume. A remarkable character who could have been
invented by Kipling but was instead significantly ignored by him,
Hume was a controversial figure trusted by both educated Indians
and English officials until his ideas for Indian reform grew too
radical, and, troubled by his failures on behalf of the natives, he broke
ranks with the British through personal service to Indians and finally
through a retreat into mysticism (Martin 53–78). Hume's pamphlets
in the 1880's brought upon him the wrath of officials who thought he
aimed at becoming "the Indian Parnell" (Martin 321). (Kipling
had also been accused by the English of consorting too closely with
the natives.) But Hume's commitment to the cause, which galvanized
Indian resistance and the leadership of W. C. Bonnerjee, G. S. Iyer
and P. Mehta among others, resulted in the first Indian National
Conference (1883) and (during the years of Kipling's earliest stories,
1884–5) the birth of the Indian National Congress.

Kipling's early fiction records his struggle with representing the
voices and landscape of India at a time when the bureaucracy at
Simla and state repression were so severe that officials feared an
unprecedented cross-class revolutionary outbreak (Majumdar 1965:
531; Wedderburn 1913: 101). If Kipling's Indian fiction ignores the
realities of the rise of Indian Nationalism and the existence of men
like Hume, it refracts its material reality and helps construct (as
Wurgaft and others suggest) the ways in which Colonial India saw
itself. And for that, Kipling is a creator of history – not merely a
"parasitic reflector of historical fact" but rather part of a "complex
textualized universe in which literature participates in historical
processes and in the political management of reality" (Howard 1986:
25). Kipling's India was at once the land of the Other and of "Mine
Own People," the source and subject of his inspiration and the object
for mediation. For Kipling (to paraphrase Bakhtin) India was a
multiplicity of conflicting, contending languages whose meaning

could only be understood in the context of its dialogic and untidy relationship to its many social communities. To his friend and editor, Kay Robinson, he writes:

> Would you be astonished if I told you that I look forward to nothing but an Indian journalist's career? Why should I? my home's out here; my people are out here; all the friends I know are out here and all the interests I have are out here. Why should I go home? ... I am deeply interested in the queer ways and works of the people of the land. I hunt and rummage among 'em; knowing Lahore City – that wonderful, dirty mysterious anthill – blindfold and wandering through it like Haroun-al-Raschid in search of strange things... I'm in love with the country and would sooner write about her than anything else. Wherefore let us depart our several ways in amity. You to Fleet Street (where I shall come when I die if I'm good) and I to my own place where I find heat and smells of oil and spices, and puffs of temple incense, and sweat, and darkness, and dirt and lust and cruelty, and, above all, things wonderful and fascinating innumerable. (*KP* 17/25: April 30, 1886)

The split here between the "I" who hunts, rummages in and loves the physical India and the "you" who departs for Fleet Street reflects, more than epistolary convention, Kipling's division between his Indian night self that had to be abandoned on the streets of India and his English day self that in fact did depart eventually for Fleet Street. But the strength of the letter-writer's voice reflects the strength of his resistance to the Fleet Street self, which, refusing to be silenced, haunted the voices of his other narrators – and sometimes his other, narrower, writerly self that judges and categorizes Indians as if they were specimens marked for the London Ethnological Society: "The main road teems with magnificent scoundrels and handsome ruffians; all giving the on-looker the impression of wild beasts held back from murder and violence, and chafing against the restraint. The impression *may* be wrong; and the Peshawari, the most innocent creature on earth, in spite of History's verdict against him; but not unless thin lips, scowling brows, deep set vulpine eyes and lineaments stamped with every brute passion known to man, go for nothing" ("The City of Evil Countenances," *CMG* April 1, 1885 in Pinney 1986: 84). So too, the languages of his characters and his narrators seem to live (as Bakhtin would say) "a tense life on the borders of someone else's thought, someone else's consciousness" (1973: 170), and as more recent theorists might add, always slipping out of the author's, the narrator's, and reader's urge to control, and

sliding towards doubt and self-contradiction. His characteristic
willingness to leave a story open, incomplete, and gasping for
resolution is precisely the mechanism that puts the reader into action,
that compels us into question and ambivalence, wondering where we
stop in the process of reading the story's schizophrenic splitting
between oppositional skepticism and imperial faith. His great
triumph, which he chooses to attribute to his "Personal Daemon," as
he remembers it over fifty years later, is the ability to "think in
another man's skin" (*SM* 209). That thought does not compel him
towards identification, but leaves him, his narrator, and his reader in
a dialogic relationship with the character, able to feel the par-
ticularity of the other's voice, yet distant enough to situate that voice
in a larger, multiple, and different cultural context.

The problem in reading Kipling (after we break away from
received ideas of his "absolute barbarism" and "Hooliganism") is
understanding the complexity of his attitude towards imperialism
and the unified individual subject as agent. In contrast to his family
back in England as representative of the metropolitan (Moore-
Gilbert's term) colonial mind, he mocks and fragments the idea of
either India or of colonial identity as fixed, while recognizing the
importance of fixity in imperial mythology – a contradiction registered in the two quotations from his letter and his newspaper sketch
above. So too, his authorial stance towards that Other is self-
conscious in its recognition of the narrator as constructed by a system
whose unitary racist voice he often mindlessly echoes. Yet that same
narrator leads us towards a diversity of cultural experience that is
frequently forbidden, dangerous, otherworldly or exotic. Kipling's
newspaper stories were wildly irreverent and diverse in their stance
towards colonial problems, reported in voices that ranged from the
clinically factual to the coy, playful, cynical, parodic and satiric. But
his letters written at the same time are less playful and more
thoughtfully didactic in their efforts to mediate English reactions to
India. To his cousin, Margaret Burne-Jones ("Wop"), he writes in
1885:

I do want you to understand Wop dear that, immediately outside of our own
English life, is the dark and crooked and fantastic and wicked and awe-
inspiring life of the "native." Our rule, so long as no one steals too flagrantly
or murders too openly, affects it in no way whatever – only fences it around
and prevents it from being disturbed ... My experiences of course are only a
queer jumble of opium dens, night houses, night strolls with natives;

evenings spent in their company in their own homes (in the men's quarter of course) and the long yarns that my native friends spin me, and one or two queer things I've come across in my own office experience. The result of it all has been to interest me immensely and keenly in the people and to show me how little an Englishman can hope to understand 'em. I would that you could see some of the chapters of Mother Maturin and you would follow more plainly what I mean. (KP F3: Nov 28, 1885).

Other sections of this letter juggle contemporary colonial clichés ("We spend our best men on the country like water and if ever a foreign country was made better though 'the blood of the martyrs' India is that country"), with a more disturbed awareness of the effect of Imperialism on Indian agency: "If anything goes wrong from a quarrel to an accident the natives *instantly* fly to a European for 'orders.' If a man's dying in the road they won't touch him unless they have an Englishman to order 'em." In providing a sense of cultural context for his earliest stories, these passages also offer evidence of Kipling's paradoxical and plural relationship with an India which was at once an alien, "strange," and "queer" object, and a familiar, "wonderful," and beloved subject. The many voices that struggle against the efforts of the ironically singleminded Kipling narrator suggest the complexity of Kipling's intervention in colonial society.

Kipling's first four stories, written between 1884 and 1885 introduce us to the plurality of voices struggling to represent the colonial encounter with India. But more importantly they reinscribe ambivalence and anxiety as part of the defining discourse of colonialism and of the contradictions within it. They prepare us for his ubiquitous narrator whose attempts to impose an exaggeratedly monologic, recognizably official colonial stance on an embedded story creates the slippery and oppositional strategy that marks Kipling's work. That strategy also inevitably exposes in varying degrees the denied desire of the narrator. What interests me in these early stories, then, is first, Kipling's representation of the problem of knowing colonial India, and then, the resistances inscribed both in the narratorial voice and within the diversity of forbidden voices that, though mocked, judged or condemned by the authorial narrator, mediate the ambivalence of the colonizer's uncertainty towards the constitution of the self and the Other. Finally, I am interested in how these stories subvert and carnivalize official hierarchy. Bakhtin's theory of the carnival contrasts the official social order with the repressed disorder of subordinate festivity. The excess of carnival is specifically opposed to social discipline. My point is not that Kipling's tales are exactly Rabelaisian carnival, but that, like carnival, their excess and their transgression function in opposition to the desired imperial need for perpetual order and stability. Each of these early Kipling stories externalizes a fear of disorder, a transgression of social and individual control, a shocking encounter with a repressed and denied materiality that exposes the illusion of colonial order.

Kipling began his career as a writer of fiction with an odd story called "The Gate of the Hundred Sorrows," written during the summer of 1884 when, eighteen years old and alone in the family home in Lahore, he had taken drugs to relieve the stomach pains and sleeplessness with which he would be tormented for the rest of his life. A short dramatic monologue, it is significant because it introduces the Kipling narrator, certain habits of narrative, and key strategies that inform Kipling's later works. To begin with, we have split narration opposing the narrator who has survived and the narratee who has not. The distant and ironic narrator introduces the tale with a perfunctory frame: "My friend Gabral Misquitta, the half-caste, spoke it all between moonset and morning, six weeks before he died; and I took it down from his mouth as he answered my questions. So: – ." Misquitta's rambling, indeterminate narrative follows the contours of thought of a mind blasted by opium, living in the increasingly narrow and discarded borders of colonial life. He begins by describing "The Gate of the Hundred Sorrows," the opium den in which he lives, and Old Fung-Tching, who originally established the house, five years ago. Misquitta lives on the sixty rupees a month his aunt willed him. He dimly recalls the days when he had a job, "on a big timber-contract at Calcutta," making either three hundred or three hundred and fifty rupees a month, and remembers that he once had a "wife of sorts," who died of grief when he took to the "Black Smoke." He describes the ten original residents of the house, of whom only five remain: himself, a "Chinaman," a half-caste woman called the Memsahib, another Eurasian, and someone who may be Persian. He vaguely grumbles about how the services have deteriorated in the house since Fung-Tching died and his nephew Tsin-ling took over, and speculates about the order in which he and his four companions will die. "Well, it doesn't matter," he concludes. "Nothing matters much to me – only I wish Tsin-ling wouldn't put bran into the Black Smoke."

This early story, a sensational sketch of a bit of Indian lowlife, reflects his fascination with the fallen Other and the journalistic impulse in many of Kipling's early sketches for the *Civil and Military Gazette*. Its strategy of narrative recursion, by repeating the original act of narration, appears to turn a chaotic slice of life into narrative permanence and truth (see Spence 1987: 188–210). And this is but one of the many ways in which Kipling struggles to communicate the "truth" about fictional characters as well as the fictionality or incompleteness of real characters because all he will give us is a partial and incomplete glimpse of a colonial moment of inversion of hierarchy which he abandons without comment or closure.

The essential story, an embedded story, a "metanarration," or framed tale, will always signify the narrator's suppressed desire, will raise questions about the implications of his involvement in the lurid tale, and about the relationship between the self and the Other, between the narrator and his storytelling double who goes farther than the safe, rational and controlled narrator would dream of going – frequently over a literal or metaphoric abyss from which there is no return. The conflict between the language of the narrator and the narratee prepares us for later more elaborate conflicts between the languages of the colonizer and the colonized. The narrator who survives psychologically and ideologically will either be as coldly official and perfunctory as this narrator, or will betray the cost of his denial and splitting. At any rate, the insistence on denying connection between the impersonal, administrative, journalistic public self and the personal, creative, daemon-ridden outlawed and private self suggests the characteristic colonial problem of denied connection with the colonized object (even when the site of colonization is the self) and prepares us for the competing voices in most Kipling texts. The narratee is also characteristic; a half-caste, he is an external embodiment of what Kipling himself internally feared and celebrated. As Kim and as Mowgli, Kipling praises Allah for giving him two separate sides to his head. Those separate sides, invisible to outsiders, are none the less firmly balanced, and when the pressures mount, can be counted on to privilege the English side and transcend the perils of uncanny India. But the half-caste is different in that the balance betweeen the two halves of his castes are not as predictably harmonized as in the essentially unified Kim.

The basic plot involves a descent into an Indian nighttown and a return for one of the two Englishmen. All Kipling's stories will involve variations of this configuration, one that allows the colonial engagement with and mastery over the Other who is simultaneously desired and denied. Certain characteristic motifs in setting (the entryway to the "other" world) and character (those who display the stigma of such entry, or the "mark of the beast") also appear here for the first time. If all Kipling's opening sentences are set up for subsequent amplification, reexamination, interrogation or dissolution, the opening sentences of both the frame and the embedded tale set up a self-negating dialectic. The storyteller sets up a situation that denies his implication in the telling of the tale: "This is no work of Mine." Misquitta, the half-caste, begins by describing a gate: "It lies between the Coppersmith's Gully and the pipe-stem seller's quarter, within a hundred yards, too, as the crow flies, of the Mosque of Wazir Khan" (*PTH* 201). But he undercuts this apparent certainty by defying anyone else to find the gate "however well he may think he knows the City." That uncertainty is intensified in the second paragraph which declares that the gate "isn't really a gate though. It's a house" (*PTH* 201). Here the narrator's unacknowledged identification with Gabral Misquitta is accomplished through their mutual associations with "the house" that both have entered, in which the narrator has spent all night questioning the dying man. The reader will enter the world of Kipling's stories through this story that is no story, through a gate that is no gate but a house of a hundred sorrows, just as the drug dependent author will allow the narrator to serve as mediator between himself and the half-caste addict. The gate signifies a penetrable boundary between the world of the narrator – European, intact, and masterful – and the previously unheard and silent world of the narratee who, by being privileged with speech, has the last word in the discourse. The inner city contains several other images that will recur in Kipling's Indian stories: a one-eyed man, a mutilated hand ("both his middle fingers were gone"), disease and death, alcoholism, and murder. This is not exactly what Bakhtin would call "carnival," but it is a type of Kipling story that, like carnival, releases images and voices otherwise suppressed by the official imperial machinery; the act of choosing to remember and transcribe such a story makes it in effect an inverse story of the narrator's desire.

The cast of characters who inhabit "the gate of the hundred

sorrows" include "an English loafer – Mac-Somebody I think."
That English loafer will return in "To Be Filed for Reference" as
McIntosh Jellaludin, the former Oxford scholar now an addict and
married to a native woman, who gives the narrator a manuscript
about Mother Maturin – the title of the epic about India Kipling
himself began to write in 1885 and abandoned incomplete. The
dialogic relationship between the narrator and the inner story is
defined here and elsewhere by such intertextual allusions. I use
Bakhtin's concept of "dialogism" not to limit, but rather as a
convenient term that embraces colonial splitting, the unlimited and
yet entangled transaction between law and transgression, and the
conflict and ambivalence between desire and rejection of the
distanced Other (Kristeva 1987: 120).

The gradual decay of the gate and its occupants is metonymically
associated with the narrator who, simply by being there, questioning,
and recording, is identifying himself with the divided, half-caste
Gabral; and the story ends without closure, by interrupting a fantasy
of death with a *non sequitur*. The indirect effect of telling a story that
is no story about a failed derelict is to establish distance and desire
between the narrator and the narratee: storytelling, naming, and
framing become a way to master and conquer the fear of succumbing
to desire. Because this story gives the last word to the dying half-caste
whose memories occupy a liminal space between his own memories
and those of the dead Fung-Tching, its effect is more unsettling than
other Kipling frame tales whose narrators can bravely descend into
tales told by derelicts, and then return to the safety of the frame to
reestablish their stance of partial alliance with the reader and with
the official system. But even in those tales we see forced moments of
closure whose very awkwardness makes them both a tribute to and a
gesture of resistance against objects of desire.

Kipling's second short story, "The Dream of Duncan Parrenness,"
was written shortly after the first, and published when he was
nineteen years old in the December 25th issue of the *Civil and Military
Gazette*. Although it is a very short story, he admitted (in a November
1884 letter to his aunt) taking three months to write it: "only six
pages long but I've never fallen in love with any tale of my own
fashioning so much – not that it has any merit" (quoted in
Carrington 1986: 94). Like the earlier story, its significance lies in its
different and more complex problematization of knowledge of the
unitary self manifested through the narrator's undercutting of his

own veracity, through its elaboration of descent into an underworld (here a dreamworld), and through the dialogizing and splitting of opposing selves.

Here, however, the split is not between the narrator and narratee, but between the waking world of the "Writer in the service of the Company and afraid of no man" (the narrator) and his dreamworld in which he encounters "a more deadly terror than I hold it has ever been the lot of mortal man to know," and that deadly terror is himself. More daring than the earlier narrator, Duncan Parrenness here tells his own story and confronts the personal nightmare rather than displacing it onto another.

But the story presents an added problem with a narrator whose archaic and visionary style belies his opening statement "heaven knows how unhandy the pen is to me who was always readier with sword than inkhorn" (*LH* 290). The odd disjuncture between the drunken soldier and his style combines, in the opening sentence, with an image of mutilation that is subordinate, but metonymic to his identity as a man: "Like Mr. Bunyan of old, I, Duncan Parrenness, Writer to the Most Honourable the East India Company, in this God-forsaken city of Calcutta, have dreamed a dream and never since that Kitty my mare fell lame have I been so troubled" (*LH* 290). Like John Bunyan, Kipling too is writing a pilgrim's progress about the passage of a colonialist's soul, but he will ironically reverse the journey which this time will lead not towards salvation, but rather towards damnation of the innocent soul and salvation of the administrative self. Although Kitty the horse will not be mentioned again, its name will be displaced onto another representation of his inadequacy, also female, his unfaithful fiancée. Her memory then provokes a sequence of associations with other troublesome women he has failed with, or who reminded him of failures of character in himself.

His dream is preceded by drunkenness occasioned by a party given by the Governor-General – a situation that establishes the narrator's alliance with the colonial system and with the administration. Both drunkenness and dream involve disintegrating boundaries and invite the reader and dreamer into the uncertain but signifying unconscious where they will encounter the uncanny vision of the future self repressed and contained within the dreamer. But whereas in other stories that alliance ensures the narrator's mastery and control, here Kipling seems to acknowledge that the price for that necessary mastery might be barrenness and death. The narrator's drunkenness results in exposure of otherwise concealed aspects of his character, and in the return of the repressed – the repressed as the uncanny and grim knowledge of his future self as master colonialist. What we see here and in so many early tales is Kipling's production of the colonizer as suspect and unstable subject, a dreamer, abuser, and a drunk whose knowability is invisible to the imperial machine.

Before the dream itself his drunkenness leads to split responses to the waking world: a meek sentimentality opposed by nasty, megalomaniacal, and unmotivated aggression directed at the most victimized creatures he can find – his servants (we will see this gesture repeated in later stories). The sequence of his thoughts is revealing. A misty reverie on his inebriated state precedes mother-ridden penitences that recall the coarse drunken jests of the evening as the sort he would not have liked Mother to hear; recollections of Kitty, his fiancée who has jilted him for another, and of the beautiful but married Mrs. Vansuythen significantly blur with that of the larger India, "this land [that] had so burnt and seared my mind with the flames of a thousand bad passions and desires, that I had aged ten months for each one in the Devil's school" (*LH* 291). If he has thought that his condition can be blamed on the country, his dream will reveal the contrary.

The words that connect his waking with his dream are the last words he uses to define his identity – "Writer in the service of the Company and afraid of no man" (*LH* 292). These words, repeated by the stranger he finds at the foot of his bed, begin the process by which he is made to realize the price for acquiring such fearlessness and invulnerability. Reminiscent of the Jamesian double in "The Jolly Corner," this stranger with his face marked, lined, diseased and scarred, turns out to be his future double. But this is a self that demands and gets paid the life-denying price of the young Duncan's trust in man, his faith in women and finally his "boy's soul and conscience ... a far more terrible loss than the two that I had suffered before." It is also a future self that is to be identified with the colonial administrators of India: "I took note, as well as I could, that his face was somewhat like mine own grown older, save when it changed to the face of the Governor-General or my father, dead these six months" (*LH* 292). The significance of these images that melt into each other suggests that the older self is to the younger, what the Governor-General is to India – a master administrator. In fact, one of the promises the older self makes to the younger is that he will probably grow up to be Governor-General. But for this he must pay a great price.

In addition to his youthful trust in man and faith in woman, he takes "from out of my very heart," his "boy's soul and conscience," a loss he describes as the most painful of all because it robs him of the last vestige of decency that would allow him to repent of his wrongdoings once sober. Once he loses these, he finds in their place a "deadly coldness of the heart." This image will later be metonymically displaced onto the country he governs, which will be described as "a heartless Government" ("On the Strength of a Likeness," *PTH*). The loss of heart, soul, and conscience is described in terms of an initiation to manhood, the movement from innocence into experience, from the "Imaginary" into the "Symbolic," a fall into Otherness, into Governor-General-hood, or into "the-name-of-the-father." This story, then, compels the displaced imperial narrator to occupy two positions at once, to destabilize his unitary self as source of authority, and to see colonial authority as both power and loss, as self and as Other. As with so many other Kipling stories and novels, this too is a tale of loss, of the terror of loss, of how the colonialist mediates his anxiety over losing his place in the Imperial machinery; his fear of self-loss displaced and "named" as a series of lost women – his mother, his fiancée, Mrs. Vansuythen, and of course, his lame horse Kitty; these losses provoke his compensatory knowledge that though he can't have mothers, he can occupy the place of his Father/Governor-General in the colonial system of authority. For the young Kipling protagonist growing up is the sudden knowledge of the real, administrative, masculine social system to which he belongs, which must therefore come between himself and his boyish desire (inevitably gendered as female).[2] For Kipling, as for Freud and Lacan, civilized adulthood is based on repression, self-division, and alienation from one's childhood self. But Kipling's dream story reaches out to its cultural moments in history that determined its fears: it is dialogized too by the dreamer's abusive relation to his silent, native servants, by an India where his official function is finally as useful as the last image in the story.

The narrator's skepticism towards this passage into adulthood differs markedly from the narrator's approval in later stories like "The Brushwood Boy," in which the boy is rewarded with marriage and a place in the system. Here the reward is bitterly ironic and is revealed in an image in the last line of the story: "When the light came I made shift to behold his gift, and saw that it was a little piece of dry bread" (*LH* 295). This is the Kipling narrator's first explicit glimpse of meaninglessness, of life without desire, that he sees through the defenses of dream, and of a mannered and stylized language that is both Biblical and visionary. It is significant too that the glimpse occurs simultaneously with his loss of what he perceives as the natural and the innocent. In the Kipling canon, we can perhaps read this story not only as a story about the subjectification of colonial adulthood, about the price culture exacts from nature for allowing such a passage, but also as a story about the simultaneous origins of meaninglessness. The image of dry bread combined with the puns implied in the narrator's name – drunken Duncan meets the barrenness in Parrenness – suggests the nature of the dreamer's inheritance as he proceeds to fulfill his arid mission in India. The dream has revealed to us, if not to the dreamer, the illusion of power and free agency in a system that has trapped the colonizer in its web of rules long before he dreams of its effects.

At the end of the year that marked the meeting of the first Indian National Congress, Christmas 1885, Kipling, his parents and his sister published *Quartette*, a slim collection of fiction and verse, from which two stories would be reprinted – "The Phantom Rickshaw" and "The Strange Ride of Morrowbie Jukes." These stories are variations on the first two stories he wrote and enlarge our understanding of the symptomatic anxieties of colonialism. Like the narrator of "The Gate of the Hundred Sorrows," the narrator of "The Phantom Rickshaw" tells a story of a man whose fate he is determined to avoid. A far more elaborate frame, however, added after the original publication, emphasizes the problematic relationship between colonial power and individual desire. And, like the first stories, "The Strange Ride of Morrowbie Jukes" is also a dream encounter with the Other, with a space and setting that is a libidinized India with all of its attendant terrors of powerlessness and regression. As in the earlier story, gratuitous acts of violence to the Other provoke the return of the repressed; and here too the price of the journey is the loss of a horse and the mirrored presence of other mutilated men.

The epigraph to "The Phantom Rickshaw" is equally appropriate for all Kipling frame tales where the world of darkness and dreams is invested with fears of regression that the narrator is determined to avoid: "May no ill dreams disturb my rest / Nor Powers of Darkness me molest." Because of its longer frame, this story reveals more clearly the psychological and ideological significance of the narrator, and the conflict between the narrative voice and the embedded story that it chooses to retell. The embedded Kipling story is typically a tale of lurid action told by a narrator whose connection with the story itself is marginal because he is frequently a man defined by inaction, a newspaperman whose meditations preceding the reported action raise disturbing and unacknowledged questions about himself and his story. Although the center of interest in a Kipling story appears to be the foregrounded sequential tale at its heart, that story needs to be read in its dialogic relationship to the oblique and often strange narrative matrix that contains and inflects it.

Kipling's construction of the ambivalent colonizer is seen through his narrator's admitted power to occupy dual positions – to simultaneously distance himself from the inner story of the Other while inadvertently revealing his vulnerability. The narrator defines himself as a social type in alliance with others who aid in defining his social function, thereby guaranteeing his sanity and continuing service to empire. His function as a storyteller is to frame and thereby foreground those against whom he opposes himself. But his allusions, rhetoric, and imagery dismantle the oppositions and implicate him in the story of failure he chooses to remember and rewrite. By projecting onto the narratee that which he fears, denies, and represses in himself, the narrator makes of the inner story a mirror of the outer frame, both reflecting and contradicting what the outer story implies. The incident chosen for retelling is always a source of displaced personal or political anxiety for the narrator. What makes these stories so compelling is the way in which the narrator, despite his stated intentions, fails to provide a unified and ideologically coherent story. That characteristic stylistic incoherence suggests connections between its narrative inconsistencies and the contradictions of its larger social context. "The internal politics of style (how the elements are put together) is determined by its external politics (its relationship to alien discourse). Discourse lives, as it were, on the boundary between its own context and another, alien, context" (Bakhtin 1981: 284). Macherey would call such a dialogic relationship its "historical defect" (1978: 238) created by the collision between the narrative voice and the colonial enterprise it chooses to describe. And Homi Bhabha would read the politics of style in terms of the contradictions of a discourse in which mastery, though asserted, is always slipping away. That historical defect, slippage, or "repertoire of conflictual positions" (Bhabha 1986) will reveal itself vividly, not only in these two stories, but in almost all Kipling's stories about India.

"The Phantom Rickshaw" demonstrates the early Kipling's characteristic narrative approach to the unresolvable disturbance at the heart of the story. Caught between his rational disbelief in ghosts, his faith in all that is visibly knowable, and his unacknowledged fascination with the world of dreams and darkness, the narrator distances himself from implication in the story first by removing himself into the safety of margins. From that decentered perspective he tells the story of a young Englishman caught between his forbidden desire for a married woman and his legitimate desire for unmarried Miss Mannering. His choice of propriety and legitimacy results in the death of the married woman who returns as a ghost to haunt him into madness and death.

The narrator's immediate link with the narratee is that he commits the same act he advises Pansay to commit – the act of writing as mastery over fear: "I suggested that he should write out the whole affair from the beginning to end, knowing that ink might assist him to ease his mind" (*MK* 27). What Pansay fears is made obvious in the story; but what the narrator fears is less obvious and is suggested only through the nervous and oblique frame. The opening sentence introduces the narrator's declared interest in knowledge constrained into anecdotes, epigrammatic and detached from the subject. It also reveals his divided consciousness that would like, simultaneously, to explore and repress knowledge of the absent subject of the story – India. This opening sentence reads: "One of the few advantages that India has over England is a great Knowability" (*MK* 26). The problem of "knowing" India – a recurring obsession and subject for parody in Kipling – is so absurd and outside the scope of narrative undertaking that its very possibility is suggested and negated by shifting the issue from an external historical site to an insider's private realm of possibility. The problem of knowledge is removed by being, as it were, controlled, contained, and "colonized" by the narrative idiom which will domesticate the problem from the historical and political into the private. The reader is moved, in narrowing, concentric circles, from macrocosmic India, to the Englishmen in India, to the microcosmic case of one solitary English mind that disintegrates in India.

The connection between "knowledge" and breakdown undercuts easy equations between Kipling's limited epistemology and imperial morality. Alan Sandison (1967: 61ff) and other readers deprive Kipling's texts of irony and contradiction when they ignore the underside of his "explicit appreciation of the Indian Empire's great knowability" (Sandison 62). Kipling himself was of course an early ethnographer of the behavior of the colonizer (and the colonized) on the plains and hills of India.[3] His commitment to such an inquiry was in part a critique of Western ethnocentricism, and in part a willingness to construct India as "a circus of competing systems of meaning" (Bivona 1990: 73). Kipling wavered in his stance towards Hegelian reappropriation – the ideal of knowledge as a means to divest the objective world of its strangeness and its Otherness. A recurring scene in many stories is that of a figure of authority – a Strickland or a Major – collapsing into hysteria after struggling to solve a problem in knowledge. In "The Mark of the Beast," for instance, after Strickland uses his knowledge of Indian metaphysics and colonial power to regain the soul of Fleete, he suddenly and "without warning, went into an amazing fit of hysterics. It is a terrible thing to see a strong man overtaken with hysteria. . .and I laughed and gasped and gurgled just as shamefully as Strickland, while Fleete thought we had both gone mad" (*LH* 190). One of the few flights of liberation from the official constitution of the unified colonial subject and his monitored behavior in this society is what such Kipling figures in the jungle often resort to – weeping, laughter, and madness. All three are reactions to boundary situations, a defiance of the limitations and rules placed on everyday behavior by the rigidities of this dislocated and constrained Anglo-Indian culture (see Plessner 1970: ch. 5).

In "The Phantom Rickshaw" and other early tales, we see demonstrated the mechanism of self-destruction ironically contained in the heart of the system, the minotaur produced by the colonial system – the colonized human mind that is the fragmented, all-too-human victim, rather than master, of all it surveys. To adapt Eagleton's colorful image, colonialism "gives birth to its own gravedigger, nurturing the acolyte who will one day stab the high priest in the back." (Eagleton actually says this about capitalism in *Criticism and Ideology*, p. 133.)

To return to that first sentence and to the question it raises, what allows India its "great Knowability?" We are told that "after five years' service a man is directly or indirectly acquainted with the two or three hundred Civilians in his Province, all the messes of ten or twelve Regiments and Batteries, and some fifteen hundred other people of the non-official caste. In ten years his knowledge should be doubled, and at the end of twenty he knows, or knows something about, every Englishman in the Empire, and may travel anywhere and everywhere without paying hotel-bills." The universal truth of the opening sentence is immediately undercut by the second, not, as in Jane Austen, by a narrator playing ironically with her own omniscience, but by a narrator whose control over his stance is uncertain and untrustworthy. The answer to the problem of how to know India is answered by its contrary, how not to know it; and the apparently charming irony (which is in fact a skeptical strategy) lies in realizing that by "India" the narrator really means "every Englishman in the Empire." Such a strategy is the basis for Kipling's (and the historicist's) awareness that all knowledge is contaminated and contained by its context. By the end of the story, however, that initial irony is turned on its head when it is revealed that every Englishman in the empire is metonymically his own "India" – unknowable, dark, irrational, and self-destructive. If the first paragraph of the frame so far has reflected the narrator's concerns about knowability, subsequent paragraphs reflect other anxieties that characterize the Kipling narrator: acceptance into the houses of others, illness and disorganization, fears of breakdown, the dark unknown, and the connection between literature and sickness. Each of these anxieties will find its nightmarish repetition in the inner story that the narrator chooses to tell.

The fear of expulsion from inner circles is thematized in all Kipling's early fiction and influences the form and substance of his narratives. Narratorial knowledge itself is both characterized and made suspect by such fears. The second paragraph, for instance, qualifies the largess and idealism of the first ("every Englishman ... may travel anywhere ... without paying hotel bills") by restricting colonial generosity to an "Inner Circle." "If you belong to the Inner Circle" and are "neither a Bear nor a Black Sheep" the narrator assures us, then "all houses are open to you, and our small world is very, very kind and helpful." The intensifiers in the sentence alert us not only to the falsity of their excess, but to the desired inner sanctum that excludes and opposes the Bear and Black Sheep. And if we underscore this social opposition with its biographical subtext – of

Kipling who called himself "Black Sheep" in that undisguised autobiographical fiction of his early years, "Baa, Baa, Black Sheep," then we see the fragmented and conflicted economy of colonial discourse with its tension between the wish for mastery and the counter-reality provided by its historic context and the more personal context of the psychic life of the displaced colonizer.

The desire for "a house that is open to you" is charged with a specific "lack" for Kipling, who felt expelled as a child from his parental home India, and ever after searched for houses open to him that he could call "his very own" (cf. the chapter in Kipling's autobiography titled "The Very-Own House"). That private desire has its ideological extension in his introjection of colonized lands as legitimate homes for alienated Englishmen; the entire world, as it were, becomes fit hunting ground for "the very-own house." Our narrator must be wary of becoming a Black Sheep (like the younger Kipling, or Pansay, or McIntosh Jellaludin) or a Bear (Baloo the Bear in the *Jungle Books* is the voice of knowledge through experience) lest he be expelled from the ultimately desired open house that is the "imaginary" India of the mind. This too is part of what Bhabha would call the "'unthought' across which colonial man is articulated ... that results in the splitting of colonial discourse so that two attitudes towards external reality persist; one takes reality into consideration while the other disavows it and replaces it by a product of desire that repeats, rearticulates 'reality' as mimicry" (*October* 1984: 132).

That acceptance within a circle, in spite of trouble, breakdown, and trauma, leads to an inexplicable unity between man and man, provides the basis for the next moment of mimicry in this frame. We are told a side story about Rickett of Kamartha who falls ill while visiting the home of Polder of Kumaon, whose household is for six weeks totally disorganized by this unexpected and unwelcome intrusion. But curiously, the consequence of this unwanted interruption is a bond of eternal obligation by the host to his guest. Polder proceeds to send the little Ricketts boxes of gifts and toys every year, an unexpected inversion of gratitude from the host to the guest. The conclusion the narrator draws from this incident is as false as the opening sentence, yet reveals a homologous connection between desire and ideology in the hope that India will, like Polder, feel an eternal obligation to the intruding Englishmen: "The men who do not take the trouble to conceal from you their opinion that you are an incompetent ass, and the women who blacken your character ... will work themselves to the bone in your behalf if you fall sick or into serious trouble" (*MK* 26). This fantasy provides a model for the loss of colonial agency in process of mimicry.

The problem of representing imperialism as charmed circle and as family affair opens up the possibility of expulsion from its charms, and consequently loss of power and agency. The miming of power is further exposed in the next paragraph where the inadequacy of linguistic representation is displaced from the discourse of the narrator to the doctor who will treat Pansay's breakdown in the inner story. The narrator's language grows coy and ornamental at this point as he describes the hospital the doctor keeps in addition to his normal practice as "an arrangement of loose boxes for Incurables ... a sort of fitting-up shed for craft that had been damaged by stress of weather. The weather in India is often sultry, and since the tale of bricks is always a fixed quantity, and the only liberty allowed is permission to work overtime and get no thanks, men occasionally break down and become as mixed as the metaphors in this sentence" (*MK* 27). The brittle imagery and self-consciousness of this discourse not only provides an analogy between the construction of a breakable metaphor and the fragile identity of the colonizer, but is also an effort to cover up the real problem of a mental breakdown through a code language that reaches out of the text to connect with the reader's schoolboy cleverness and divert attention from the issue of private and public cracks in the paragraph and the story. Yet the narrator later undercuts the implications of his own language by ascribing coy, clichéd reactions to the doctor whose diagnosis reads: "Pansay went off the handle ... Overwork started his illness, kept it alight, and killed him, poor devil. Write him off to the System." In contrast with the doctor, the narrator offers his own more disturbing theory: "There was a crack in Pansay's head and a little bit of the Dark World came through and pressed him to death" (*MK* 27). The cracks that run through Pansay are also the fault lines in the story, the language, the self and the system that draw attention, once again, to Kipling's profound ontological skepticism about the colonial self and its agency.

The narrator establishes himself as Pansay's healer by caring for him during his final sickness and by suggesting that he use, as the narrator does, writing as therapy. Pansay's own story is about a self divided between loyalty to two mutually exclusive alternatives

represented by two love affairs, two lives, and the inner split within
him once he recognizes a reality other than the one he chooses to
inhabit. His manuscript begins with a description of the fatal sea
voyage from Gravesend to Bombay during which he meets the wife of
an officer, Agnes Keith-Wessington, whose passion he soon discovers
"was a stronger, a more dominant and – if I may use the expression
– a purer sentiment than mine" (*MK* 29). Both fall desperately and
unreasoningly in love. But once they arrive in India, Pansay's "fire of
straw burned itself out to a pitiful end" (*MK* 29); his love is replaced
by nausea, hate, and eventually by a new love for a younger, single
woman. When Mrs. Wessington dies, Pansay declares himself to be
"the happiest man in India." He thinks he has conquered and
outlived his fatal passion. But instead, he has simply underrated the
powers of darkness about to molest him. When the ghost persists in
appearing to him in the most unexpected and embarrassing public
places, Pansay is presumed by others to have either the "DTs" or
epileptic fits.

But the unexpected twist towards the end of the story occurs after
Pansay has gone through an intense night of the soul exploring
"thoroughly the lowest circles of the Inferno which it is permitted
man to tread on earth ... watching myself faltering through the dark
labyrinths of doubt, misery and utter despair ... then my two selves
joined, and it was only I (half crazed, devil-driven I) that tossed in
my bed ... 'But I am in Simla,' I kept repeating to myself. 'I, Jack
Pansay, am in Simla and there are no ghosts here,'" (*MK* 43). And
as later in *Kim*, here too he will resort to the multiplication tables "to
make quite sure that I was not taking leave of my senses." The
division between the world of multiplication tables and the world of
spirits is repeated in other dimensions of the story. The sea voyage
that had fostered in Pansay a love that was both "desperate and
unreasoning" was an appropriately unstable setting for the kind of
"Imaginary" relationship he sets up with Mrs. Wessington. But once
on land, he enters the domain of the system, of the "Symbolic," and
the split between the two selves leads first to a total rejection of the
Imaginary (sea) love for the married woman, and then to a Symbolic
(landlocked) realignment with the more appropriate Miss Kitty. His
inner split, acknowledged in the moments he explores his personal
"Inferno," is repeated in the split in the narrative when he sees what
others do not, when he watches himself, when he is punished for his
alienation from his former self, and finally, when he happily

accommodates himself to a double life. Now rejected by his fiancée and condemned by polite society, he begins to move in the world of ghosts where he redefines his values, declaring that his new relationship with Mrs. Wessington was "in some indefinable way a marvelously dear experience" and wonders whether he was in life to woo a second time the woman he had killed by his earlier neglect and cruelty.

Like so many of Kipling's early stories, the story of Pansay (a significantly infantile and feminine name) is about a man's struggle to evolve a stable, unified identity in India. Torn between the self-on-sea and the self-on-land, Pansay is split into two selves that watch each other suspiciously. Whereas in "My Own True Ghost Story" (also published in *The Phantom Rickshaw*) Kipling laughs at non-rational presences and reasons them away, here, the entangled encounter with the Other and the unseen that slips from mimicry into menace reflects Kipling's anxieties about control over the colonial self and its empire and prepares us for what Bhabha calls "the twin figures of narcissism and paranoia that repeat furiously, uncontrollably" in scenes of colonial power where history turns to farce (*October* 1984: 132).

In some ways, perhaps, this story is a reworking of the other side of the fantasy governing "The Dream of Duncan Parrenness," that administering India involves confronting the terrifying cost of power: the relinquishing of ties to women and mothers, the fall into lone adulthood, the threat of forbidden love, the exposure of the "unreasoning" and vulnerable self, and the persistent demand for repression and self-denial for civilization to proceed with its discontents. The ideological context behind this characteristic Kipling story, therefore, is the recovery of the masculine self so that the work of empire can continue. To defend the self against internal and external assaults, one needs consistently to be wary of the return of the repressed, of love, passion and drugs – all gendered, along with desire, as female and Other – which confuse and blur the clear lines of boundary defining the function of the colonialist within the system. The imagery too follows a familiar gendered configuration that we will see in later stories – the sea and the land, the ship and the club, horses and carriages, love and work, madness and passion versus multiplication tables, and finally, a journey with the phantom into the sphere of love and the irrational (what he will later call "the Road to En-Dor") which is also the journey to death.

The compulsion to repeat a story of madness, disintegration and death is on an unconscious level a disguise for human failure and perhaps for "the sharper pain of exclusion by history" (Jameson 1981: 238); and the telling of a ghost story preserved in a dead man's manuscript is perhaps a disguised means of transcending or evading the historical context by moving into the imaginary and the recursive. The private fear made explicit in the story is the loss of control over a unified imperial self; the public fear that remains unacknowledged except in the narrator's marginal comments in the frame, is the loss of a place in the workings of the empire, the loss of admission into homes, and the loss of home-empire-India. The story itself offers no way to connect the private fear of loss of self or subjectivity with the public fear of loss of empire. Structured as it is on the contradiction between the frame and the embedded story, neither the narrator nor Pansay can find a way out of his impasse. So too the contradiction between the false domestic reassurance of the frame and the domestic nightmare of the inner story poses an unresolvable dilemma artificially closed by the formal device of the frame. And finally, the narrator's repetition of Pansay's story paradoxically confirms his fear of losing the defining boundary of the imperial family. His own loss of "original" location is repeated in his obsession with increasingly menacing tales of boundary loss. The colonizer needs no native Other on whom to project threat: it lies within the self or it is gendered in terms of female otherness and the metaphysical world. Both frame and tale must expel feminine desire into the margins, but what remains is a shadow of a man haunted by that expelled Other, who will return to haunt him in life as empire has returned to haunt England after his death.

The anxieties of mimicry and menace in the construction of the colonial Other, the colonizer's fears of self-loss, and the carnivalization of colonial history as farce find their nightmarish apotheosis in "The Strange Ride of Morrowbie Jukes." The most disturbingly metaphoric of Kipling's earliest attempts at fiction, it encloses a totalizing vision of a democratized India as a city of the dead and as a black hole in Imperial reality. By invoking and then inverting the hierarchies of colonial discourse, the story becomes a nightmare "carnival" that encodes hysteria in mimicry and fantasy (see Stallybrass and White 1986: 175) and compels the imperial subject to depend for his very life on the good will of disgustingly smelly Indians whom he has hitherto excluded, abused and marginalized. The story is also a paradigmatic scenario for Fanon's (and later Homi Bhabha's) construction of the positions and oppositions of colonial discourse with its continual chains of other stereotypes (Bhabha 1986). The colonized Indians in this fantasy fulfill all the colonizer's split and contradictory expectations: once he starts to recognize the native as his "natural protector" (*MK* 11), the Englishman is treated mercilessly, reduced to impotence, and made – literally – to eat crow.

Set in a pathologized India represented as one large gaping hole filled with figures of life-in-death, this is Kipling's most undisguised allegory of transgression and colonial powerlessness. It is about a fall into an ultimate Indian orifice, a gap between life and death filled with holes, symbolic filth and the dead who did not die. Kipling's diary for the year 1885 (see Pinney 1990) tells us that the story was written during a time when the nineteen-year-old Kipling was suffering from weeks of insomnia, stomach cramps, and depression. In that state of bodily vulnerability and psychic alienation he wrote the ultimate colonial nightmare about the collapse into the tyranny of material equality with the lowest of the natives – a situation charged with disgust and paranoia. When first published in *Quartette* (1885), the story lacked the frame added for its later publications when he characteristically used a narrator to mediate between the reader and his tale of terror. The resolution or at least end to the tale awkwardly and artifically opposes the thrust of the ending anticipated by the events in the story by using a *deus ex machina* – ironically an Indian servant who becomes the instrument of the Englishman's salvation. The strange ride, while pointedly different from the bitter self-critique of Duncan Parrenness, also reminds us of other Kipling journeys that take their protagonists over a threatening landscape only to teach them how not to immerse themselves in its destructive elements, not to see the material conditions of conflict, not to understand the problematic productions of the imperial system – journeys that promise in exchange for such blindness and restraint the rewards of social reconciliation. The frame and the artificial closure both serve as ideological screens that mediate the extremity of colonial hysteria.

As in "The Dream of Duncan Parrenness," the protagonist's encounter with unknown India and subsequent hysteria is provoked by his assault on the natural – he shoots a dog and suspends its carcass outside his tent to warn other dogs who instead devour the body. That which is outside the tent (the baying dog) proceeds to further threaten the inside occupant who then determines to "finish him off." The conceptual divisions and symbolic values of colonial society that the story transgresses and mutates are those between the civilized inside and the uncivilized outside. The white master as paranoid and passive victim of native (and natural) intransigence sees himself victimized by the land, its animals, and its people.

The sequence of events and the underlying fears in these stories remind one of Kafka's "The Country Doctor." The doctor's journey into his psychic past is also provoked by an unexpected act of aggression. "You never know what you're going to find in your own house," he is ironically reminded after he kicks open the door of his uninhabited pigsty to release the enormous horses and their sexually violent groom (p. 149). The combined forces of the savage groom and magical horses released from his pigsty drive Kafka's doctor through a regressive journey to a forced confrontation with his own paralyzing impotence, his own denied and excluded gender – that of the mother's wound. The doctor, who defends himself against his own ailment by healing others, finds the metaphoric signs of his own wound in the worm-infested, rose-red wound in the body of the boy whom he is called to cure, but whom he is powerless to help.

Here in "The Strange Ride of Morrowbie Jukes," some twenty years before Kafka, Kipling writes of an engineer, who as builder and constructor finds the signs of his inner fears in a foul and hellish hole filled with the living dead and the disintegrating dead, and who in the role of master colonizer finds himself at the mercy of mocking natives who deny the hierarchy of the colonial system. But the village of the dead is not only projection but also introjection, a gendered cavity, a libidinized India democratized to self-destruction and destined to further emasculate the already maddened colonizer.

The story is embedded in a frame narrated by a teller who subverts its reliablity from the start. As the voice of society and administrative authority, the narrator vouches for the sanity and reliability of the narratee Morrowbie Jukes, yet sabotages the veracity of his tale. He opens with the line "There is no invention about this tale," but continues: "And, since it is perfectly true that in the same Desert is a wonderful city where all the rich money-lenders retreat after they have made their fortunes...and drive sumptuous C-spring barouches, and buy beautiful girls, and decorate their palaces with gold and ivory and Minton tile and mother-o'-pearl, I do not see why

Jukes's tale should not be true. He is a Civil Engineer, with a head for plans and distances and things of that kind, and he certainly would not take the trouble to invent imaginary traps" (*MK* 3).

The unsettling play with invention and reality, truth and imagination, evolve into more rigid categories familiar to colonial homophobic and racial anxiety as splittings between white men and natives are mapped onto splittings between the "manly" and "unmanly." Like the narrator, Morrowbie Jukes also indulges in the ordering of himself and others in terms that conflate morality, gender and race. "Moping" for instance is an "unmanly" weakness as opposed to the "determination to slaughter" which is naturalized as "merely the semi-delirious notion of a fever-patient," one that struck him at the time as being "eminently practical and feasible" (*MK* 4).

The colonial paranoia about India as the source of illness and alienation, of natives as degenerate gangs who need surveillance and control dominates the narrative events as the story begins. Jukes' opening sentence blames the entire occurrence on "a slight attack of fever," but from the language describing the setting we know that he believes he has in fact been assaulted by India – represented by the "desolate" country, howling animals, his sense of his own "misfortune," his knowledge that he is in some way at the mercy of "exasperating ... gangs" of coolies. The slight attack of fever that unmans him into a hysterical determination to slaughter the animals is the starting point of a dreamlike journey into a pathologized India. The passage describing his journey reenacts a precarious fantasy of omniscience reminiscent of the kinds of dreams Kipling recalls in his autobiography.

In one moment ... we were flying over the smooth sandy soil at racing speed. In another we had passed the wretched dog, and I had almost forgotten why it was that I had taken the horse and the hog-spear.
  The delirium of fever and the excitement of rapid motion through the air must have taken away the remnant of my senses. I have a faint recollection of standing upright in my stirrups, and of brandishing my hog-spear at the great white moon that looked down so calmly on my mad gallop; and of shouting challenges to the camel-thorn bushes as they whizzed past. (*MK* 4–5)

The full moon, the baying dogs, the fever, and his irritation combine to deprive him of "the remnant of my senses," to ride "like a thing possessed, over what seemed to be a limitless expanse of moonlit sand." In this delirious, semi-conscious, twilight state, Jukes recounts events that stage his fears of regression, disintegration, helplessness, and total annihilation. He and his horse fall off an edge, into a hole, and wake to find themselves in a timeless world, a crater of death in life with no exit, in a situation that is a repetition with variation of his prenightmare state, as well as a repetition of the ultimate nightmare to be repressed – the nightmare of colonial history. The story will reenact the struggle between the colonizer and the colonized, the oppressor and the oppressed, with the difference that within this carnivalized struggle, the oppressed are destined to be the winners. The space into which Jukes falls will occasion the collapse of conventional oppositions on which colonial civilization relies.

Morrowbie Jukes' defense against the hysteria of occupying a common materiality with the native, a common hole, diet and destiny, is that of the engineer and ethnographer as imperialist – to control by empirical facts, knowledge, and measurement. He precisely reports a mechanically accurate description of the insides of the horseshoe-shaped crater of sand he discovers he has fallen into: the height, the degree of the angle of the slope, its length and the measurements of its varying widths, the construction of "the series of eighty-three semi-circular, ovoid, square and multilateral holes, all about three feet at the mouth" that run around the bottom of the crater. In other words, he begins his narration with that which is most accessible to rational understanding, that which reduces the nightmare quality of the experience to quantifiable and comforting order – like the multiplication tables in "The Dream of Duncan Parrenness" and in *Kim*. The thrust of the events in the story, however, casts all categories of social order into doubt by producing through the reconstituted "republic" a political travesty that fixes and stereotypes the native both as incomplete presence *and* as menacing power.

The "agencies of disgust" that provide the nightmare material of this tale are the normally repressed aspects of racist discourse. Jukes is overwhelmed by filth, by the "sickening stench ... fouler than any which my wanderings in Indian villages have introduced me to" (*MK* 6). The stench emerges from tunnels which eventually give life to sixty-five human beings who give the impression of "a band of loathsome fakirs," whose "filth and repulsiveness" are beyond all description. Each of the senses will be assaulted in turn, as after smell and sight will come touch (his violence upon others), taste (he will be

forced to eat crow), and hearing. He hears the sound ▒▒▒▒▒▒ g
totally alien to the native's expected behavior towar▒▒ ▒ ▒▒▒▒▒ –
laughter: "The ragged crew actually laughed at me – such laughter
I hope I may never hear again. They cackled, yelled, whistled, and
howled as I walked into their midst; some of them literally throwing
themselves down on the ground in convulsions of unholy mirth"
(*MK* 7). Jukes' reaction to this ridicule, contempt and "chilling
indifference" is a repetition of his earlier behavior towards the dogs
and of the larger colonial behavior towards the insubordinate native.
Fear is transformed into loathing, disgust, and hysterical aggression
as he proceeds to beat on "those nearest ... with all the force I could.
The wretches dropped like ninepins, and the laughter gave place to
wails for mercy; while those yet untouched clasped me round the
knees, imploring me in all sorts of uncouth tongues to spare them"
(*MK* 7). If the constitution of the colonial subject depends on
excluding the Other who is imagined as unclean and internalized as
disgusting, Jukes is forced to confront the fragility of boundaries that
collapse like ninepins around him. But, as Stallybrass and White
contend, "disgust always bears the imprint of desire," and the
marginalized inevitably return as objects of nostalgia and fascination
(1986: 191).

The fear of the Other's mastery over language returns in the
evolution of the babble of uncouth tongues into eloquence – the
unexpected, disruptive and disrespectful voice in English of one
Gunga Dass whom Jukes recognizes as the Brahmin government
servant who has changed beyond recognition into a "withered
skeleton." In spite of his physical change, Dass still retains his power
over language. His only mark of recognition is a "crescent-shaped
scar on the left cheek – the result of an accident for which I was
responsible" (*MK* 8). The scar, the past, their jobs as "servants" to
the government, and their skill with language all connect the
Englishman to the repellent Indian. The third voice embedded into
this story then is that of Gunga Dass, whose story begins with an
appropriately disturbing line shattering even further the structures of
differentiation on which the Englishman has built his life. "There are
only two kinds of men, Sar. The alive and the dead. When you are
dead you are dead, but when you are alive you live." Gunga Dass
mimics the sort of master-English mocked and feared by Englishmen:
he can make bad puns in English, a skill that Jukes recalls because "it
is seldom that a Hindu makes English puns" (*MK* 8). By reminding

the Englishman of the inversion of power, by taking control of his money, his life, his horse, and his language, Gunga Dass makes Jukes eat colonial crow.

Even the landscape terrorizes Jukes by turning into quicksand and almost swallowing him up. The entire story, therefore, seems structured on psychological and social elements feared and repressed that return to haunt the trapped Englishman. His "reeking village" is a place of no-exit where the dead who do not die are sent to live. This is where the once presumed-dead Brahmin makes all the rules: he prescribes the diet of eating crows and chapatti, he takes all Jukes' money, he kills Jukes' horse, he introduces to Jukes his English double – the Englishman who had gone mad and been killed by Gunga Dass in the act of trying to escape the crater. "This place," Gunga Dass tells him, "is like your European heaven; there is neither marrying nor giving in marriage" (*MK* 12). And when Jukes sees the horrifying image of his dead horse killed by the natives, Dass explains in a discourse parodying that of the master colonizer that eating horse is better than eating crow, and that as a community of equals, they were to partake in the communion of eating it: "greatest good of greatest number is political maxim. We are now Republic, Mister Jukes, and you are entitled to a fair share of the beast. If you like, we will pass a vote of thanks. Shall I propose?" (*MK* 18).

Disempowered by the natives, Jukes sees before him nightmare images of his mutilated self, first his horse and then the Englishman. Beneath the English officer's rotten khaki hunting clothes, his body contains a "hideous cavity," a "gaping hole," and a plan of escape. The vision of this Englishman killed in the act of trying to escape is, like the dream double in "The Dream of Duncan Parrenness," a mirror of the self destroyed by those whom he has once controlled. And Morrowbie Jukes who, before the journey, considered moping an "unmanly" weakness, now acknowledges: "I was as completely prostrated with nervous terror as any woman." A metaphoric and gendered India as vaginalized space has swallowed and unmanned the colonizer. For an Englishman bred into a sense of class and hierarchy, the closeness, oneness and equality in this enclosed space is a nightmare of democracy: "Yes, we were a Republic indeed! A Republic of wild beasts penned at the bottom of a pit, to eat and fight and sleep till we died." Deprived of social resources, Jukes, like his dead double in the burrow, begins to go mad: "I acted as one mad. I hurled myself against the sand-slope. I ran round the base of the crater, blaspheming and praying by turns. I crawled out among the edges of the river-front ... in an agony of nervous dread ... and so fell, spent and raving, at the curb of the well" (*MK* 10).

At once a personal, political and historical nightmare, the representation of colonial despair is shaped by infantile rage at entrapment and by political anger at loss of control:

> Here was a Sahib, a representative of the dominant race, helpless as a child and completely at the mercy of his native neighbours. In a deliberate way he set himself to torture me as a schoolboy would devote a rapturous half-hour to watching the agonies of an impaled beetle, or as a ferret in a blind burrow might glue himself comfortably to the neck of a rabbit. (*MK* 13)

The story may of course be read as a metaphoric night journey into the self reflecting the anxieties of regression, loss of control, and the fear of "slipping backwards" into a hole surrounded by quicksand. Politically, however, this is also the colonizer's nightmare of a "crisis in authority" (Gramsci's term), where madness and death are the only answers to the revolutionary absence of established hierarchies of race and class. But unable to handle the implications of his nightmare vision (Jukes knocked down senseless by Gunga Dass), Kipling introduces a *deus ex machina* at the end – rescue by a servant, followed by a return to daytime safety and the club. This is the sort of forced closure and ideological screen that we will see in many Kipling stories, the sort of resolution and reconciliation with the system that differentiates this story from Kafka's "The Country Doctor," which, by risking the implications of self-encounter, ends with the Doctor naked, at the mercy of unknown elements, and permanently lost in space and time.

These early stories introduce us to Kipling's multiply fragmented habits of narration as a way of retelling and releasing certain fears created by the schizophrenic system common to colonial life: his first four stories plug their anxieties into the impossible demands made by the imperial machine whose monolithic productions of masculinity, character, and desire excluded the kinds of experiences, anxieties and desires which provided the material for Kipling's fiction.

CHAPTER 4

The worst muckers

"No one can accuse young Cottar of runnin' after women, white
or black," the major replied thoughtfully.
"But, then, that's the kind that generally goes the worst mucker
in the end."

("The Brushwood Boy," DW 263)

In the Indian stories I mention in this chapter, I want to give a sense
of Kipling's worst fear – going "worst mucker" amid the multiple
tyrannies and invisible structures of everyday colonial life. Both
Victorian and imperial systems of education placed inordinate
emphasis on the body as the site to be disciplined by sexual and class
power. The colonizer's body is (as Foucault reminds us in another
context) also society's body and therefore a political reality that
must be schooled into order and harmony. Joseph Bristow, the most
recent of critics to draw attention to the education of English
schoolboys during the age of empire, reminds us of the conflation of
"culture," games, sports and moral values, and of the assumption
that "culture" was a defense against excess, vulgarity and division
(1991: 8ff). The colonizer's body, in particular, is a miniaturized
model of the society that needs to be disciplined, tamed and
domesticated. So too, the body of the Other. As Susan Stewart
eloquently puts it in her discussion of freaks, "The body of the
cultural other is ... both naturalized and domesticated in a process
we might consider to be characteristic of colonization in general.
For all colonization involves the taming of the beast by bestial
methods and hence both the conversion and projection of the animal
and human, difference and identity. On display, the freak represents the naming of the frontier and the assurance that the wilder-
ness, the outside, is now territory" (1985: 109–10). The revolt
of the colonial body through hysteria, unacceptable sexuality,
or permanent breakdown is the sort of impermissible, freakish,

78

behavioral excess that found its way into many of Kipling's Indian stories.

The narrator seems compelled to repeat for us stories of breakdown, of transgression that meets with defeat, of small efforts to connect that meet with yet other breakdowns, and of the larger effort to presume connections with another person or country that meet with further breakdown. Why this fascination with breakdown, with going "worst mucker?" I see it as Kipling's way of internalizing the unacceptable, the terror of annihilation or boundary slippage in the troubling structures of gender, race and identity. Repeated collapse under excessive pressure is, in a way, the repressed text lying just beneath the surface bravado of such poems as "If" in which the narrator is told to force

> ... his heart and nerve and sinew
> To serve your turn long after they are gone,
> And to hold on when there is nothing in you
> Except the Will which says to them: "Hold on!"

These are stories in which boys *cannot* keep their heads about them when "all about ... are losing theirs." (Incidentally, to carry the point to an absurd literalism, Carnehan carries Dravot's decapitated head with him in a sack until he loses it at the end of the story "The Man Who Would Be King.") It is also Kipling's way of fictionalizing the internal, of aestheticizing through repetition, of circumscribing the unbearable and thereby preventing it from becoming reality. Another way to understand Kipling's representation of traumatic breakdown may be found through Deleuze and Guattari's readings of Kafka's resistance to power through rhizomatic lines of escape, through fragments, through transformation and becoming animal-bug-mouse-human: "No, freedom was not what I wanted. Only a way out; right, or left, or in any direction; I made no other demand" ("Report to an Academy" in Deleuze 1986: 13). The politics of the rhizomatic suggests patterns of endless connections between the weakest links and the strongest powers; these alternate but compatible ways of dealing with psychic, historical and cultural stress allow me to theorize Kipling's multiply determined struggle with his impasse between childhood desire and adult oppression in terms of repetition as defense, and in terms of lines of flight from anxiety, fear and domination.

Kipling's lines of flight from the oppression he both fled and desired led in two antithetical directions: towards the animal and the childlike (*The Jungle Books*) and towards the forbidden (as in the love stories), or alternately towards reintegration in the system, towards deterritorialization and reterritorialization. But the efforts of English-men towards escape from the strangleholds of the colonial system with its police and surveillance fail. And so the stories I have chosen appear to challenge the authority that gives birth to them, not by offering a viable alternate voice, but by taking a certain grim pleasure in witnessing the world's greatest imperial power collapse at its human joints.

As in the earlier stories, these tales are all reported by a self-conscious narrator, who, by ironizing his own reticence, opens up new spaces for knowing and representing colonial ways, and who records these events as if he were an ethnographer recording the breakdown of a tribe. His authoritative voice controls the story with moral platitudes, with displays of esoteric oriental knowledge, and with cynical social insights that establish his voice as essentially superior to that of the embedded Other whose story will necessarily be one of subjection and aborted escape. The desire for knowledge itself, thematized not only in the Kipling narrator, but also in a variety of protagonists, ethnographers, and most significantly police-man Strickland, illustrates the Foucaultian idea of the production of knowledge by power relations: "the turning of real lives into writing is no longer a procedure of heroicization; it functions as a procedure of objectification and subjection" (Foucault 1977: 191). And the unitary voice of the narrator struggling to see and to know reminds us of the unitary and centralized power of the Imperium that, like the panopticon, gazes, surveys, classifies, and objectifies its subjects into permanent captivity. But Kipling's narrating voice, constrained and ironized, seems to resist the official imperial stance by the limitations of its worn and often weary language, its clichés that alternate with bitter cynicism.

The "worst muckers" in Kipling's tales are sometimes those who transgress boundaries liberating themselves from their place in colonialist hierarchy, inverting the order of class, race and gender; inevitably they include those who involve themselves with native women; and most terrifyingly they are the ordinary colonialists who fall into panic, nameless terrors, madness and death. "At the End of the Passage" (1890), for instance, describes the effect of isolation, heat, sleeplessness, stress, overwork and monotony on the lives of a few Englishmen who meet to play a weekly game of whist at the home of Hummil, an assistant engineer. All are aware of the dangers of isolation, of allowing an acquaintance to drop out of sight for even one short week: "The players were not conscious of any special regard for each other. They squabbled whenever they met; but they ardently desired to meet as men without water desire to drink. They were lonely folk who understood the dread meaning of loneliness. They were all under thirty years of age, – which is too soon for any man to possess that knowledge" (*LH* 139). All fear the powers of dreams and darkness which drive too many colonialists to their death. Yet the men envy the early death of one Jevins known to have recently shot himself in the head. Hummil, the man who has reached the end of his passage, dies of fear, haunted and hunted in his sleep by "a blind face that cries and can't wipe its eyes, a blind face that chases him down corridors" (*LH* 152). We are made to understand his fear as the terror of regression: "He had slept back into terrified childhood... he was flung from the fear of a strong man to the fright of a child as his nerves gathered sense or were dulled." After the last man leaves, Hummil is left to "face the echoing desolation of his bungalow" (*LH* 154), and the first thing he sees standing before him is an apparition of himself. That spectre follows him through the day, sits before him at dinner, and the next time the other three friends come to visit, they find him, a ghastly look still in his eyes, dead. Their diagnosis is that he died of fright: "He was scared to death ... Look at those eyes! For pity's sake don't let him be buried with them open!" (*LH* 156). The uncanny fear uncovered by the unnatural and fragmenting experience of living in alien colonies is the fear of perpetual loss emblematized in the image of the blind, weeping childhood self that returns with the full force of the repressed to threaten the fragile power erected by the system.

Kipling's troubled representation of the colonial system is reflected not only in the disturbed early fiction this chapter will consider, but in his unsettling newspaper sketches on the Government. Here we see a curiously gendered construction of not only the imperial subject but the imperial machine. On September 3, 1886, for instance, a sketch written by the now twenty-year-old Rudyard appeared in the *Civil and Military Gazette* (now part of the Kipling Papers at Sussex) titled "A Nightmare of Rule." It begins:

Now, because IT was a thief which took and restored not again – not once
but twelve times yearly – and wrote vain tales, and wrought confusion in
places and brewed anger among men, I said: – "I will go forth and will not
rest until I find the Government of India; and I will straightway disembowel
IT and force IT to disgorge. Needs must that IT is somewhere to be found
concrete, and therefore vulnerable.

The rest of this nine-paragraph sketch follows the narrator in quest of
the "Government" through an allegorical landscape in which the
searchers find fragments of deceptive signs. IT is not to be found in
the streets, in the Anjumans (associations), in the Milky Way of
Lesser Lights, or on the plains. Finally, the Mahatma, the Greybeard
of the Himalayas, constructs "the dread circle of the Wheel within
the Wheel, and the crooked Line of the Inexplicable Course of
Action" and when the revelation comes, the Mahatma proclaims to
the narrator's shock that "IT is a Woman." And the story ends with
the following lines:

And we saw Hands that were not the hands of men, which turned the Wheel
within the Wheel and drew staight the crooked Line of the inexplicable
Course of Action, and pulled the Great Wire and the Lesser, and made plain
the book of the Unholy Job.
    Lastly there fell from the Clouds a Powder-puff and a Fan, and a left-
hand Shoe in white satin, whereof the number was Two, and the heel two
and a half inches. And the Mahatma, trembling, laid aside these things
reverently, for he said: –
    "We have seen a visible God."
    Thus was it that we found the Government of India – the IT that we set
forth to destroy. But we let IT go. (Kipling Scrapbooks 28/3)

The tone, nightmare imagery, biblical style, and use of the upper case
remind us of the curious schoolboyish mockery characteristic of the
unstable slippery narrator in Kipling's earliest fiction. Adrian Poole's
fine reading of Kipling's stylistic quirkiness in his use of the upper
case as "symptomatic of a deep irresolution in his work, a refusal to
do justice to the difficulties of belief and doubt" (1989: 135) is
perhaps true. But here the capitals also emphasize the magisterial
absurdity of an absence that can only be named as an IT that is no
government but an empty signifier – a powder puff of a feminine
presence that is therefore an absence.
    The emptiness that is the sign of the lack or of the female is part of
the gendered structure of colonial consciousness and culture. The
denigration of the feminine is also part of what Ashis Nandy refers to

as the cultural damage colonialism did to British society (1983: 32).
It valorized the least humane parts of British political culture, "de-
emphasized speculation, intellection and *caritas* as feminine, and
justified a limited cultural role for women – and femininity – by
holding that the softer side of human nature was irrelevant to the
public sphere. It openly sanctified – in the name of such values as
competition, achievement, control and productivity – new forms of
institutionalized violence and ruthless social Darwinism" (p.32).
The "worst muckers" are those who reflect the stresses of their
society by transgressing colonial imperatives, by behaving in ways
that are emotionally or culturally deviant, and by capitulating to
uncertainty, to introspection, and to the siren call of feminine desire.

Kipling's fallen colonizers are cultural reminders of nineteenth-
century anxiety about the fluidity of sexual and racial Otherness, an
anxiety that insulates itself by excluding that which is deviant, dirty
and effeminate. In constructing both the self and the stereotype as
fixed reality, the colonizer's desire for pure masculinity and pure
origins (I adapt Bhabha's terminology here) is always threatened by
its rupture or division. The end of the century was the age of paranoia
for a culture that externalized its own fears and saw itself under seige
by immigrant hordes of effeminate, inefficient and physically
undesirable aliens (see Rosenthal 1984: 131ff), by the degeneration
of empire and the mongrelization of the white race. Victorian myths
of manhood and of empire as paternalistic enterprise informed ideas
of character as key to colonial superiority. These ideas were
popularized not only by Samuel Smiles but more importantly by
Kipling's friend Lord Baden-Powell, constructor of "boy nature,"
architect of the masculinist ideal, founder of the Boy Scouts, and
holder of the patent on English character as defense against external
peril. The hidden agenda in his code, as Rosenthal demonstrates, is
the self-interested voice of the middle class defending its right to
established privileges while justifying the inequalities of the class
system (p. 9). The models for the ideal appearance of the Englishman
specifically excluded those who were stunted, narrow chested,
excitable, easily wearied, or inefficient – qualities associated with
women, with the lower classes, and with Jews. "Boy nature,"
Rosenthal tells us, was a class construct designed for the lower classes
in order to refashion them to conform to middle-class interests.
Character and the Boy Scout code aimed at instant denial of
individualism, thought and emotionality in favor of corporate loyalty

and acceptance of public school values. What is apparent in the boys
who blow their brains out in the uncertainty of the tropics is that they
have not learned to "play the game" according to the Boy Scout
codes of pluck and determination that translated skills on the cricket
field to the battlefields of empire. The construction of weak, broken
white men who fall prey to the sexuality of white or native women is
also the externalization of the colonizer's private nightmare, of their
own bodies as fetishized lack – a space in which race, class and gender
oppositions are shown to be interdependent and interlocked.

"In the Matter of a Private" (*ST* 1888–9) and "Thrown Away"
(*PTH* 1888) are both, on the surface level, stories of warning against
the daily pressures that destroy the fragile English "character" and
body in India. But they are also stories that imply possibilities of
escape from the colonial system. In that sense, we might, if we choose
to, consider these and other Indian stories in terms of a contrasting
diptych representing, as it were, "the misery of everyday life" with its
routine tasks and humiliations, and "the power of everyday life"
with its continuity, its endurance, its lurking power of adaptation,
resistance and escape (Lefebvre 1971: 35). Each is enclosed in an
elaborate frame in which the narrator's voice mimics the voices of
social authority with more uncertainty than it does in the earlier four
stories. Resistance to colonial expectations takes on a variety of
forbidden forms – alcoholism, hysteria, murder, and suicide.

As with Kipling's other stories, the epigraph to "In the Matter of
a Private" illustrates a point that the narrator refuses to make
explicit – the incompatibility between the power implied by public
codes and the misery of private reality:

> Hurrah! Hurrah! a soldier's life for me!
> Shout, boys, shout! for it makes you
> jolly and free.   ("The Ramrod Corps")

The story, however, reverses this expectation and shows, instead, that
the promise can drive a simple "Tommy" to insanity and violence.
It tells of the hysterical collapse of one Private Simmons, pushed to
the breaking point by his station in India, particularly by his fellow
campmate Private Losson whose many abuses include a trained
parrot whose insults include the call "Simmons, ye *so – or*" (or
"Simmons you swine"). The stresses under which this lower-class
Tommy operates are those to which Mannoni alerts us in *Prospero and
Caliban: The Psychology of Colonization*. Competitiveness and victimi-

zation translate into a vision of the world as a battlefield of power, destruction and aggression. Simmons, whose boyish innocence turns into hatred and insanity, is a far more disturbing portrait of the private than are the later more idealized (though still divided) and higher caste soldiers we see in the works of the 1890s, such as "The Brushwood Boy." The stresses on Simmons are meticulously detailed and begin with the external pressures of heat and dust, the sense of powerlessness and aloneness combined with the forced claustrophobic intimacy of army life, and the awareness of the constant threat by hostile others more assertive, more aggressive and more dangerous than oneself. Whereas Losson's attacks on Simmons are real, Simmons reenacts Losson's aggression through repetitive fantasies: "Sometimes he would picture himself trampling the life out of the man, with heavy ammunition-boots, and at others smashing in his face with the butt, and at others jumping on his shoulders and dragging the head back till the neckbone cracked." As the heat continues and tempers wear away more quickly, Simmons' hatred builds as he stays awake while Losson sleeps, and as the parrot continues to mock him, one night the thin boundary between reality and fantasy wears away and Simmons snaps.

He grabs a gun, kills Losson, and goes on a rampage in which he threatens to shoot anyone who approaches him. For this Simmons gets hanged, an occasion that allows all the moralists to come out of the woodwork. Some attribute the outbreak to alcohol, others to the Devil, while the "intelligent publicists" write "six beautiful leading articles on 'The Prevalence of Crime in the Army.'" The collision between the mad, unexpected, unpredictable act and the voices of order and rationality who wish to impose a single meaning on this overdetermined, multileveled scene of destruction is repeated in the formal collision between the narrator and the tale and between the conscious intention of the narrator and his unconscious fascination with the denied meaning of the story. No one sees him as the self-destructive heart of the imperialist enterprise. Simmons himself accepts all schools of thought and hopes that his fate will serve as a lesson to his companions in the army. The frame narrator, however, concludes the tale with a cryptic paragraph: "But not a soul thought of comparing the 'bloody minded Simmons' to the squawking, gaping school girls with which this story opens," thus drawing the reader's attention to his metonymic mode and obliquely to the absence of coherent interpretation in which all participants collude.

Kipling's recurring themes of boundary loss and of gender, subjectivity and selfhood under siege persist on several levels in this story. It opens with three long paragraphs on what the narrator calls "one of the quainter spectacles of human frailty... an outbreak of hysterics in a girl's school." It then proceeds to describe how one girl's giggle gets out of control, turning into an animallike "'*Honk, honk, honk,*' like a wild goose, and tears mix with laughter" only to lead to the next girl's similar affliction and collapse. The narrator then draws an analogy between the convent and the army, whose mother superiors and colonels "would be justly shocked at any comparison being made between their charge" – because this would amount to an unthinkable boundary breakdown between gender constructions. But, the narrator adds, it is a fact that soldiers too can be worked up to a "dithering, ripping hysteria." The effect of the analogy is clearly, once again, to threaten the demarcation of the soldier and of empire as unassailably masculine and aggressive, to say that this soldier can collapse into unmanly feminine loss of control. What the narrator (and others) are attempting to do is to find a term for a problem that no one in the system or in the army is willing to name. The unnamable problem is inadmissible and unacceptable to the code of the soldier, but is nonetheless real, and our narrator tries to deal with the efforts of others to define it. He objects, for instance, to the hysterical soldier being called "a brute":

Thomas isn't a brute ... he really ought to be supplied with a New Adjective to help him to express his opinion; but, for all that he is a great man. If you call him "the heroic defender of the national honor" one day, and "a brutal and licentious soldier" the next, you naturally bewilder him, and he looks upon you with suspicion. There is nobody to speak for Thomas except people who have theories to work off on him; and nobody understands Thomas except Thomas, and he does not always know what is the matter with himself. (*ST* 77)

But after all his efforts, the narrator is no better at naming than are the others, and he lapses into lame comparisons between the broken Simmons and the hysterical schoolgirls. Here the story and its narrator draw attention to its own inability to name – to its own hole in the narrative, and to its own silence. Yet the narrator seems to struggle with the contradiction between the desire to plug the soldier into the heroic, national apparatus and the opposing, resisting reality of the undefinable "feminine" male. In attempting to name the unnamable, he can only compare that unconscious aspect of the soldier to his caricatured negation – a schoolgirl falling into a giggling fit. The outrageous comparison violates the repressive code of the soldier by inverting its demands, exposing its potential absurdity by uncovering the feminine giggling schoolgirl under the uniform of the Tommy.

The analogy might be read as the narrator's own awareness of the pressures that compel an escape from masculinity or as narratorial evasion of the actual problems exposed by the event. Breakdown in the colonizer is homologous to breakdown in the system whose burdensome complexities rest on the fragile shoulders of such ordinary, yet characteristic Englishmen. But the analogy also reveals the hidden underside of masculine imperialism that relied on rigid and absolute definitions of "Manhood" as defined by sports, exercise, strength, hard work, and stoicism. The effeminate man is a nightmare of lost gender demarcation, and insofar as self is masculine and empire, it heralds the decline of the British Empire. This particular breakdown reminds us of many others also caused by isolation, victimization, and power-relationships sanctioned by a system that deprives the European of his normal resources: "but a man of any profession cannot read for eight hours a day in a temperature of 96° or 98° in the shade, running up sometimes to 103° at midnight. Very few men, even though they get a pannikin of flat, stale, muddy beer and hide it under their cots, can continue drinking for six hours a day. One man tried, but he died" (*ST* 76). As John McClure writes, the only categories of human relationship available to the colonizer as a consequence of his public school education were "dominance and submission" in a "terrible negative community." The negativity is also the result of homoerotic and homosocial affections simultaneously encouraged and denied by the masculinist community. And the impotent, unessential soldier explodes into destructiveness as a reaction against his invisibility, his denied need for a viable life and for a place in the community (McClure 1981: 18–20).

Committed as Kipling is to the reconstitution of gendered roles and the family in such institutions and groups as the army, the school, the Masonic lodge, or the club, his ambivalence is seen in such tales of resistance to that group-making impulse that demonstrate the pathology of the fraternal construct. These stories also suggest the problem of the construction of the imperial subject whose vulnerability and hysteria are but symptoms of the contradictions in the larger system. The breakdown of one reflects the fragility of the many, and private personality becomes a means to understand the larger society. The contradiction between the idealized strength of the system and the weakness of its link is confronted only obliquely and dismissed and resolved through flippant analogies, schoolboy heroics, and the ritualized celebration (a wedding) of the man who overpowers Simmons. The narrator himself lacks the conceptual vocabulary to account for what he knows must be accounted for – this explosion at the heart of the system that exposes for a split second its fatal flaw. And in that lack is an absence of knowledge, an admission of failure, characteristic not only of the Kipling narrator, but of the system he so ambivalently defends.

If all knowledge is political, then the Kipling narrator's knowledge of the colonial subject is charged with the power of the writer who knows that writing itself is a desperate gesture of survival against odds. To survive in India, the narrator and the colonial subject must be constantly on guard, learned in Indian ways, a master of Indian disguise, wary, observant and cautious. The chief threats to their rigidly defensive stance are many, but primarily they fear disintegration in the mysterious and chaotic nature of the land, particularly as it is manifested in the complexity of alien India, the Byzantine bureaucracy of colonial India, and the intrigues of colonial women. The compulsion to rework this fear in various modes through the distinct voices of the detached, knowledgeable and ambivalent observer and the victimized participant is part of Kipling's uneasy strategy of mediation with power relations in colonial India.

The failure of mediation with the overarching, masculinist system is revealed in eruptions of violent irrationality in stories that simultaneously confront and deny what they confront – the intolerable loneliness and misery produced by the imperial system. "Thrown Away," one more searing story of everyday colonial life, is a parable of a "Boy" who comes out ill-equipped to handle displacement and challenge. Its biblically detached tone establishes immediate boundaries between the teller and the "Boy" who isn't even given a name since he represents legions of sheltered, pretty, petted boys who come out only to die in the colonies. Lacking balance, restraint, or the armor of humor, the Boy takes all his losses (gambling, friends, women, and identity) too seriously, we are told. Some carelessly cruel comment made by a woman seems finally to have been "*the* thing that kicked the beam in The Boy's mind," and he withdraws first into isolation and then into suicide.

Of particular significance here as elsewhere in Kipling's narrative strategy are the contradictions between the narrative voice and the tone in this merciless tale of suicide. Related by a narrator-reporter equipped with a weary, cynical knowledge of colonial life, the voice is armored and defensive, though an oppositional, resisting discourse is created by a second voice – that of an older more experienced major who admits more vulnerability and access to private feeling than the Kipling frame narrator normally permits. The slippery voice of the narrator is at first efficiently detached, then coyly poetic in its elaborate metaphors and analogies, then scientifically empirical in its effort to understand this behavioral phenomenon unique to the colonies – suicide as the answer to social stress. My point here is that the official bureaucratic language adopted by the narrator conceals implication in the suicide at the heart of the story even as it reveals the impossibility of privacy and subjectivity in an act as private as suicide.

The opening sentence introduces the omnisciently announced universal truth that will implicitly be turned into unanswerable questions by the story's end: "To rear a boy under what parents call the 'sheltered life system' is, if the boy must go into the world and fend for himself, not wise" (*PTH* 16). The implication here is that the world offers no shelters, that it is a bullring of hostilities (as in Kipling's poem "If") for which the man/child must be prepared through savage schooling from his earliest years. The second paragraph develops an elaborate analogy whose inappropriateness draws attention to the narrator's inadequacy to deal with the subject: "Let a puppy eat the soap in the bathroom or chew a newly-blacked boot. He chews and chuckles until, by and by, he finds out that blacking and Old Brown Windsor make him very sick; so he argues that soap and boots are not wholesome... If he had been kept away from boots, and soap, and big dogs till he came to the trinity full-grown and with developed teeth, consider how fearfully sick and thrashed he would be!" (*PTH* 16).

After the oblique and oracular introductions, the actual story is introduced with yet another omniscient sentence made especially ironic by its eerie Wordsworthian echo: "There was a Boy once who had been brought up under the 'sheltered life' theory; and the theory killed him dead" (*PTH* 16). Because he has not learned to play the game and been systematically desensitized to humiliation and hostility, and because he has not been prepared to be "cut off from the support of his parents," and because he was unprepared to have "no one to fall back on in time of trouble except himself," he takes too many things too seriously. The narrator then interrupts the narrative again to offer a homily on the preferred perspective in colonial posts:

Now India is a place beyond all others where one must not take things too seriously – the mid-day sun always excepted. Too much work and too much energy kill a man just as effectively as too much assorted vice or too much drink. Flirtation does not matter, because everyone is being transferred, and either you or she leave the Station, and never return. Good work does not matter, because a man is judged by his worst output, and another man takes all the credit of his best as a rule. Bad work does not matter, because other men do worse and incompetents hang on longer in India than anywhere else ... Sickness does not matter, because it's all in a day's work, and if you die, another man takes over your place and your office in the eight hours between death and burial. Nothing matters except Home-furlough and acting allowances, and these only because they are scarce. (*PTH* 17)

These lines display characteristic contradictions in the narrator's discourse: they set up a merciless backdrop for the imperial enterprise, and they accept a stance at once unconcerned, distant, and cynical; it therefore comes as no surprise to the reader that boys blow out their brains rather than put up with the unrelenting indifference and hostility of such a system. The school for officers' sons that Kipling attended as a boy promised a different fare, as does Kipling's 1893 essay "An English School." There he remembers a wayward boy "cured" in the army after being "sent off on a little expedition alone where he would be responsible for any advice that was going, as well as for fifty soldiers" (Pinney 1990: 192); and recalls the joyful roar of students singing

> We are not divided,
> All one body we,
> One in faith and doctrine,
> One in charity.   (in Pinney 1990: 187)

"Thrown Away" selects different evidence. The unified roar of the song, as it were, is disrupted by dissenting voices. Now Kipling chooses the ironic voice of an embittered narrator whose knowledge gives him the power to see but not feel the anxiety of the fallen. He chooses a discourse designed to repress the specific and the private, to contract and reduce into manageable metaphors overwhelming problems that are then ruptured by the reality of an individual act – a drunken explosion, a hysteria, and a suicide. And so the movement from "one must not take things too seriously" to "nothing matters" is a movement from cynicism to nihilism, from one system of using knowledge to another. To blur real social distinctions is to deny them value; and once the narrator has deprived the colonial situation of value ("one must not take things too seriously"), he can retreat into false universalities and decadent nihilism ("nothing matters"). But the narrator's recognition of meaninglessness as defense interlocks with the suicide's inability to survive the loss of "meaning," and the narration therefore admits patterns of contradiction. The narrator's self-consciously cynical stance collides and connects with the other voices: that of the major, the silent, poignant one of the dead Boy's letter, and the polyphony of laughter and tears that interrupts the shaky authority of the troubled narrative.

These different voices are released when the narrator and the major discover the Boy's mutilated body. The major breaks down and weeps uncontrollably ("like a woman") but the narrator, though touched, continues with the business of clearing up the mess. After the two men decide to stage a fake, but more comforting death by cholera for the benefit of his family, and after they substitute for his "dreary and hopeless and touching" letters some of their own more appropriate and untruthful ones, both men collapse into hysterical laughter: "The laughing-fit and the chokes got hold of me again, and I had to stop. The Major was nearly as bad." Their uncontrollable laughter following the major's uncontrollable weeping repeats the loss of control at the heart of the story that the frame narrator tries to contain and repress. Laughter and crying, as Plessner has shown us, are both subversive eruptions of the body over which, momentarily, the mind has lost control. Both draw attention to the borderline relationship of people to their bodies, of the body to the social system, of being a body to having a body, of outside environment to inner selfhood. Both involve a struggle between the self and its physical existence in which the self loses control to the physical body. But whereas laughter is directed outwards at others, weeping is directed inwards towards and about ourselves (Plessner 1970: 56–69). Each uncontrollable act in the behavior of these survivors also becomes a visible and public substitute for the invisible, private, and uncontrollable suicide concealed in the folds of this story.

The narrator, the major, and the Boy expose the problem of living dual roles, of various forms of collapse into the cracks of the imperial structure. Their varying ways of silently resisting the system (to which they also submit) mirror each other: whereas the major can willingly identify with the Boy's feelings by weeping, the narrator defends himself against that possibility through grotesque and excessive laughter. A mirroring, doubling effect can be seen in the relationship between the narrator, the older major and the Boy himself. The Boy's suicide reminds the major of his past fears ("He said that he himself had once gone into the same Valley of the Shadow as The Boy, when he was young and new to the country; so he understood how things fought together in The Boy's poor jumbled head" [*PTH* 23]); and the major's collapse into tears reminds the narrator of his own vulnerability, against which objectifying laughter is the only defense. Both the Boy and the major, then, in varying degrees threaten the working defenses the narrator has erected against the possibility of privacy, regression and self-loss. But because the narrator seems determined to repeat and also to expose the contrast between himself and the suicide, the story of the Boy becomes the outward sign of the unacknowledged fears of the narrator. The narrator and the major finally conquer their fear through writing falsehoods which conceal the truth of the suicide's letters that would have given his life and death some form of agency and subjectivity had they not been destroyed. The final story we read, however, is a fiction that empowers the narrator and the major and that includes both laughter and weeping as subversive and rupturing strategies for survival.

Crossing over into the territory of the native, becoming native or even gaining "too much" knowledge about the Indian nighttown, but most dangerously entering the fatal liaison with the native woman were yet other ways for the "worst muckers" to transgress against the rigid boundaries enforced by colonial organization of social life. Kipling's letters and autobiography repeatedly identify the scene of writing with nighttime wanderings through the labyrinthine back alleys (gulleys) of Lahore in which he is both separated observer and accepted participant. His autobiography of course briefly mentions his insomniac wanderings through streets "when the night got into my head." But his letters of 1884–8 document more elaborately his pleasures at being part of native life. In one of several lengthy, serialized, funny, and informative letters to his cousin Margaret Burne-Jones, the nineteen-year-old Kipling tries on one day (November 28, 1885) to present the nobler view of the Englishman sacrificing himself for the good of India. But on the following Wednesday (this letter is written over a five week period) he writes in an alternative voice:

I have endeavoured to put forward feebly the fact that the English have the welfare of the natives at heart. One year out here would show you how much truth I have *not* written. Then you demand: – Have we any interests in common? *Werry* few dear old Wop – the bulk of us – d — d few. And 'faith if you knew in what inconceivable filth of mind the peoples of India were brought up from their cradle; if you realized the views – or one tenth of the views – they hold about women and their absolute incapacity for speaking the truth as we understand it – the immeasurable gulf that lies between the two races in all things you would see how it comes to pass that the Englishman is prone to despise the natives – (I *must* use that misleading term for brevity's sake) ... Underneath our excellent administrative system; under the piles of reports and statistics; the thousand of troops; the doctors; and the civilian runs wholly untouched and unaffected the life of the peoples of the land – a life as full of impossibilities and wonders as the Arabian nights. I don't want to gush over it but I do want you to understand Wop dear that, immediately outside of our own English life, is the dark and crooked and fantastic, and wicked: and awe-inspiring life of the "native." Our rule, so long as no one steals too flagrantly or murders too openly, affects it in no way whatever – only fences it around and prevents it from being disturbed. I have done my little best to penetrate into it and have put the little I have learnt into pages of "Mother Maturin" – Heaven send that she may grow into a full blown novel before I die. (*KP* F3: 3–4)

This extract draws attention to Kipling's acknowledgment of what he does *not* say and to what he sees. Earlier in this letter he reveals his understanding of the "native" as construct as he assures her that there is no such thing as the Indian "native." "When you write 'native' who do you mean? The Mahommedan who hates the Hindu; the Hindu who hates the Mahommedan; the Sikh who loathes both; or the semi-anglicized product of our Indian colleges who is hated and despised by Sikh, Hindu and Mahommedan. Do you mean the Punjabi who will have nothing to do with the Bengali; the Mahratta to whom the Punjabi's tongue is as incomprehensible as Russian to me; the Parsee who controls the whole trade of Bombay and ranges himself on all questions as an Englishman; the Sindee who is an outsider; the Bhil or the Gond who is an aborigine; the Rajput who despises everything on God's earth but himself; the Delhi

traders who control trade to the value of millions; the Afghan who is
only kept from looting these same merchants by dread of English
interference. Which one of all the thousand conflicting tongues,
races, nationalities and peoples between the Khaibar Pass and
Ceylon do you mean? There is no such thing as the natives of India;
any more than there is the 'People of India'" (*KP* F3: 2).

   This catalog of kinds of natives is an ethnological trick that creates
the illusion of mastery and knowledge – an illusion that Kipling is at
pains to undercut by insisting that the "native" is a false category.
Yet he can't resist the temptation to catalog. So too, his acknowledged
desire to "penetrate" the "awe-inspiring life of the 'native'" is
charged with the erotics of transgression that must be denied and
repressed as the price for power.

   Of all the aspects of native life impenetrable to the colonizer, the
body of the Indian woman served as the most forbidden zone of
transgression. In Kipling's love stories or stories of miscegenation
where the Englishman goes "worst mucker" by either loving or
living with a native woman, the marginalized and otherwise silent
native female is idealized and denigrated, given presence and voice,
yet finally erased. The punishment meted out to the native woman
for her role in the seduction is usually mutilation or death. The
production of the role of "Englishman as native-lover" plays out, in
part, an explicit political and cultural interest in preserving the
European against local contamination. But since the narrator (and
Kipling himself) admit to their own recurring fascination with the
contamination, the position of the author is at best finally ambivalent.

   In "Beyond the Pale," a story of an ill-fated affair between the
Englishman Trejago and a beautiful fifteen-year-old widow, both the
narrative stance and the structure seem at pains to repress the
unknowable problem at the heart of the labyrinthine gulleys of India
– the problem of the native woman as subject. The narrator, however,
acknowledges no such problem. He appears to have so mastered the
matter of India that he can announce "much that is written about
Oriental passion and impulsiveness is exaggerated and compiled at
second-hand, but a little of it is true" (*PTH* 131); his fascination with
the protagonist is clearly their kinship in "knowing too much" about
Indian life. Yet the narrator appears to rewrite the story of native
tragedy into a Victorian advice story designed to help young
Englishmen in the tropics: "This is the story of a man who wilfully
stepped beyond the safe limits of decent everyday society, and paid

for it heavily. He knew too much in the first instance; and he saw too much in the second. He took too deep an interest in native life; but he will never do so again" (*PTH* 127). "Trejago knew far too much about these things... No Englishman should be able to translate object-letters" (*PTH* 128). The problem of excessive knowledge contains within its dominant and hegemonic frame the horror of excessive desire and excessive lack: the tale ends with the gruesome vision of the girl's arms held out in the moonlight – "both hands had been cut off at the wrists, and the stumps were nearly healed" (*PTH* 131). The girl's amputation further objectifies her into a fragment, a lack, a part object of what was once almost whole, and for the reader, she is now marked by horror. Her mutilation makes her "less" than the other characters (and readers) and costs her the reader's interest in seeing her as worthy of Trejago's love. Her amputation is only mildly repeated in the wound Trejago suffers. Trejago, who swiftly heals, is "reckoned a very decent sort of man" who pays his calls regularly. "There is nothing peculiar about him, except a slight stiffness, caused by a riding-strain, in the right leg" (*PTH* 131). The story must end with a lie, with a denial of knowledge, and with symbolic castration that is his punishment for attempted escape from the system and for transgression into native life.

The gendered geography of the setting conflates the body of the female with the landscape of the city. The setting is a "trap," "deep away in the heart of the city" – a space that "ends in a dead-wall pierced by one grated window," which by the end of the story will be permanently walled over. Kipling's romance reenacts the fantasy family affair between India and England and blames the end of the affair on the "unreasonable" jealousy of the Indian girl who refuses to share the Englishman's devotion to club and culture. Although the story uses the cliché of "falling in love" to reenforce a fantasy of equality and to efface the power relationship between the ruler and the ruled, Kipling's narrator displays the inequality in the characteristic discourse of love: Bisesa is a "child" with "little feet, light as marigold flowers, that could lie in the palm of a man's one hand" (*PTH* 131); she is "an endless delight," as "ignorant as a bird" whose reactions to his daytime affairs "seemed quite unreasonably disturbed." But it is she who determines the end to the affair and it is she who accurately predicts that no harm will come to him no matter what her fate.

Confusions of gender, sexuality, knowledge, and geography create problems of fixing meaning in this story. The subject/narrator is empowered by his knowledge to pursue the eroticized object of sexual desire – the native woman who is troped as child of India. The politics of this Orientalized relationship are constructed by eroticizing the childlike, the passive, and the animal which opens the space for the colonizer who must of course master, domesticate and control. Trejago achieves his desire in piercing through the forbidden barrier that is her room though his quest leads him finally to a dead end. But she, the child with roseleaf hands, is victimized by her very gender into a sexuality and object position that mutilate her. She is thrice victimized, first by her own society that incarcerates the wife and widow, and then by her affair with Trejago, who objectifies her into the obscure object of Oriental desire, and finally by her uncle who reminds her of her status as partial being by amputating her hands. At Trejago's final visit, "someone in the room grunted like a wild beast, and something sharp – knife, sword, or spear – thrust at Trejago in his boorka." At the end, the slightly wounded Englishman rages and shouts "like a madman between those pitiless walls" (*PTH* 132); and the native girl is walled forever into a borderline space between the human and the nonhuman, life and death, culture and chaos, embodying the absence, darkness, beastliness, and castration that the European fears will be his lot if he goes beyond the pale. Her missing hands repeat the trope of other gaps – the mysterious house that cannot be found, the missing front door, the effaced and the hidden cause of the tragedy in the serialized conquests of the girl by native patriarchy and English imperialism. Trejago and the narrator repeat the trope through their final lack of knowledge of what the story means: he "does not know" what became of the girl, he "does not know" where the front of the house of his beloved is, and he cannot get "poor little Bisesa" back again. "He has lost her in the City where each man's house is as guarded and as unknowable as the grave; and the grating that opens into Amir Nath's Gully has been walled up" (*PTH* 132). Two forms of gendered desire, the lack and the thrust, collide and meet with destruction. Finally, then, the tropes of Kipling's story mutilate the desire of the reader, the narrator, and the native subject for further knowledge.

Structures of forbidden sexuality and desire, troped in terms of mastery and pleasure, fetishize the woman in order to counter male fear of self loss; these structures are part of a familiar nineteenth-century colonial discourse that fetishizes the Other as fixed stereotype. The colonial object and the native woman, then, are both objects to be recognized and disavowed, appropriated and defamiliarized. Transgressing the body of the forbidden woman as desired lover was treated again in 1891 ("Without Benefit of Clergy") and in 1893 ("Love-o'-Women"). The more involved the English protagonist, the greater his suffering and punishment. But the narrator's attitude towards the love in each story is marked by varieties of ideologically determined figures. In "Without Benefit of Clergy," the details of Ameera's life, background, appearance, and destiny are all charged with Orientalist anxieties. The native "wife" has been "bought" from her mother by Holden the Englishman; she is introduced to us sitting at his feet, "a woman of sixteen, and she was all but all the world in his eyes" (*LH* 116). Her mother is described as "the withered hag" (*LH* 116), again an Orientalist stereotype of the Eastern beauty as one who ages easily and hideously (this happens at the end of "Lisbeth" and most horrifically in Rider Haggard's *She*). But famine, drought, fever, and cholera combine to kill first their child Tota and then Ameera who (like She) gradually dissolves from beautiful desired body to a corpse, even as the rain dissolves walls, roads and graves; and the house that enshrined their love is burned by the Municipality who will instead build an English road, "so that no man may say where this house stood" (*LH* 137).

In "Love-o'-Women" the syphilitic soldier dies in the arms of his "Diamonds-and-Pearls" murmuring "I'm dyin', Aigypt – dyin'" (*MI* 323) – words that idealize the degraded object of desire who is about to enter a brothel but chooses death over life without her man. In this moment of fusion in death we see also Kipling's version of the connection between idealization and degradation: the love is idealized in Shakespearean language to defy the law but degraded by the reader's awareness of the real physical corruption that contradicts the apparent idealization of the final unifying consequences of desire.

The most famous story in which personal and political desire collide at the boundary of a native woman's body and cause for the Englishman a fate worse than death is, of course, "The Man Who Would Be King" (December 1888). In one of his letters to his "sweet and trusty Wop," his cousin Margaret Burne-Jones, which he began on January 25, 1888 and concluded on March 24, 1888, Kipling includes two personal anecdotes that will find their way into the frame of his best known allegory of empire. Both are worth quoting at some length to give the flavor, not only of the similarity between his letter writing prose and that of the Kipling narrator's, but of the escape routes from the private nightmares of the insomniac Kipling and from the larger colonial system available to Kipling as journalist:

Since November last I have been a vagabond on the face of the Earth. But such a vagabondage! Did I tell you how the *Pioneer* took me over and bade me go out for a month into Rajputana – the home of a hundred thousand legends and the great fighting men of India. They gave me did my generous masters Rs 600 a month and paid my Railway expenses. Ach Himmel. Was there anything like that dissolute tramp through some of the loveliest and oldest places upon the face of the Earth. I wrote a series of letters called "Letters of Marque" – by the way it is running still – and I railed and rode and drove and tramped and slept in Kings palaces or under the stars themselves and saw panthers killed and heard tigers roar in the hills, and for six days had no white face with me, and explored dead cities desolate these three hundred years, and came to stately Residences where I feasted in fine linen and came to desolate wayside stations where I slept with natives upon the cotton bales and clean forgot that there was a newspapery telegraphic world without. Oh it was a good and clean life and I saw and heard all sorts and conditions of men and they told me the stories of their lives, black white and brown alike, and I filled three note books and walked "with death and morning on the silver horns" and knew what it was to endure hunger and thirst. (*KP* F5: 2)

And on January 27, in the third serialized continuation of the same letter, Kipling describes an impending meeting at a Masonic Lodge which reminds him of a "fantastic tale" he wants to tell "mon amie," also called "the Wop of Asia":

Last month I was right away on the other side of India; not 400 miles from Bombay. Now I am less than 300 from Calcutta. You can see the stretch on the map. When I was on the borders of Bhilwarra (look that out on the map) I met a man who was also a mason. "Ships upon the sea" are nothing compared to our meetings in India. He said to me "A friend of mine is coming across the Empire from the East (Assam way) touching at Bombay and going Home. I cannot stir from here to meet him though he will pass within less than 300 miles. Your road towards the Great Indian Desert will cross his, if you go by such and such a train, just on the borders of the sands, if he keeps to his timing. Take me a message, to which I do not wish to write." The message was perfectly unintelligible to me and would, I imagine, have been equally so to any man who did not know to what it referred. My brother gave me this message and I went up and up northwards from the western side of India till I came to a junction on the edge of the desert and was set out of the train at five on a bitterly cold winter's morning with all the stars blazing overhead and a wind fit to cut you in two blowing off the sands. The Calcutta train – i.e. the train from Agra bearing the Bombay mails came in and a man in one of the carriages opened a window and looked out sleepily. I didn't want to go threshing all down the train – there were three Englishmen on it, in search of my unknown, so I went towards the window and behold, it was the man I was told to find; for he also (doesn't this sound mad?) was also a brother of mine. I bent over him and gave the message and he said sleepily: – "Tha'anks. I know what it means. You needn't repeat it. Tha'anks." Then I went away and the Calcutta train went off to Bombay and I set out into the desert on my journey. Now *remember* I didn't know the name of the man who gave me the message. He didn't know mine. I didn't know the name of the man who received it and he didn't know me. Wasn't it odd and out of the world? I felt like the Camorri and the Brothers of Mercy and all sorts of veiled and mysterious things for at least five minutes. (*KP* F5: 4)

The Kipling Papers at Sussex also contain another odd letter (1890) alluding to this story from Kipling to a Dr. Taylor inviting him to bring his daughter and Miss Dravot to a visit. Mrs. Hill adds a memorandum to this letter that reads as follows:

When "The Man Who Would be King" was germinating in R. K.'s mind – one day, lunching at Belvedere House, he suddenly demanded names for his characters. Mr. Hill responded, "Well, the most distinctive name I ever heard was that of a missionary whom I once met in the Himalayas – Peachey Taliaferro." Kipling seized that at once and turned to me. Of course I could think of nothing unusual. "Well," said he, "Who were the most prominent men in your home town?" "Dravot and Carnehan," I replied – and the names struck his fancy. The young lady mentioned in the letter written to my father in 1890 was the daughter – interesting that he should have actually met her. (*KP* 16/2–5: 97)

"The Man Who Would Be King" is Kipling's most powerful allegory of empire and kingship, a story of control, desire and subversion, of authority and its discontents, and of the "worst muckers" as world makers and destroyers. A small compendium of his most characteristic concerns, it is enclosed in one of his more elaborate frames that invites the reader to read the lurid embedded tale in its dialectical relationship to the oblique and strange matrix that contains it. The incident chosen for retelling is, as always, a source of displaced personal and political anxiety for the narrator who assumes a stance at once invulnerable, distant and ironic, but whose rhetoric inadvertently reveals his vulnerability and collusion.

The bare outline suggests a cautionary colonialist allegory about two daring, swashbuckling adventurers who, finding India too confining for their grandiose ambitions, decide to travel to remote, icy, and forbidden Kafiristan in order to become kings. Dravot's and Carnehan's conquest of Kafiristan, accomplished with twenty Martini rifles, a knowledge of British military drill, and a mystique of divine right based on a garbled, half-forgotten version of Masonic ritual, sounds remarkably like a seedy version of the British Raj. That their downfall is provoked by Dravot's hubris encourages us to read the story as a treatment, in schoolboy-thriller form, of Kipling's recurrent "Recessional" theme: England can retain its divinely given right to rule only so long as it retains moral superiority, a "humble and a contrite heart." The partiality of such a reading is demonstrated by the fact that it omits the most important character in the story – the narrator – who compels us to reread its meaning through the complex negotiation between the embedded adventure and the frame. The disturbance in this narrative is created by the collision between its central romantic myth and its distancing realistic, ironic frame whose narrator tempers his dispassionate perceptions of the adventurers with an elegaic and religious sentimentality. The narrator's stance relativizes his relationship to the embedded tale, distances itself from the quest of the adventurers, yet appears incapable of detaching itself from collusion in its implications. That ambivalence, so typical of Kipling, exteriorizes cultural and historical conflicts between the desire to colonize, connect and possess (country and woman) and the warning against such desire, between the glorification of imperial adventure and the cynical debunking of its origins in greed, self-aggrandizement, and childlike games of power.

Typical of Kipling's narrative strategy, the world of "The Man Who Would Be King" is radically divided. Although the initial and fundamental opposition between "Man" and "King," between the human and his politically symbolic function, is announced in the title, the larger opposition in the story is between the world of the narrator – realistic, seasoned, ironic – and that of the adventurers – romantic, flamboyant, and "mad." The duality makes some parts of the story more dreamlike than others, as if the narrator were the waking self and the embedded tale a dream, a journey into archaic fantasies charged with desire, romance and unreality. The denied and forbidden aspects of character not accessible but desired by the narrator find expression in the daring of the two bombastic and misguided adventurers whom he glorifies and exoticizes by myth and romance. If this structure, however, would seem to imply a liberating confrontation with the repressed leading to a cathartic resolution of contradiction, the story never realizes that promise. By enveloping the tale in romantic religiosity, Biblical language and the mythology of Freemasonry, Kipling seems to evade and transcend the social and political. Analogously, he displaces the problem of invasion, lawlessness and power in the story away from its historical immediacy to the personal; yet he represents that displacement in terms of the overdetermined contradictions of imperial mythology. By displacing the reader's attention from history onto the individual act in order to "manage" and defuse deeply political crises with substitute gratifications, the story becomes a version of what Jameson might call "the modernist project" (1981 : 266). The theme of the story appears to be an anticolonialist allegory in which the adventurers are an absurd parody of the British in the third world; yet its apparent absurdity is subverted by imagery and language that idealize the imperial mission. And the distance of the frame, which appears at first to counter the inner, individual and subjective experience, finally supports it through its own neutralizing of irony with compassion.

The conflict between the realistic frame and the romantic story for which it provides a matrix, its two conflicted modes and genres, is partially generated by the historical contradiction of imperial culture: the myth of imperialism is disrupted by the very principle that created it – by colonial man who is neither god nor king, and by the colonized country (Kafiristan) that has already a power, a native presence, and a mother lodge which cannot tolerate the reality of the man beneath the myth.

The doubleness and splitting of the narrator mirror the splitting of the colonial enterprise into agencies of protection and power, of subjugation and powerlessness. The narrator's office and life are invaded by the two adventurers who overpower him with their physical presence and demand his submission to their wishes; but his powerlessness is only temporary because he and his writing will survive into the permanence of recorded fiction. It mirrors too the splitting of Dravot from the ordinary man to the symbolic and divine God-King, a moment that is illuminated by Pierre Bourdieu's reading of political fetishism, "the process in terms of which individuals constitute themselves... as a group but through this process lose control of the group in and through which they constitute themselves" (1984–5: 57). Dravot as political fetish consecrates himself with the mystery of leadership through strategies of language and action that ritualize his power. In Bourdieu's scheme, his splitting of the self is necessary to achieve "the oracle effect" through which the individual extinguishes himself in the service of the transcendent and symbolic self. The movement from man to king involves a conversion through which the ordinary person must die so that the symbolic moral person can be born (p. 63).

Whereas the outer story is told by a man about men, the inner story is a temporarily realized dream of heroism and kingship. The man who would be king, Dravot, focuses on the end product – kingship – as the basic unit of his economy around which all else must revolve. But he grows blind to those who grant him that kingship and upon whose labor his status depends. And it is that blindness to his people, to their expectations of him as king, that leads him to his fatal mistake – the marriage that exposes him as a man – a category which his kingship was designed to conceal. The impossible contradiction he is now faced with is quite simple: he cannot be both man and king and must therefore die. Ironically, however, these polarities have been generated by his own desire and are as radically incompatible as those other binary oppositions that the convenient closure of the frame seeks to transcend – native and ruler, the individual and society, nature and culture, the unconscious and the conscious.

The frame narration creates an almost Brechtian estranging effect, at once alienating the reader from the subject matter and compelling her, in spite of the disturbing ambivalence of the narrator, to think about the political dimensions of the enclosed tale. The daring, swashbuckling, romantic adventure into Kafiristan is in part a projection of a narrator who cleaves to the security of margins, of offices, of bureaucracy, and of second-hand reporting of the forbidden adventures of others. But it is also what a Jameson might see as the nostalgic fantasy of an empire in crisis, creating for itself a myth of origins and trying to discover a cause for the still to be dreaded future – the fall of the British Raj. The story of two crazy adventurers will become signs for the tragedy of colonialism: crucified by the men over whom they rule, their end will justify and glorify the means they use to attain it.[1] But it will also be a sign of the Kipling narrator's deepest fear which repeats itself with variations in poems and stories and dreams – the fear of literally and figuratively losing one's head; the story, then, is also an effort to master a recurring fear of self-loss.

The opening paragraph sets up the story's structure of values and voices. The world to which the narrator introduces us is one already structured by unifying tropes of family and social grouping. Although it is a hierarchical world made up of brothers, princes, beggars and kings, the epigraph would seem to suggest a transcendent design available through the Freemason law of equality: "Brother to a Prince and fellow to a beggar if he be found worthy" (*MK* 244). The narrator's attraction to such a law is based not on his observation of its internal contradiction, but rather on his understanding of the obvious truism, that what lies beneath one's social disguise is impossible to assess: "I have been fellow to a beggar again and again under circumstances which prevented either of us finding out whether the other was worthy" (*MK* 244). More significantly, he is attracted by transcendent metaphors, by language that extends reality into new dimensions and possibilities (a sort of linguistic colonization), by the analogy between family and class structure, an analogy that can only be sustained by metaphor and not by social or political reality. But the metaphors of Freemasonry, like the metaphors of empire, share the lure of imaginary unity and transcend real political and economic divisions through rituals that deny the absence of "brother-hood" between the colonizer and the colonized, the rich and the poor, or democracy and dictatorship. The first paragraph, then, introduces a problem of language and metaphor that contains the contradictions between social institutions or law and life ("The Law, as quoted, lays down a fair conduct of life, and one not easy to follow"), but fails to pursue the implications of the dilemma. Rather, the narrator allows himself to be absorbed by the metaphor, to soften his skeptical tone, until the last elegiac sentence of the paragraph which resonates with religiosity and myth: "But today, I greatly fear that my King is dead, and if I want a crown I must go and hunt it for myself" (*MK* 244).

The rest of the frame is a flashback divided into four scenes recalling the four encounters between the narrator and the adventurers. The shifting stance of the narrator from his initial sense of connection, to detached doubt and distrust, to his eventual reluctant admiration and pity is analogous to the movement of the inner story and also to the change in the initially doubtful stance of Carnehan towards the grandiose dreams of Dravot. The first meeting with Carnehan in the train establishes sufficient kinship to lead the narrator to agree to pass a message on to Dravot at the Marwar

Station. The second meeting takes place in the narrator's office late one hot, tense, and anxious night, when Dravot and Carnehan appear with the "contrack" outlining their plan to become kings of Kafiristan. The third meeting occurs the next morning at the town square where the two men, disguised as mad priest and dumb servant, display their facility at deceiving native mobs and at concealing the reality of aggression (rifles and ammunition) under the guise of selling whirligigs to the Amir. Carnehan's story will use the image of the whirligig repeatedly to suggest the unconscious understanding of the deadly implication of the Great Game as it evolves from play to massacre. The last time the narrator meets Carnehan some three years later, the giant who had thought "India isn't big enough for such as us" (*MK* 252) is now a shrunken, ragged, whining shadow who returns after crucifixion, clutching the decapitated, crowned head of Dravot and survives only long enough to tell his tale to the narrator.

The bonds connecting the narrator as journalist with the adventurers begin with the most obvious, their mutual attraction to India, to travel, to politics and to secret clubs: "He was a wanderer and a vagabond like myself... He told tales of things he had seen seen and done... We talked politics – the politics of Loaferdom, that sees things from the underside where the lath and plaster are not smoothed off – " (*MK* 245). And the bond of Freemasonry is the hook that connects the narrator with Dravot and their later lives. The deeper connection making the adventurers doubles for the narrator is their gift for story telling and their profession, which is an unlawful version of his restrained double life. The newspaperman's job takes him to "the dark places of the earth, full of unimaginable cruelty, touching the Railway and the Telegraph on one side, and, on the other, the days of Harun-al-Rashid" (*MK* 247). But whereas the narrator survives such descents into the dark, the adventurers will not. Like them, he too is fascinated with disguise, with power and with kings: "I did business with divers Kings, and in eight days passed through many changes of life. Sometimes I wore dress-clothes and consorted with Princes and Politicals... Sometimes I lay out upon the ground and devoured what I could get, from a plate made of leaves, and drank the running water, and slept under the same rug as my servant. It was all in a day's work ... Then I became respectable and returned to an Office where there were no Kings" (*MK* 247–8). The similarities between the narrator's language and Kipling's letter, between the narrator's meeting with the adventurers and Kipling's meeting with the "brothers" while travelling across India, remind us of the personal sources of fiction and of his investment in the secret societies, clubs and systems of homosocial bonding that were part of the ideology of empire as family.

The narrator's complaints about the heat, sickness, world politics, and working conditions are repeated in caricature by his storytelling double, Carnehan, who suffers from some of the same distress but reaches different conclusions: "We have been all over India, mostly on foot. We have been boiler-fitters, engine-drivers, petty contractors ... and we have decided that India isn't big enough for such as us" (*MK* 252). Flirting on the edge of danger, fantasy and dream, the narrator's voice is a recurring call to restraint, to stay one's hesitating foot at the edge of the abyss in order to survive self-loss and ascend into the authority of authorship.

The immediate appeal of the vagabonds to the narrator is their ambition, their dream, and their action. In contrast to the narrator, who labors and struggles and sweats thanklessly into the night transforming trauma and distress into palatable newsmatter for the leisure class, Peachey and Dravot are shapers and controllers of destiny, builders of dreams and empires. When they reappear in the narrator's life at three o'clock one hot, tense and anxious morning, clothed all in white, they appear almost as dream figures emerging out of his unconscious. Larger than life, we are told that they were not only too big for India but for the office: "Dravot's beard seemed to fill half the room and Carnehan's shoulders the other half" (*MK* 252). What they share with the narrator is a sense of defeat by India ruled as it is by a displaced establishment in competition with each other ("they that governs it won't let you touch it" [*MK* 252]). Because they wish to move from the margins of society into its centers, from being vagabonds to kings (their aim is to "Sar-a-whack" Kafiristan) they decide to pursue their megalomaniacal illusions of power and grandeur into creating an empire: "We shall be Emperors – Emperors of the Earth!" Their announced plan is a familiar one: "We shall go to those parts and say to any king we find – 'D'you want to vanquish your foes?' and we will show him how to drill men; for that we know better than anything else. Then we will subvert that King and seize his throne and establish a Dy-nasty" (*MK* 252–3). The adventurers, therefore, overcome their sense of defeat by history and class through aggression, cunning and conquest. The narrator trails along their tracks admitting certain connections with them, undercutting others, and finally establishing the authority of his mode over theirs by the fact of his sensibility and survival.

The dynamics between Carnehan and Dravot are a variation on the pattern of opposition set up between the narrator and the adventurers. Dravot the overreacher and visionary is to Carnehan – the cautious worker and the voice of restraint and practicality – what both men are to the narrator. They pay as little heed to his warnings as Dravot pays to those of Carnehan. At first happy to play what appears to be a continuation of their earlier game with whirligigs and concealed rifles, Carnehan later admits, "I knew he was thinking plans I could not advise about, and I just waited for orders" (*MK* 268). But when Carnehan questions his decisions and his order to arrange a marriage for him with a native woman, it is too late for Dravot, who has by now internalized the illusions and the oracular rhetoric of kingship and power: "You are my people, and by God ... I'll make a damned fine Nation of you, or I'll die in the making!(*MK* 267) ... I won't make a Nation ... I'll make an Empire! these men aren't niggers; they're English!" (*MK* 269). Dravot's desire to marry is a violation not only of his contract with Carnehan, but of an unspoken code of imperial male bonding that surpasses the love of woman.

Just as the narrator's apparently ethical awareness of problems of lawless imperialism is subverted by his language and his allusions, so too Carnehan's awareness of Dravot's hubris is averted by his elevated language and imagery. These conflicted languages reflect Kipling's ambivalence towards his subject matter which shapes itself into competing voices, frames, and modes. Carnehan's early childlike language describing their methods of subversion ("Dravot he shoots above their heads, and they all falls down flat. Then he walks over them and kicks them, and then he lifts them up and shakes hands all round ... Then a lot of men came into the valley, and Carnehan and Dravot picks them off with the rifles ... " [*MK* 262]) contrasts with the later more ornate and biblical language of appropriation and kingship. The flatness of the earlier passage, for instance, denies the horror of violence and death and slides into another language of denial – that of the Old and New Testaments. Now wanton killing of "enemies" is followed by an absurd sacramentalizing ritual: "For each dead man Dravot pours a little milk in the ground and waves his arms like a whirligig, and 'That's all right,' says he" (*MK* 262). This ritual is followed by further biblical pronouncements which, increasingly for Carnehan, serve to sanctify their actions: "and Dravot says: 'Go and dig the land, and be fruitful and multiply,' which they did" (*MK* 262). After acts of colonization described simply as "firing into the brown of the enemy" (*MK* 264), Carnehan crowns the moment by saying to his Chief, "'Occupy till I come'; which was scriptural" (*MK* 264).

As Paul Fussell has pointed out, their imperialist enterprise begins in the language of the Old Testament, with allusions to the accounts of creation, the history of early Hebraic kings, and the harmonizing of the tribes of Israel, and ends in the language of the New Testament. Carnehan begins his story by swearing: "It's true ... True as gospel. Kings we were, with crowns upon our heads – me and Dravot." During his arbitrations over land wars between villages, Dravot is peacemaker, judge, destroyer and creator, the first Adam and the second: "And Dravot says, 'Go and dig the land, and be fruitful and multiply,' which they did"; "'That's just the beginning,' says Dravot. 'They think we're Gods ... They were a poor lot, and we blooded 'em with a kid before letting 'em into the new kingdom'" (*MK* 263). Eventually, their kingdom will be built upon a rock under which is concealed the Masonic mark that makes them also into Gods. Their closest and most loyal friend among the priests and chiefs is Billy Fish; they perceive their people as "The Lost Tribes, or something like it"; Carnehan uses arguments from the Bible to dissuade Dravot from taking a native wife: "The Bible says that Kings ain't to waste their strength on women" (*MK* 271); and most lurid of all, Carnehan, marked by stigmata, is punished by crucifixion followed by a resurrection ("it was a miracle that he wasn't dead" [*MK* 271]), after which he returns to civilization to spread the word through our narrator.

But I want to add to Fussell's observations a political dimension that suggests Kipling's perhaps unconscious recognition of the strategy through which kingship separates, isolates, sacramentalizes, and demonizes the man. During the final crisis over desire for a wife, Dravot and his flaming red beard grow to signify ambivalently charged associations: "he went away through the pine-trees looking like a big red devil, the sun being on his crown and beard and all" (*MK* 270). By this stage in his evolution, Dravot has monopolized and appropriated all meaning and power into himself. He becomes what Nietzsche might call the Antichrist whose hypocrisy consists of living the lie of representing others (Bourdieu 1984–5: 62). But the connection of the demonic with the emblematic color of the British Empire is almost immediately transcended by sentimentality after Dravot's death when the whole narrative is bathed in nostalgia for the man who was once a King – a moment celebrated in the hymn Peachey sings as he shambles out of the narrator's office:

> The son of man goes forth to war,
> A golden crown to gain;
> His blood-red banner streams afar!
> Who follows in his train?

Whereas the allusions to the Bible sanctify their venture, and those to Freemasonry transcend the divisions between the colonizers and colonized by presuming archetypal unities,[2] the self-divided Kipling would for other reasons, too, be attracted to an order that encourages the further division between inside and outside. By emphasizing universal brotherhood and a commonality that was nonpolitical and nonreligious, the order attempted what a Kipling was too ready to do – transcend and thereby avoid political and religious division and strife. And so a youthful Kipling would congratulate himself on presuming to have broken barriers in India by associating with natives within a lodge. Just such a division (a point earlier made by Fussell) is celebrated in "The Mother-Lodge":

> Outside – "Sergeant! Sir! Salute! Salaam!"
> Inside – "Brother," an' it doesn't do no 'arm.

If all plot involves the unfolding of blocked and resisted desire (Brooks 1984: 12), the logical source of narrative desire in Kipling must be found in the narrator who diffuses and represses motive, interest and intention through his worldweary stance and defensive discourse, and who drives the denied object of unconscious desire into the central embedded story. Yet he suggests the direction of this desire in the nostalgia of his opening paragaph's final hypothetical clause – "I greatly fear that my King is dead, and if I want a crown I must go hunt it for myself" (*MK* 244) – a clause which also contains the metonymy that moves the narrative and "can never quite speak its name" (Brooks 1984: 56). The story that began with acknowledgment of fear and desire ends with a nightmare image of that desire fulfilled – the image of crucified Carnehan carrying the decapitated, shrivelled head of Dravot with a crown: "He fumbled in the mass of rags round his bent waist; brought out a black horsehair bag embroidered with silver thread; and shook therefrom on to my table – the dried withered head of Daniel Dravot! The morning sun that had long been paling the lamps struck the red beard and blind sunken eyes; struck, too, a heavy circlet of gold studded with raw turquoises, that Carnehan placed tenderly on the battered temples."

At this point my reading leaves unanswered how the ending resolves the conflict between individual desire and social reality. Social and economic realities are controlled and embodied in the voice of the narrator and later Carnehan when he warns Dravot against giving in to his desire for a native wife. The moment of Dravot's kiss signifies not only his inability to restrain desire, but the racist and political implications of that lawless desire: the Englishman has violated the boundaries proper to his place in the ruling class. But that gesture, accompanied by his proprietary but lower-class responses that provoke and accompany the kiss, complicates the social model and codes that collide against each other here:

"She'll do," said Dan, looking her over. "What's to be afraid of, lass? Come and kiss me."...

"The slut's bitten me!" says he, clapping his hand to his neck, and, sure enough, his hand was red with blood. (*MK* 274)

Dravot's desire tests the social code that he has violated with the marriage, and the kiss momentarily allows us to hope for his unifying bond with the natives and for his continued control over them and his bride, but then returns us to the frame with its grotesque image of Carnehan and the surviving narrator/reporter. Although both the narrator and the adventurers work through a desire that can never be fulfilled (Brooks 1984: 98), the significance of the quest romance is in the effect of again remembering, repeating, and working through the conflict over a desire that must be fulfilled even as it is thwarted and contained (Frye 1957: 193). Through his restraint and acquired knowledge, the frame narrator delivers us from the anxieties of illicit desire and conflicted social reality: he suggests a way to live that will allow the colonialist to exert yet contain his desires for power and control – by remaining discreetly in the margins exerting authority through authorship and transforming life into print. The inner story, however, reveals the workings of his repressed desire for "a crown" and for forbidden adventure that necessarily implicates the seeker in power which leads to isolation, self-deception, and tragedy. A frame that contains and controls the inner tragedy is an appropriate form for an ideology that masks the dangers of its own enterprise in comic rhetoric and that transcends its own contradictions with mythology. The anxieties that accompany real kingship and imperialism are confronted on levels that are at once ordinary and symbolic, private and political, with the profound recognition that when power is fetishized into the symbolically sacred, it must destroy its human source. This dream journey to power, kingship, divinity, crucifixion, death, and return, takes the restrained newspaperman not only into forbidden desires and alien territories, but also towards dangerously prophetic insights into the self-destructive mechanisms of imperialism. And Kipling's narrative tests the extent to which the desire unleashed by the mythology of imperialism can violate its sustaining social system and unspoken cultural codes.

The Kipling narrator/reporter's wanderings through India result in stories of loss and of horror, of collapse into gaps and holes that literalize lack and absence. The wounds of India mirror concealed wounds in Englishmen that, formed in childhood, reopen in India. The tiny wound on little George Cottar's thumb in "The Brushwood Boy," for instance, is an appropriate example of the secret lack and injury that, though insignificant and irrelevant to the manifest events in the story, is nonetheless mentioned and repressed, only to return later to haunt and destroy other colonizers in other stories. So too that which is named as fearsome, undesirable or objectionable in one part of his work, for instance, often returns – and this is a central feature of the metonymic mode – to haunt another part of his fiction as ambivalent object of obscure desire. Trejago will be wounded in the groin and his lover will have her hands cut off at the wrists; Fleete will be turned into a beast ("The Mark of the Beast" *LH*) and Otheris will go temporarily mad ("The Madness of Private Otheris" *PTH*). It is easy to explain these wounds in terms of English education, of repressed sexuality and denied homoeroticism, of Kipling's childhood, or of a system that victimized its children in schools that concealed ruthlessness with rigidity and discipline. But Kipling's texts refuse to allow such single explanations for events that signify multiple possibilities of competing political, social and psychological meanings.

In "Bubbling Well Road," first published in 1888, though collected later in *Life's Handicap* (1891), the narrator-protagonist gets lost in a grassy jungle where he discovers an eerie, haunted well guarded by a strange priest whose face displays evidence of torture at the hands of his local rulers: "He is a one-eyed man and carries, burnt between his brows, the impress of two copper coins. Some say that he was tortured by a native prince in the old days" (*LH* 266). Although, by the end of the story, the narrator is safe, the episode has aroused in him an uncharacteristic surge of irrational anger: "I heard the Well laughing to itself alone in the thick grass, and only my need for his services prevented my firing both barrels into the priest's back ... Before I left I did my best to set the patch alight, but the grass was too green. Some fine summer day, however, if the wind is favourable, a file of old newspapers and a box of matches will make clear the mystery of Bubbling Well Road" (*LH* 269). The irrationality of the narrator's desire to fire "both barrels into the priest's back" and to set fire to the place in order to clarify the mystery of the well is compounded by the absence of a narrative solution to the conflicts in the story. The tale itself becomes, as it were, a black hole that laughs at the narrator's (and the reader's) desire for explanation, clarification and resolution.

The Kipling protagonist, character, or narrator who is mutilated physically and psychically is also the mutilated victim of a flawed colonial power structure, of his powerless position in the bureaucracy, and of the clubs and the women whose slightest wiles could drive a man either to suicide ("Thrown Away") or into an abyss ("At the Pit's Mouth"). The "preface" to *Life's Handicap* attributes some of the stories to "Gobind the one-eyed" holy man. The subtitle to the volume, "Being Stories of Mine Own People," is appropriate because half the stories are about the mutilated, the dying, and the hopelessly defeated.

The problem of failure and going "worst mucker" in India is confusingly conflated with class and sexual desire in "The Man Who Would Be King." But the connection between failure and transgressive knowledge is nowhere as explicit as in "To be Filed for Reference," the last story in *Plain Tales from the Hills*. Here, the Oxford scholar McIntosh Jellaludin (clearly a different caste from the earlier vagabonds), now perpetually drunk and "past redemption," cared for by his native woman, is evidence of the cost of miscegenation and transgression of class and race boundaries. Narrated by the Kiplingesque reporter, this is the only story in which the author, by referring to a work-in-progress, uses another artist as a double. The book on which the Oxford educated scholar, now gone native, has been working for seven years is *The Book of Mother Maturin*, the subject of Kipling's epic novel about Anglo-India which he began writing in 1885. It was never published because, so his biographers tell us, his parents disapproved of its contents.[3] That novel, the product of Kipling's nightwalking knowledge of the bazaars and gullies of Lahore, repressed and censored by his most beloved authority figures, reappears here as the last will and testament of a broken, alcoholic writer, who has traveled even further than his author into the Indian night.

The story recalls the narrator's friendship with him and McIntosh's last request that he come and help him die. On this last day, he bequeaths to the narrator what he had long promised, "the materials of a new Inferno," that might someday make him "greater than Dante": "This ... is my work – the Book of McIntosh Jellaludin, showing what he saw and how he lived, and what befell him and others; being also an account of the life and sins and death of Mother Maturin ... My only baby! ... You will treat it brutally, I know you will. Some of it must go; the public are fools and prudish fools. I was their servant once. But do your mangling gently. It is a great work, and I have paid for it in seven years' damnation" (*PTH* 240–1). The narrator, "a Virgil in the shades," is a man who is never truly lost, who has never really "reached the uttermost depths of degradation," and whose "soul" has not cavorted "with the Gods." Measured against Jellaludin, even Strickland, the erstwhile Kipling hero, is laughed at as "an ignorant man," ignorant because only degradation can help one understand the lower depths. But the price of such knowledge is complete alienation from colonial society, marriage to a native woman, and alcoholism. After Jellaludin's death, Strickland helps the narrator to sort out the papers, which Strickland feels are the work of "an extreme liar," and which the narrator decides to expurgate. The story ends with the self-referential line "If the thing is ever published, some one may perhaps remember this story, now printed as a safeguard to prove that McIntosh Jellaludin and not I myself wrote the Book of Mother Maturin. I don't want *The Giant's Robe* to come true in my case" (*PTH* 241). Too much knowledge about India tests the boundaries of the social system, victimizes both the knower and the known, the fictional and the real author, and ironically looks ahead to the powerlessness of Kipling himself to author his ultimate epic about India.

The story is about a self split three ways – the narrator, Strickland, and Jellaludin – in its perceptions of India. The first is the safest, the second and third are fantasy selves for the first: Strickland is the invulnerable policeman, whose disguises and knowledge of the streets see him through all challenges, but only in the early stories. In later stories, he will marry a nice English girl who plays the organ in a church, have a baby, play golf, and become part of the system. Jellaludin is the nightmare of the fallen self, the nightwalker who realizes that there is no turning back to English ways. He is, as Jonah Raskin phrased it, Kipling's own night self (see Raskin 1971: 57), the self he described in his autobiography in language that connects him fictionally with both Strickland and Jellaludin:

Often the night got into my head... and I would wander till dawn... Sometimes, the Police would challenge, but I knew most of their officers, and many folk in some quarters knew me for the son of my Father... Much of real Indian life goes on in the hot weather nights. (*SM* 59)

The difference between the Kipling frame narrator and McIntosh Jellaludin is that McIntosh descends, finds underground escape routes from the Imperium, becomes a nativized Englishman, disrupts the System and lives the Indian night, whereas the Kipling narrator confines himself to functioning within the social system in the margins and frames of his stories, frames that grow increasingly elaborate in form and troubled in voice in proportion to the disturbance of his subject matter. Whereas the wanderings into "real Indian life" are the experiences that give birth to the "McSomebodies" of his early stories ("The Gate of the Hundred Sorrows"), Kipling's later stories will be about characters who, like the narrator, affirm their identities through the ascent from rather than the descent into the destructive element.

CHAPTER 5

The bridge builders

In his introduction to *The Portable Kipling*, Irving Howe identifies what he calls the "specter" that haunted Kipling's imagination as "breakdown of authority: at first the authority of public life, but in his later work that of private life as well." Kipling's attitudes towards authority were as divided as his attitudes towards India and himself: it is at once something he desired and fled. The frame of narratorial authority in his early stories is always disturbed by and implicated in the tale it chooses to tell. The authority he relies on to guide his daily life is fractured in his art, where he recognizes that it has no essence outside of the social groups that construct hierarchy and recreate received images of imperial power. Through his narrators Kipling acknowledges the power of the various institutions to know but not to control the behavior of their subjects. But he also articulates the power of "stalkying" – the authority to defy the system through superior and crafty individualism – the "heroism" of a T. E. Lawrence or an Oliver North who can transcend the laws of ordinary morality and function beyond the control of external policing powers. As Isabel Quigley and others have observed, Stalky is produced by imperialism: "the very adjective 'imperial' applies to him because to function at all such a man needs devoted followers, childlike admirers to whom he seems godlike, unquestionably right" (*Stalky & Co.* p. xxvi).

The problem of authority raises the specter of Kipling's relation to imperialist hegemony, to the combined strategies that created "a mythology of Imperialism" (Wurgaft 1983), to "the collective national-popular will" (Gramsci 1971), to the state apparatus (Althusser 1971), or to the "micro-powers" (Foucault 1977) that enter all aspects of social life. Kipling's stories are surprisingly inconsistent in their surface reactions to discipline, authority, and punishment. The power of imperialist discipline had shaped not only

Kipling's childhood by subjecting him to physical abuse and a brutal version of Christianity, but had also shaped the institutions of language, education, industry, law, and business in India. Yet Kipling's stories often celebrate or give voice to rebels against the system. These stories are unsettling precisely because their effect is to disconnect readers from the social norms whose presiding surveillance they expect to encounter.

Insofar as his early stories tarnish and problematize the image of colonial service, of authority over self and empire, and speak in a language alien to the literati, who heard in him the voice of the vulgar commoner, Kipling's stories about India are a type of "minor literature," or "that which a minority constructs within a major language" (Deleuze 1986: 16). Martin Green has drawn an analogous division between England's denial of its "minor" literature of action, adventure and imperialism, within which Kipling is a "minor" oblique, ironic, and oppositional voice, in favor of its "major" "literature-as-a-system." He suggests that we compare Kipling to Brecht, Kipling's early stories to Brecht's *Man Equals Man* (1927) and *Threepenny Opera* (1928), to understand the similarity in their angry protest against social and political hypocrisy (Green 1984: 44–5). Although they seem trivial, the incidents chosen in Kipling's stories are necessarily political because the slightest Simla flirtation reverberates across the plains: an incidental comment is enough to make a boy blow his brains out, an argument makes another soldier go berserk, and a thoughtless affair leads to the loss of one more "pillar of empire" as he goes crashing into a pit. This tightly enclosed familial world of the British in India leads to stories that sound like parables, to allegories and to fables that take on a "collective value" giving voice and agency to marginalized figures of empire – subalterns, builders, vagabonds, engineers, dreamers, and fallen men and women.

The stories of the 1890s were written during turbulent times of imperial self-examination and expansion: although Britain had rejected Henry Morton Stanley's overtures to be drawn into the Congo, it had entered the scramble for Africa by annexing Lagos in 1861, followed by new interests in the Niger basin, the Northern Territories of the Gold Coast, Sierra Leone, Zanzibar, Uganda, and Kenya. Cecil Rhodes sending his armies to take over Southern Rhodesia in 1890, General Kitchener invading the Sudan and defeating the Mahdi in 1898, and the disastrous Boer war, provoked in part by Cecil Rhodes' investments in the diamonds and gold recently discovered in South Africa, all respond and contribute to Kipling's anxieties about the constitution of "character" needed to sustain the trials of imperial power.

Whereas Kipling's fictions of the 1890s are mostly stories of triumph over adversity, his personal life during these years was marked by trouble, change, and loss. These were the years of his painful departure from India, his travels to South Africa, Rhodesia, Australia, and New Zealand, of his marriage to the American Caroline Balestier, his growing friendship with Milner and Rhodes, his efforts to live in the United States, and the deaths of his best friend Wolcott Balestier and of his "best-beloved" six-year-old daughter Josephine. His determination to author his life is shaken by bankruptcy, quarrels with publishers over copyright laws, prolonged fights with his brother-in-law Beatty, and illness and deaths. Meanwhile the empire fought to survive against the growing nationalistic movements in India (never to be mentioned in Kipling's fiction) and a variety of small and large wars all over Asia and Africa.

Kipling's return to London was strained by an overwhelming sense of loss, by homesickness, by alienation from Englishmen and women of all classes, except from women of the London slums (see A. Wilson 1979: 148–50), and by a general hostility towards English literary society. He wrote to friends in India: "There are five million people in London this night and, saving those who starve, I don't think there is one more heartsick or thoroughly wretched than that rising young author known to you as - Ruddy" (Carrington 1986: 189–90). And to his Lahore *Civil and Military Gazette* he sent "In Partibus" which contained the following verses:

> The Sky, a greasy soup-tureen,
> Shuts down atop my brow.
> Yes, I have sighed for London Town
> And I have got it now:
> And half of it is fog and filth,
> And half is fog and row.
> ...
> But I consort with long-haired things
> In velvet collar-rolls,
> Who talk about the Aims of Art,
> And "theories" and "goals,"
> And moo and coo with womenfolk
> About their blessed souls.   (Rutherford 1986: 470–2)

Except for *The Light that Failed* (1891), into which he poured undisguised anger and self-pity, Kipling's stories of the 1890s, for the most part, seem to free themselves from the authority of the frame narrator, from recurring tales of breakdown and disintegration, and from the fragile hold on identity by actors on the imperial scene. Although more centered in storytelling subjects (Findlayson, Georgie, Kim), these later tales nevertheless conceal the threat of breakdown within stories that only appear to resolve the protagonists' personal and ideological conflicts. Findlayson's bridge could collapse, as he could into terminal hallucination. So too Georgie, the brushwood boy, wins authority over his dream self by confronting it albeit in a drama that is at once fragmentary, conflicted, and contained in dreams policed by Policeman Day.

As some of the more suggestive of his titles in the 1890s remind us, these are stories about power, agency, and survival through compromise, and about the disguised conquest of nature/India/jungle by culture/England/imperialism. "The Bridge-Builders," "The Ship that Found Herself," and "William the Conqueror" (titles of stories in *The Day's Work*, 1898) are all about subjects – a man, a ship, a woman – learning to empower themselves against hostile odds. The other stories in this volume prepare us for later stories about the strength of the English countryside, about the rewards awaiting the good colonialist when he returns "home," about the triumph of the day's work over the night's fears and dreams, about the power of the machine, and about the rage for order in the face of anarchy. *The Jungle Books* (1894–5), about an English boy, Mowgli, raised by animals, is about the course of his survival, education, and "natural" leadership among the alien breed. John McClure sees Kipling diagnosing imperial problems in the 1880s and presenting a method for "perfecting the Imperial mold" in the 1890s. I want to extend McClure's thesis by suggesting that distance turned India into the picturesque and the pastoral, and that Kipling's use of the blurred and distant focus became a way to find what Roger Sales calls the famous five "Rs" of pastoralism: "refuge, reflection, rescue, requiem and reconstruction" (1983: 15). Pastoral allows Kipling to domesticate his increasing anxiety about authority, and to manage his nostalgia for his lost childhood so entwined with his lost India.

The focus of this chapter is on the first and last stories Kipling chose to structure *The Day's Work*; each reproduces fragments of his own interpellation and dialogizes the contradictory discourse of imperial authority with the imagined "voice" of a mythologized India whose arguments against English authority are at once predictable and provocative. In his stories of the 1880s, authority rests in the unstable voice of ironic narrators, in stories of collapse, disintegration, and the breakdown of authority over the self and others; but the presence of the subordinate voice belonging to the denied self or to others is, whether marginalized or centralized, nevertheless recognized and heard. The recurring figure of authority in these stories is the often suspect, ironic, almost absent, and occasionally stable frame narrator who hears and records the story of another; or it is policeman Strickland who will solve the mystery of Imray's disappearance, but not before acknowledging the validity of the native's revenge by giving it a hearing. The problem with the voice of the subaltern, the native or the "Other" as reproduced by Kipling is the degree to which that voice has been deformed and produced by the other voice of authority. The writer's dialogues, therefore, are not necessarily "dialogic" in Bakhtin's sense of the term, because all apparently conflicting voices are guided and shaped, unconsciously perhaps, by the interests of the class in power and are active imaginings rather than reflections of voices. The problem for the critic, then, is to recognize the ways in which all colonial representations are active imaginings shaped by ideology rather than the unambiguous reflection of voices. The voice of the author and of the narrator in Kipling's tales, by its very determination to separate itself from the fate of the other whose story he will expose, is marked by the hegemony of the larger imperial mission.

Kipling the insomniac, however, walked through the nights of Lahore and through serialized worlds of dreams. The time when, as he called it, "the night got into my head" was also the time of knowledge and creativity for this writer who created those night-stalkers Kim, McIntosh Jellaludin, Trejago, John Holden and Strickland. A profound conflict between loyalties to two different worlds underlies the overdetermined bridge that Kipling uses to resolve symbolically, and necessarily unsatisfactorily, the personal and historical contradictions constituting his world view. And Kipling's acknowledgment of this problem dialogizes the imperial project at the center of his stories, and uses, in the stories of the 1880s, the imagined voices of subalterns, suicides, prostitutes, native workers, and gods to decenter the framed control of the English narrator. The stories of the 1890s, however, while acknowledging some forms of alternative voices, defuse the presence of India by containing its unpredictability in metaphor and abstraction, by allegorizing the opposition first into Indian Gods and then into absence. In the last story of the volume, "The Brushwood Boy," for instance, Indians are mentioned twice in passing, once only as spectators watching a game; and then as the silent unnamed "enemy" in a "little winter campaign": "Cottar nearly wept with joy as the campaign went forward ... [they] cheerfully cut their way ... they crowned and cleaned out hills full of the enemy with the precision of well-broken dogs of chase" (*DW* 271). The increasing marginalization of Indian natives in his stories is analogous to the eventual marginalization of the boy's dream life once he returns to England and to the reification of the dream.

"The Bridge-Builders" is an allegory of the argument for empire building with a twist – mythologized India is allowed a voice in the proceedings, and somewhat predictably, her Gods permit the scaffolding to survive. The story centers on the English engineer Findlayson, who after long years of work constructing an elegant suspension bridge over the Ganges, faces the threat of its destruction by floods. Refusing to leave, he takes the opium and toddy offered by his native foreman, Peroo, and plunges into a dreamworld where he hears the Indian gods debating the work of the English. When he awakes, he finds the flood has abated and realizes that the gods have, in spite of much debate, allowed his work to stand. That the resisting forces of night (ancient India) finally give consent to the constructions of day (empire) feeds into the hegemonic agenda of the author who saw himself as a bridge between the two worlds, who, himself a nightwalker, was destined to do the work of day, and who, in a world divided also between the Sons of Mary and the Sons of Martha, was a true Son of Martha:

It is in their care in all the ages to take the buffet and cushion the shock.
It is their care that the gear engages; it is their care that the switches
  lock.
It is their care that the wheels run truly; it is their care to embark and
  entrain
Tally, transport, and deliver duly the Sons of Mary by land and main.
  ("The Sons of Martha" *Verse*: 380)

The mechanical and industrial images here are metonymies for empire, and these Sons of Martha would also bear the burden of the

White Man which was to "reap his old reward: / The blame of those ye better, / The hate of those ye guard." Elliott Gilbert reminds us that the title of the book refers both to John 9:4, and to the sentence alluding to it from Carlyle's *Sartor Resartus* which Lockwood Kipling had carved over his son's fireplace in Vermont: "Work while it is called day, for the night cometh wherein no man can work" (Gilbert 1970: 126). Here, as elsewhere in Kipling, day work is couched in biblical language so that the subject is sanctified before it can conflict "dialogically" with its nighttime opposite. So too in the story, the work of bridge building is inserted into the playground of the Indian gods who appear to engage in a carnivalesque subversion of imperial hierarchy. But the work of bridge building is the hegemonic project of English dominion. And when posited against the decentralizing forces of the Hindu Pantheon, Kipling permits a temporary carnivalesque interrogation of such power which must then be suppressed into dream.

The poles in Kipling's Indian world – night and day, Indian gods and English engineers, chaos and order, water and land – are connected and transcended by the gods, and by empire with its emblem, the Kashi Bridge. Although such dualism was apparent in the earlier stories of *Plain Tales from the Hills* and *The Phantom Rickshaw*, the problems of power, domination and colonization now appear to shift from the cities of dreadful night to the playing fields of the gods. By so shifting the focus, the problem transforms from the social and personal to the mythic. The language and tone are also transformed from the personal to the detached. By transferring the level of attention from men to gods, Kipling assumes (as T. S. Eliot tries to assume in other contexts) the voice and authority of universal and supposedly primitive truth. This undifferentiated truth, heard in the decision of Krishna, justifies the questionable work of the colonizer. The shift of responsibility from the ordinary, the personal and the social to the mythic covers and deflects the unresolved conflicts that underlie the complex colonial enterprise that must often disguise power as responsibility and as service.

Divisions and dualities inform all levels of the story. Structurally, the story is divided into two almost equal halves between the bridge builders and the opium dream of Findlayson, the chief engineer, who sees and hears the Hindu gods argue the fate of the bridge. Geographically, it is divided between the bridge (occupied by creatures of the present, the workers) and the island (inhabited by creatures of the past, the gods). The gods are divided between the more earthly gods who side with the bridge and the more ethereal who don't. The workers are divided into English and native, and those two groups subdivided between master and apprentice. And Findlayson, after the opium, finds himself split between soul and body, fighting to connect the two lest he lose himself: "Findlayson had already escaped ... was circling high in air to find a rest for the sole of his foot. His body – he was really sorry for its gross helplessness – lay in the stern, the water rushing about its knees. 'How very ridiculous!' he said to himself, from his eyrie; 'that – is Findlayson – chief of the Kashi Bridge. The poor beast is going to be drowned, too ...' To his intense disgust, he found his soul back in his body again, and that body spluttering and choking in deep water. The pain of the reunion was atrocious, but it was necessary, also, to fight for the body" (*DW* 21–2). So too, the river is both a mere passage of water to be overcome and it is Mother Gunga in irons. And Hitchcock is at once Findlayson's assistant, "a magistrate of the third class with whipping powers" (*DW* 8), and a "cub," a "colt" whom Findlayson has chosen because of "his rawness to break to his own needs" (*DW* 7).

The bridge itself, described in the second paragraph of the story, is a construct ambivalently divided between natural energy and technology, between its source in the river Ganges, and its use in the imperial enterprise.

Findlayson, C. E., sat in his trolley on a construction line ... and permitted himself to think of the end. With its approaches, his work was one mile and three-quarters in length; a lattice-girder bridge, trussed with the Findlayson truss, standing on seven-and-twenty brick piers. Each one of those piers was twenty-four feet in diameter, capped with red Agra stone and sunk eighty feet below the shifting sand of the Ganges bed. Above them was a railway-line fifteen feet broad; above that, again, a cart-road of eighteen feet, flanked with footpaths. At either end rose towers, of red brick, loopholed for musketry and pierced for big guns, and the ramp of the road was being pushed forward to their haunches. The raw earth-ends were crawling and alive with hundreds upon hundreds of tiny asses climbing out of the yawning borrow-pit below with sackfuls of stuff; and the hot afternoon air was filled with the noise of hooves, the rattle of the drivers' sticks, and the swish and roll-down of the dirt ... In the little deep water left by the drought, an overhead-crane travelled to and fro along its spill-pier, jerking sections of iron into place, snorting and backing and grunting as an elephant grunts in the timber-yard. Riveters by the hundred swarmed about the lattice side-

work and the iron roof of the railway-line, hung from invisible staging under
the bellies of the girders, clustered round the throats of the piers, and rode
on the overhang of the footpath-stanchions; their fire-pots and the spurts of
flame that answered each hammer-stroke showing no more than pale yellow
in the sun's glare. East and west and north and south the construction-trains
rattled and shrieked up and down the embankments, the piled trucks of
brown and white stone banging behind them till the side-boards were
unpinned, and with a roar and a grumble a few thousand tons more material
were flung out to hold the river in place. (*DW* 5–6)

The alternating rhythms of each sentence in this remarkable
paragraph reenforce the splittings and oppositions in the thematics of
the story: the reader is forced visually to look up and down, north and
south, in certain hierarchic patterns that discriminate and separate
the "raw earth-ends" from the structures the colonizer erects upon
those ends, and the swarming natives from the Chief Engineer who
sits above them. The scene is split between Findlayson, C. E., who
thinks "of the end," and the author who sees the present and makes
it into a prose poem. The ironic distance between the author and
Findlayson is important because this is to be an initiation for the
Chief Engineer who will be forced, though a crack in his world, to see
the powerful and unacknowledged world of the invisible, the
underside of his surface practicality. The paragraph is also split
between the single individual who takes credit for what he later calls
"the splendid Findlayson truss," and the indistinguishable "riveters
by the hundred" who swarm about the lattice work; between the
bridge and the river that it must hold in place; between the red Agra
stone and the shifting sand of the river in which it is sunk and from
which it rises towards the sky; between railway-lines and cart-roads
and footpaths; between towers loopholed for guns and the "raw
earth-ends" beneath; between "hundreds upon hundreds of tiny
asses" and "riveters by the hundred"; between fire-pots, spurts of
flames and the sun's glare; between water, mud, dirt and the air in
which the bridge is suspended. These splittings are each assigned a
value in the hierarchy of empire in which success, work, activity, and
power are supreme. For Findlayson, the failure of the bridge is
equivalent to the failure of life, of "everything that made a hard life
worth the living" (*DW* 17–18). And he recalls with pity and
understanding the failure of another – the time when "Lockhart's
new waterworks burst and broke down in brick-heaps and sludge,
and Lockhart's spirit broke in him and he died" (*DW* 18). The

opposition between Findlayson and Lockhart is implicitly repeated in all the other divisions and splittings in the story.

The resolution to this opposition, however, undercuts its own system of values. The survival of the bridge is not the result of Findlayson's personal success, but the decision of the Indian gods who occupy the river. The underlying political fantasy is that the structures of empire are supported by all the rulers and the ruled, the human and the divine. That fantasy is sustained by the story's contradictory value system that claims that power rests in the practical world of calculation and mathematical precision, yet raises the question "but what man knew Mother Gunga's arithmetic?" (*DW* 18). The order of hierarchy, although valued by the protagonist of the story, is gently mocked by the narrator who will compel the protagonist to see what he knows. Yet, it is unclear at the end whether or not Findlayson has learned what the native Peroo has – that "when Brahm ceases to dream the Gods go," meaning that only in dreams can one perceive divine realities, that the waking world is an illusion. Native insight, in other words, undermines colonial certainties.

That process of interrogation begins in the opening paragraphs and is announced in the distance between the eloquent, ironic, poetic voice of the narrator and the prosaic, practical language of the protagonist. The first sentence of the story alerts us to Findlayson's consciousness of English military power, of hierarchy and of his position in it. We learn that he hopes for a "C. I. E." though he dreams of a "C. S. I.," and that in less than three months, once the bridge is complete, "his excellency the Viceroy would open the bridge in state, an archbishop would bless it, and the first trainload of soldiers would come over it, and there would be speeches" (*DW* 5). The smugness of his great expectations climaxes a few pages later when he looks over the country that he feels he has changed and with a godlike "sigh of contentment saw that his work was good … *pukka* – permanent – to endure when all memory of the builder, yea, even of the splendid Findlayson truss had perished" (*DW* 6). Findlayson's self-satisfied meditation is interrupted a few pages later by the narrator, who introduces a further disturbance into our earlier perceptions of the bridge builders: "So the bridge was two men's work – unless one counted Peroo, as Peroo certainly counted himself" (*DW* 8). Peroo, the experienced native ex-sailor and world traveller, "worth almost any price he might have chosen to put upon his services," is not paid his true value by his master, but is by the narrator, who removes him from the social and fictional margins to which he is relegated in the first third of the story and moves him centerstage. That move undergirds the ambivalence of the story even as it destabilizes the ethnocentric assumptions on which the colonial enterprise rests.[1]

Only Peroo understands the metaphysical implications of the building of the bridge: "Look you, we have put the river into a dock, and run her between stone sills ... We have bitted and bridled her. She is not like the sea, that can beat against a soft beach. She is Mother Gunga – in irons" (*DW* 11). Whereas a Findlayson only smiles at Peroo's use of the "we," the narrator informs us of Peroo's strength, skill, and knowledge: "No piece of iron was so big or so badly placed that Peroo could not devise a tackle to lift it ... It was Peroo who had saved the girder of Number Seven pier from destruction ... There was no one like Peroo, serang, to lash, and guy, and hold, to control the donkey-engines, to hoist a fallen locomotive craftily out of the borrow pit ... to strip, and dive, if need be, to see how the concrete blocks round the piers stood the scouring of Mother Gunga ... 'My honour is the honour of this bridge,' he would say ... " (*DW* 9). Thus, unlike Findlayson, he can combine an admiration for the technology of the English ("I like sus-sus-pen-sheen bridges that fly from bank to bank" *DW* 10) with a reverence for the nonrational ("Mother Gunga is Mother Gunga, and when I come back to her banks I know this and worship" *DW* 11). That combination, of course, is an extension of the political fantasy that imperialism can spawn such happy hybrids as Peroo and Gunga Din.

The argument between the gods, or the dream within the dream, takes place on an island where the flooding river has carried Peroo and Findlayson. Mother Gunga (the crocodile) argues that she has lost her freedom since "they have chained" her flood, and prays for the other gods to help "take this yoke away" (*DW* 29). But the gods are divided in their response to her plea. Whereas Kali (the tigress) and Sitala (the ass) have helped the river by spreading sickness and death among the workmen, Hanuman (the ape) and Ganesh (the elephant) would like the work to continue. Hanuman likes bridges, "remembering that I also built no small bridge in the world's youth," recalling the bridge described in the Ramayana, built of an army of monkeys that allowed Rama to cross from India into Ceylon to rescue his wife Sita. Ganesh, the god of good fortune, has also fed on the work of the builders because they have profited his "fat money lenders." He is perhaps the most cynical of the gods: "It is but the shifting of a little dirt. Let the dirt dig in the dirt if it pleases the dirt" (*DW* 26). Ironically, the gods who support the bridge builders are wrong in their assumptions. Ganesh's distant and dehumanized perception of men as dirt recalls the distant perspective of the colonial Chief Engineer at the beginning of the story. The common man is reduced to a metaphor – a swarm, dirt, the unnamable masses thought of only in numbers – "five-thousand," or "the half-hundred," or "the hundreds." Bhairon, the god of the common people, is significantly drunk, implying the lack of control the common man has over his destiny. His endorsement of the bridge builders is predictably thoughtless in its assumption that their "fire-carriages" will increase the number of pilgrims who will come to worship him. Kali is right when she assumes that the native workers will lose their faith in Mother Gunga once they see that she avenges no insult: "they fall away from her first, and later from us all, one by one. In the end, Ganesh, we are left with naked altars" (*DW* 26).

Krishna, the Well-Beloved of the gods, the only one who chooses to walk on earth as man, finally settles the dispute. Speaking for the common people, "*my* people – who lie under the leaf roofs of the village yonder," he pleads for an end to human destruction. Unlike the other gods who change shape and live in their own divine island, Krishna has made his own bridge from the divine to the earthly and it is therefore only he who understands the dual threat because he alone can see as man and as god. Krishna identifies the motives that underlie the plurality of voices and demystifies them: "Bhairon is drunk always. Hanuman mocks his people with new riddles... Ganesh thinks only of his fat traders; but I – I live with these my people" (*DW* 30). Accepting the new realities, he informs the gods that some of their suspicions are right, that the people will pay fewer dues to the gods, that they will forget their altars, that they will worship the new more powerful gods made visible by their fire-carriages in place of the older invisible ones. He predicts that at the end, the great gods will become "little Gods again – Gods of the Jungle – names that the hunters of rats and noosers of dogs whisper in the thicket and among the caves – rag-Gods, pot Godlings of the tree and the village-mark, as ye were at the beginning" (*DW* 31–2). But Krishna will survive where the other gods will not because he walks among men as one of them – in disguise; just as in other contexts, Kim, Mowgli, and Strickland will survive where other colonialists will perish, because they will walk among the natives as one of them. They will be double agents in India as Krishna is on earth.

When Indra (the buck), father of the gods, is called to judge, he answers with a riddle, although he claims to agree with Krishna: "When Brahm ceases to dream, the Heavens and the Hells and earth disappear. Be content. Brahm dreams still." The irony in this story is clear: the gods exist as long as Findlayson remains in his opium dream. And the colonialists exist as long as the natives remain asleep. Rationality, consciousness, enlightenment will gradually awaken the dreamers, and then the gods will die. The polarities of the story finally contradict each other and create an ideological impasse. Structured on two sets of self-cancelling values, the outer and inner story contradict each other. The outer story suggests that as long as Findlayson works he will avoid the problems of a dreamer and the gods will not disturb his consciousness. The inner story says that as long as Brahm dreams the gods will not die, and that life itself is the consequence of Brahm's dream. Rationality and daytime consciousness, though limited, are opposed to creative irrationality and nighttime dream. Caught between these two polarities, the colonialist must walk an impossibly thin line to survive.

Although the recourse to mythology might imply a transcending of earthly problems, more convincingly, it suggests the deep ambivalence Kipling felt about the two kinds of experience. The English colonialist, splendid craftsman though he might be, is powerless before the flood, before the intensity and destructiveness of nature. Having constructed a political, social, and personal identity on the ability to control nature and the unconscious, he is impotent before the fury of the return of the repressed or oppressed. This paralyzing awareness of dual desires characterizes Kipling's dialogic stance to the colonial system, when he appears to deny the project of empire building, or when he falls – momentarily and in dream – into the desire to oppose the scaffolding of imperial bureaucracy. Most typically in his Indian tales Kipling represents a borderline position that incorporates, polarizes, dialogizes, and bridges the worlds of colonizer and colonized, master and slave, England and India.

In Krishna's final summation, we find a typical Kipling resolution to ideological contradiction – become a double agent, join the enemy, conquer from within by remaining distant from that to which you are committed. The conflict, which began as one between the colonizers and the colonized, between the forces of empire (the bridge builders) and the forces of India (the river Ganges and the ancient gods), ends with the native forces not merely ceasing to question the structure, but granting it fresh impetus for further efforts at bridge building. Its formal structure problematizes its internal oppositions and conflicts by twice reversing expected patterns of hierarchy – first by the fall and decentering of the engineer into his dream, which pulls onto centerstage the native voices of the gods, and then by the waking mockery of native voices against local gods. In effect, the story plays against the modernist (Eliot and Yeats) tendency to glorify the mythic past at the expense of the industrial present. Rather it appears to dialogize the relationship between myth and reality, to recognize the impossibility of the effort, and then retreat into schoolboy mockery of its own visionary descent into the India of the gods.

The last story in *The Day's Work* is "The Brushwood Boy," the most explicit of Kipling's attempts to construct a metaphoric bridge between an individual colonizer's worlds of dream and reality. Like "The Bridge-Builders," its action involves the protagonist in a descent into unconscious material that eventually conforms to, rather than challenges, the values of his waking life. It is, however, more than merely an extension of his earlier stories of nightwalking and of encounters with the repressed that always threatened to return. Kipling was himself a persistent dreamer who, in "Brazilian Sketches" confesses that in a childhood dream he wandered into a Fifth Quarter of the world and "found everything different from all previous knowledge" (see Tompkins 1959: 205). Kipling's attempts to fictionalize a frightening and private aspect of his divided life reveal also the structures of a cultural self constructed during decades that saw radical revisions in European understanding of the identity of the subject, of gender, the psyche, the child, and the "native." These were also the years during which England dealt with another split in its national psyche. Men like Admiral Beresford, William Evans-Gordon, and Arnold White, concerned with the degeneracy of sturdy British stock by foreigners, immigrants, or Jews, provoked agitation that led to the formation of the Royal Commission on Alien Immigration in 1903 (Rosenthal 1984: 144). Baden-Powell's programs of race regeneration and Boy Scout codes were but extensions of the stated aims of the National Council of Public Morals whose goal was nothing less than the spiritual, moral and physical renewal of the race: "to help to raise the quality and to maintain the purity, stability, and strength of the British race, at home and in our Dominions beyond the seas. We are out to promote the permanent racial and moral welfare of an Imperial Race-to-be" (quoted in Rosenthal 1984: 144). The invisible assumptions at the story's end are the need to renew and valorize race (we are assured that the girl is not Jewish), class (she is of the Herefordshire Lacys) and the all-male program of maturity before earning the right to marriage.

The story conflates several plots endemic to colonial fiction: the perils and rewards of journeys into the unknown, the oppositional discourse of survival and colonialism, the need to domesticate the unknown even in dreams, and the rewards of sexual self-denial.

Georgie's journey through life, which includes a series of pro-gressively threatening dream landscapes, is a paradigm of the colonialist's journey from the nursery to school to India, and back to the rewards of home and marriage. The basic configuration of the dreamscape includes entrance through a safe outer region guarded by a pile of brushwood and by a street lamp crowning a ridge of high ground, a middle region of valleys and a Sea of Dreams, and a still more dangerous interior with mysterious strangers eating amid roses and gardens in a railway station, and finally, the mysterious end of the journey – a huge house containing, in its deep recesses, a Sick Thing. The entrance to his secret world where "anything was possible" is guarded by two recurring signs – a pile of brushwood and a lamppost, clearly differentiated emblems of femininity and mas-culinity that mark the boundaries of a day world of recognizable sexual differentiation:

He would find himself sliding into dreamland by the same road – a road that ran along a beach near a pile of brushwood. To the right lay the sea, sometimes at full tide, sometimes withdrawn to the very horizon; but he knew it for the same sea. By that road he would travel over a swell of rising ground covered with short, withered grass, into valleys of wonder and unreason. Beyond the ridge, which was crowned with some sort of street-lamp, anything was possible; but up to the lamp it seemed to him that he knew the road as well as he knew the parade-ground. (*DW* 265)

Beyond these signposts lie worlds of "incommunicable delight... glorious, for he felt he was exploring great matters" (*DW* 266). More threatening elements in his unpredictable night world confront him with a road "eaten away in places" that spans ravines, runs along the edge of precipices, and tunnels its way through endless mountains. The sea, sometimes a lyrical Sea of Dreams, is often a black and angry sea that rages under a full moon and lashes at him "black, foamless tongues of smooth and glossy rollers" (*DW* 267).

The dream illustrates the ambivalence of the boy's needs – his need to explore and dare to go beyond the boundaries set by "They" and "Them," and his opposing need to control and manage the unexpected; the need to rely on another, opposed to the fear that, when the going gets rough, would-be rescuers are useless in a world filled with hostile and unknown Others. Although he loses himself on unknown seas and slips and slides across many-colored islands, rescue at first appears in the form of his brushwood girl, a figure who first comes to life out of an illustrated edition of *Grimm's Fairy Tales*, then takes on the form of a real girl he meets in an Oxford pantomime theatre. In the dreams, the girl evolves from a childhood fairy-tale princess into his boyhood's AnnieanLouise, then into his young brushwood companion.

Alternating fantasies of rescue countered by dream reality (a motif we have seen in his autobiography) control the narrative of the dream. Inland, we are told, lie dark purple downs and mysterious and ever more dangerous territories: "Sometimes he was trapped in mines of vast depth hollowed out of the heart of the world, where men in torment chanted echoing songs; and he heard this person (the brushwood girl) coming along through the galleries, and everything was made safe and delightful" (*DW* 269). More threatening than either the sea or the mines is the danger from a series of mysterious people referred to as "Them," "They," and "It." First perceived as a "mob of stony white people, all unfriendly" (*DW* 269), who sit at breakfast tables covered with roses, "They" attempt to separate George from his girl. "It" is a female, a dying Sick Thing that lies in bed in a room reached "through leagues of whitewashed passages" (*DW* 269), in a huge house "surrounded with gardens all moist and dripping" (DW 269). One endless hot tropic night, the boy and girl find themselves creeping into this huge forbidden house and discovering "It" lying in bed. Because Georgie knows that this is his moment of greatest threat, and that the least noise "would unchain some waiting horror" he is disgusted at realizing that his only companion is a mere child: "'What disgraceful folly!' he thought. 'Now she could do nothing whatever if Its head came off'" (*DW* 269). When the Thing coughs, the ceiling begins to shatter, "They" come rushing in from all quarters, and George barely manages to drag the girl through the stifling rose gardens, across the Thirty-Mile Ride, to the safety of the down, the lamppost, and the brushwood pile. By the end of the story, as George heads back for England, he dreams his familiar dreams once again. Only this time the dreams are entirely safe: the dream companion is no longer a little girl but a woman with dark hair; "They" for some dreamland reason are now friendly or unthreatening, and their Thirty-Mile Ride is accompanied by underground singing and "no panic" as they repeat their old journey from the brushwood pile through the rose-filled waiting rooms and gardens, past the house of the now dormant Sick Thing.

Whereas the dreamworld is filled with a variety of unspecified threats, in the waking world George realizes all his fantasies and desires and acquires that ultimate object of desire – Miriam ("Sounds Jewish – Miriam." "Jew! You'll be calling yourself a Jew next. She's one of the Herefordshire Lacys. When her aunt dies –" [*DW* 277]). Miriam with her class, money, and legitimate aristocracy comes trailing clouds of signification, of attendant hegemonic prejudices against Others. Miriam, with her ailing mother, is also fatherless, and, by marrying her, George will inherit not only her wealth, but the parental role that would be forbidden to him were her parents active participants in society. Marriage will therefore resolve social and familial contradictions: the son will become the father, and the working soldier will become the aristocrat. This simple and mythic outer story with its light and whimsical tone compensates for the disturbingly incomplete inner metaphoric journey into the house of the Sick Thing. The inner story also subverts the expectations raised by its form. Twin journeys embedded within a dream story might lead the reader to expect, in the protagonist, changes in perception, self-awareness, or wisdom. But our George learns primarily how to defend himself against external threat without gaining any significant insight into his hidden fears.

As in the stories of Kipling's own life ("Baa, Baa, Black Sheep" and his autobiography), this story too begins by positioning society's natural victim, the child, against the adults who guard, control, and police his behavior. Part of my intention here is to see how that victimization is resolved in another curiously absent theatre – India. On the level of dream, we watch the child explore increasingly threatening geographical areas that he attempts at first to control by naming, miniaturizing (Hong Kong and Java become tiny lilies, stepping-stones in his path), defining, and displacing, but that grow increasingly uncontrollable. On the waking level, however, we see the boy's encounters with a series of microsocieties in which the disempowered and marginalized child-protagonist gradually assumes a position of centrality and power. And the alien society he enters, India, is marginalized into nonexistence.

The story begins, "A child of three sat up in his crib and screamed at the top of his voice, his fists clenched and his eyes full of terror" (*DW* 256). His helplessness is exacerbated by the geographic isolation of his nursery – in the west wing where no one could hear him: "The nurse was talking to a gardener among the laurels" (*DW* 256). When the housekeeper, whose special pet he is, tries to soothe him by asking what it was that frightened him, the boy answers that a policeman came into the house. The dream itself does not appear terribly fearful: it is a dream of intrusion by public authority into a private, intimate space; it has its waking-life source in an actual meeting with policeman Tisdall on Dowhead that morning. But the autograph manuscript and typescript of the story suggest that the author edited what might have been most fearsome to the child. In that unrevised version the child says, "It was – it was a policeman. He came in froo the window an' ate the rug! I saw him do it!" To which the nurse replies, "Nonsense Master George. Policemen never come through windows. They live in the Garden just like Ponto. Go to sleep" (Pierpont Morgan Library). That added detail of intrusion through a forbidden entrance – the window – to eat forbidden contents – the rug – suggests why the child might wake up terrified: the next object for consumption on the policeman's menu might be himself.

That first dream of a boundaryless appetite and of intrusion into a forbidden space will later be displaced or, as Edward Said might put it, "Orientalized." India will become the place of excess undermining the rational control of the Englishman, who will in turn test his manhood, his character, and his rationality by repeatedly intruding into threatening territory that he will decode, tame, and circumscribe within manageable domains. And within his sequential dream story, he and the brushwood girl will intrude into the house of the Sick Thing "It," whose distant bedroom surrounded by gardens must be a late displacement of his own early geographically remote nursery. On one level, as in Kafka's dream story "The Country Doctor," he is himself the sick thing who fears anatomical loss or engulfment. Only now in his dreams, that distant marginal room is the central nightmare setting, and on this level that bedroom is both the beginning and end of one of his many journeys.

When we next see the boy as a child of six, we see him acquiring "a new power" which he keeps a secret – the power to shift daytime incompletion into nighttime mastery. It is the power of trans-formation and transgression that encounters literal boundary prob-lems and that his daytime life and imperial culture translates as intrusion into India. He transposes an unfinished bedtime story told by his mother into a dream in which he becomes the prince, the "pasha" and the giant-killer. Rather than fear intrusion, as he did in his first dream, he becomes the intruder entering the forbidden dreamscape through a safe outer region guarded by a pile of brushwood stacked somewhere near a beach. It is a territory casually divided between land and sea, so casually that "ships ran high up the dry land and opened into cardboard boxes; or gilt-and-green iron railings, that surrounded beautiful gardens turned all soft, and could be walked through and overthrown so long as he remembered it was only a dream" (*DW* 257). And because he is in control, he can choose not to be alone in his dreamscape as he had been in his nursery. He peoples it with playing children, and in particular with a brushwood girl whom he names AnnieanLouise, whose magic words, "'Ha!Ha!' said the duck laughing" (*DW* 257), rescue the boy from drowning by raising the bottom of the deep as he wades out with a twelve-inch flowerpot on each foot. The boy has acquired the early power to domesticate and control even the depths of the sea.

The fear of instability ("he could never hold that knowledge more than a few seconds ere things became real"[*DW* 257]) invades every narrative event in his dream; and, as in his daytime life, Georgie meets that fear with the need to control and manage structures. We see him at age seven for the first time outside his bed, outside the privacy of his home, and in an alien and grotesque world of "grown-ups" – an enormously fat man who asks if he will eat bread and cheese, a play in which people's heads come flying off, a Provost of Oriel who sleeps in the presence of others; his only comfort is a lovely little girl in black who looks like Alice in Wonderland. Of these new inhabitants, Georgie likes the last best and shows her his wound, a cut on his thumb, the result of his "most valuable possession" (*DW* 258) – a savage, triangular knife. This wound, displayed here as a sign of his triumph, is displaced in his dreams onto the Sick Thing. Other uncontrollable features in the outside world are also dismissed and internalized into his more significant inner life. The grown-ups are depersonalized into a world of "They" and "Them," and the dark girl will be colonized into his dream life to replace the earlier golden AnnieanLouise. In both worlds, the boy's identity will be defined in terms of his success in turning a wound into a triumph, threatening others into petrified objects, alien territories into manageable toys, and then surviving in spite of a world inhabited by "They," "Them," and "It." That the wound is an object of desire in real life and an object of fear in his dreams suggests the fluid and permeable boundaries between George's outer world and his inner self – boundaries that will harden with age and with the fall into authority, adulthood, and India.

The next three phases of his life – ten years at an English public-school, Sandhurst, and India – are both a program of education and a model for the construction of the gendered colonial subject. He restructures his private inner emotional life by subordinating its demands to the public and external world of school and games. Now, home becomes "a far-away country, full of ponies and fishing and shooting, and men-visitors who interfered with one's plans; but school was the real world ... And Georgie was glad to be back in authority when the holidays ended" (*DW* 260). We are also told that school defines for the boy certain boundaries between what is discouraged (dreaming and emotions) and what is encouraged (precision, accuracy, strength). During this third stage we see the boy defining a hierarchy of values to be measured against what he sees as most "real" – his school. And it is here that the outer world encroaches upon, contests, and begins its triumph against the claims of his inner life – a triumph that materializes when George returns to England to discover that his dream brushwood girl is the real-life Miriam whom he is destined to marry, thereby renouncing any need for an inner dream life. It is at this stage that we see the evolution of the Kipling daytime ideal – discipline, sexual innocence, self-control, the value of the "school mask," and the upholding of public official policy. If part of the conscious meaning of the story is that "England's wars are won on the playing fields of Eton," then George's school must take credit for his triumphs on the battlefields of empire.

His masculinist education leads to appropriate success in India, where, though he is the most loved, most sought after, and most quoted barrack authority, he learns to rely on imperial virtues that deny desire and rather feed on war and male camaraderie. In spite of all the designing ladies, George keeps free from the intrigues of the Indian outpost and from sex: "If Cottar only knew it, half the women in the station would give their eyes – confound 'em – to have the young 'un in tow" (*DW* 263). His seniors worry about his turning into a "regular 'Auntie Fuss' of an Adjutant" (*DW* 270), but fate proves him a man by sending him to fight a "real" war: "Cottar nearly wept with joy as the campaign went forward. They were fit – physically fit beyond the other troops; they were good children in camp, wet or dry, fed or unfed; and they followed their officers with the quick subtleness and trained obedience of a first-class football fifteen" (*DW* 271).

Singularly minimized during his heroic combats are personal and historical wounds, any aspect of victimization, vulnerability or oppression. India and Indians are marginalized into nonexistence. We are told, probably about the Second Afghan War of 1881, that "fate sent the change that was needed, in the shape of a little winter campaign on the border, which, after the manner of little campaigns, flashed out into a very ugly war; and Cottar's regiment was chosen among the first" (*DW* 270–1). George's distance from the reality of war, India and his inner life are reflected not only in the increasingly coy use of the third-person omniscient narrator whose voice seems only accidentally related to a boy encountering death and India, but in the curious language exemplified in the passage above. The angle from which the event is perceived is so distant that the horror of war is miniaturized into a "little" campaign, and its only significance seems to be contained within the context of sports – Cottar's regiment was chosen among the first. Those who are to be warred against, subdued, defeated, killed are neither named, sentimentalized nor romanticized. They are simply and significantly absent. And India is an empty space, an absence, that serves as a means for progressing from school to life, from the playing fields of Eton to home, marriage, and empire. The war therefore is an excuse to glorify and fortify the men into manliness: "'Now,' said a major, 'this'll shake the cobwebs out of us all – especially you, Galahad'" (*DW* 271). The experience in India allows George to construct a code of personal behavior and leadership based on public school codes that results in the nonsexual commitment to the brotherhood of empire, and in the infantilization of his men into "good children" and a "football fifteen," of a war into a "little" campaign, and of India into an absence. Maturity and character are gained by a colonization of the self – by denial, repression, and mechanization. But once this stage is accomplished, a limited intimacy is allowed:

> "There's no place like England – when you've done your
> work."
> "That's the proper way to look at it, my son." (*DW* 276)

But as other Kipling stories have demonstrated, outward success is no guarantee for survival in India; midway through Cottar's phenomenal successes with subordinates, superiors, and women in the army, a major prophesies: "but, then, that's the kind that generally goes the worst mucker in the end" (*DW* 263). The fear of going "the worst mucker," of disintegrating irrationally and publicly, of being invaded, engulfed, or petrified by threatening Others results in the elaborate development of denial and repression in the waking world, and a nightworld haunted with a sexually charged dreamscape that mirrors his deepest anxieties about authority over the self and others.

Those anxieties are provoked by areas of his waking life over which he has no control: home, England, and sex. If school, Sandhurst, and empire do not consciously threaten George (as they did Kipling), it is partly because they are made to obey the rules of his defense system and partly because he has displaced onto the language of his dreams what he finds most fearsome about those institutions. As opposed to the "real" world of games and war, home is soft, unreal, dreamlike, and relatively scary. If the only way to reconcile these two opposing worlds is through marriage to Miriam, then the main threat to that ultimate reward of union is illicit maternal love. All through his years in India, he is, unknown to himself, threatened with motherly sex from a series of married women beginning with Mrs. Elery, who complains to a Commander that he is "workin' my nice new boy too hard"; Mrs. Morrison, who admits, "I want to kiss him. Some day I think I will. Heigh-ho! She'll be a lucky woman that gets Young Innocence" (*DW* 264); the designing Mrs. Zuleika, and his actual mother back home. His most threatening sexual encounter takes place on that most unstable place, a ship at sea, where Mrs. Zuleika with her "motherly" interest speaks of "love in the abstract" (*DW* 272) and demands sexual confidences. When George arrives home, he lands into the waiting arms of yet another woman – his eager mother, who comes into his bedroom to tuck him up for the night and to ask him leading questions about his nonexistent sex life. After she discovers the incredible (his virginity), "she blessed him and kissed him on the mouth, which is not always a mother's property, and said something to her husband later, at which he laughed profane and incredulous laughs" (*DW* 276).

The sexual anxiety at the heart of this story repeats itself in the recurring flight of the boy from exposure, vulnerability, and danger to a sheltered place of security, away from the threats of forbidden, motherly relationships toward a safe, mature sexuality. The defense system he establishes against his dangerous fantasy is careful self-control under the magical protection of an internalized fantasy girl, who in his dreams keeps changing ages to remain as remote from the mother as possible. The entire journey carries an implicit Kipling theme: that we mature by escaping maternal love and being "manly" until we find a suitable love object free of maternal associations, after our colonial characters are built and tested. And someone back home is always watching, censoring, controlling our most dangerous actions, and we trust that silent watcher in the night as we do the surveillance of family and empire: so later, Miriam admits to dreaming of "another woman – out there on the sea. I saw her" (*DW* 286). The ordinary adventure story holds its tension and the reader's interest because of the potential threat as the protagonist encounters his next major test in the real world. In this story, however, the boy's triumphs in encountering worldly tests are tediously predictable. The question that remains problematic is if he can cope with and survive the threats of his unconscious life.

This obsession with the private and unconscious as a source of terror and fascination lies at the heart of the Kipling myth and informs all his tales, particularly those which, as we have seen, involve night journeys into the labyrinths of Lahore and of inaccessible India. But what makes these journeys so idiosyncratic, so typical of Kipling (rather than Conrad or Lawrence), is their guarded nature, their sense of forced continuity and cohesion that seems to repress elements of disturbance in the text. The outer journey of the wooden, predictable protagonist from England to India and back, at first jars against the inner unpredictable dream life – but only for a while. The *deus ex machina* at the end gives the reader a sense of an ending in narrative and history that is radiant with confidence. Always in Kipling, tranquility and order will be restored if necessary through hysterical insistence on forced closure.

In this story, however, the closure is charming. The brushwood boy will be saved, rescued from the dangers of his own unconscious, even from his own self – and will be rescued by a member of the ruling class: a princess. What the story leaves incomplete is the inner journey that simply stops without allowing the boy a final confrontation with the beast in the jungles of his own unconscious – the Sick Thing.

Except for the brushwood pile, all other dream elements surrounding the house have their origins in details the boy recalls of waking life. The gardens dripping with roses recall his parents' home, which he finds distant, romantic, vaguely confusing, and threatening. What George finds most threatening at home before his journey to India is his lack of control and the presence of authorities other than his own ("and Georgie was glad to be back in authority when the holidays ended" [*DW* 261]). After he has earned the rewards of the good colonialist and acquired an armor with which to journey into danger, he returns home to a new acceptance by the previously forbidding adults. His father invites him out on the terrace "to smoke among the roses," and George thinks: "'Perfect! By Jove, it's perfect!' Georgie was looking at the round-bosomed woods beyond the home paddock, where the white pheasant boxes were ranged; and the golden air was full of a hundred sacred scents and sounds" (*DW* 275). This sensual, maternal, paradisal landscape is a clear contrast to the threatening feminine landscape of his Indian dreams, filled with ravines, precipices, tunnels, black and changeable seas, and gardens overly ripe with moisture, perfume and song. The Sick Thing – fed by multiply determined, indirect, and contradictory elements – is, however, the most complex symbol in the dream. On a regressive level, the sources in real life are partly George's own mother, partly the sickly, sleepy behavior the seven-year-old George attributed to adults, and partly Miriam's invalid mother – a contribution of her mind. That the unreachable end of this otherwise delicious journey should contain a sick female figure lying in bed with an unstable head ready to fall off at the least provocation suggests that the initial incest anxiety is accompanied by a projected fear of punishment – headlessness or castration. With her vague and oppressive sickness associated with excess heat and loss of control, the Sick Thing's infantile connections with forbidden and destructive sexuality are later Orientalized and displaced onto that ultimate center of disintegration – India. As child, as fantasy princess, and

later as mature woman from a legitimate class, the brushwood girl
grows old along with George, thereby representing safe, normal
companionship and acceptable sexuality, in contrast to the life-
threatening and repellent sexuality of the Sick Thing. Thus Army,
Sandhurst, and School are also the institutionalized counterpart to
the princess: they will protect him against the House, the journey
through the abyss, or what Kipling elsewhere called "The City of
Dreadful Night."

"The Brushwood Boy" is, in some ways, the paradigmatic Kipling
story of psychic splitting and division. Within the larger polarization
between his waking world guarded by Policeman Day and his
nightworld of dreams exist many other oppositions, the most
significant between "They" and "Us." This defining of boundaries
and defenses against intrusion by others insulates the Kipling
protagonist against "unknown continents" within and without.
"Them," "They," "It," and the mob of stony white people are all
dream objects petrified by the dreamer's need to dehumanize,
simplify, and classify Others into stony anonymity in order to control
them. The division between Us and Them is also a wish-fulfilling
inner division between desire and fear, between the realm of
possibilities allowed the boy and the girl when they are a self-
contained secret unit, and the restricted realm allowed by the larger
world that contains Others.

This division haunts the story's form, imagery, actions, and
ideology. The schizophrenic fragmentation of this text into the
political world of action, war, colonial discipline, and empire and the
sexual world of dream, desire, freedom, and fear is repeated in both
the form and the ideological content. Quite simply, the work of
empire is daytime work and therefore incompatible with objects of
nighttime desire. Once that fundamental division is accepted and
assumed on a private level, then its social implications can be
expected to follow. The story of George Cottar, like that of other
Kipling protagonists, is that of a young man who has gone through
an exemplary Kiplingesque regime of repression, control, and denial
in India and can now return to England and its release from
discipline, armed against its dangers with "character." In the real
world, it will allow him to enter threatening colonized spaces like
India to test his resistance against immersion in the destructive
elements of desire or empathy for the alien Other. His reward for such
personal and ideological schizophrenia will be social reconciliation

(return to the parental English home, smoking in the garden with father, parties) and union with a significant symbol of empire – marriage to the heiress with the appropriately aristocratic lineage.

The need to control crippling divisions within the self takes on a diversity of variations in Kipling's middle and late stories. Sometimes the story is about a house divided against itself, as in "The House Surgeon," or about a ship divided between its many voices as in "The Ship that Found Herself," or a man divided against his psychic self as in "'They.'" In the first two stories, the closure is forced, confident and complete. In the last, it is wracked with agony, perhaps because houses and machines and ships, even if they serve as allegories for the self, can be manipulated into submission more effectively than people.

"The House Surgeon" (based on Kipling's own experience with a house which he rented in Torquay) is about the massive depression and anxiety that fall on the inhabitants of a house until the narrator, a "house surgeon," takes it upon himself to do some detective work and discover the cause of the problem. Its very plot suggests the optimism that underlies its premise – that such mysteries have permanent solutions that can be discovered by ordinary folk. The contrast between the fiction and the actual incident that befell Kipling and his wife is instructive because at Torquay, no solution could be found and Kipling was forced to leave the house. Here, the narrator experiences the house for the first time in the following description of the active and hopelessly inevitable approach of a depression:

I was aware of a little grey shadow, as it might have been a snowflake seen against the light, floating ... in the background of my brain ... Then my brain telegraphed that it was the fore-runner of a swift-striding gloom which there was yet time to escape ... the gloom overtook me before I could take in the meaning of the message. I moved towards the bed, every nerve already aching with the foreknowledge of the pain that was to be dealt it, and sat down, while my amazed and angry soul dropped gulf by gulf, into that Horror of great darkness which is spoken of in the Bible ... Despair upon despair, misery upon misery, fear after fear, each causing their distinct and separate woe, packed in upon me for an unrecorded length of time till at last they blurred together, and I heard a click in my brain like the click in the ear when one descends in a diving-bell, and I knew that the pressures were equalized within and without, and that for the moment, the worst was at an end. But I knew also that at any moment the darkness might come down anew; and while I dwelt on this speculation precisely as a man torments a

raging tooth with his tongue, it ebbed away into the little grey shadow on
the brain of its first coming, and once more I heard my brain, which knew
what would recur, telegraph to every quarter for help, release, or diversion.
(*A&R* 287–9)

I quote this extract at some length because of the specificity of its
details, the intensity of its pain, which contrasts ludicrously and
unconvincingly with the resolution – the lifting of the oppressive
gloom once the narrator reveals to the surviving sisters who had
owned the house that their youngest sister had fallen out a window by
accident and had not committed suicide. The narrator receives
"praise, thanks, and blessings," and everyone has a riotously happy
time playing children's games along the once-frightening corridors.

The title of the story reminds us of the fantasy of healing that
replaces the walking wounds of the earlier stories. Yet Kipling did not
choose to call this story "The House Doctor." The surgical operation
called for implies the desperate wish to hack away at one's own
unconscious. The early Kipling narrator was a reporter whose
helplessness was accentuated by the luridness of the story he chose to
retell and contain within a frame. He could not help the opium
addicts, the alcoholics, the ghost ridden, the mutilated, the one-eyed,
or the crucified characters who peopled his plainer tales. But here, the
narrator is granted new powers. He is now a searcher after truth, a
detective who gives himself the title of "house surgeon"; and
especially when the biographical dimension of the story reminds one
of the real helplessness of the writer in the face of such metaphysical
oppression, the fictionalizing of the actual event exposes the fantasy
underlying the tale: the artist has become the healer of the house that
is himself.

In "The Ship that Found Herself" (*The Day's Work*, 1894), the
once divided voices of the ship finally unite into the harmony and
unity necessary for its function: "The Steam knew what had
happened at once; for when a ship finds herself all the talking of the
separate pieces ceases and melts into one voice, which is the soul of the
ship" (*DW* 74). The parts need to learn to work together, a process
more complicated than the naive outsider understands:

"The engines are working beautifully. I can hear them." "Yes, Indeed. But
there's more than engines to a ship. Every inch of her, ye'll understand, has
to be livened up and made to work wi' its neighbour – sweetenin' her, we
call it technically." (*DW* 60)

The rest of the story involves a variety of cacophonous conflicts between the many voices of the ship each of whom wishes to take credit for being "the sole strength of this vessel," but who subdue themselves into unity once they have weathered the necessary suffering that accompanies a storm at sea. "There isn't a ship on the sea that has suffered as we have – is there, now?" asks the bow-plates of the Steam just before the many voices melt into the "soul of the ship" (*DW* 74).

"The Bridge-Builders," "The Brushwood Boy," and "The Ship that Found Herself," stories written during Kipling's stay in Vermont after his second loss of India and his bankruptcy, all seem to be stories about shoring the self against further external and internal assaults. His defense of the self, homologous to his defense of empire, of the ship, and of the bridge, was especially significant for him during these years. Newly married to an American, he was also newly bankrupt, forced into dependence on his new in-laws, in an alien land whose landscape and inhabitants threatened Kipling in unexpected ways. Angus Wilson tells us that the very openness of the farms and gardens, as opposed to England's fenced and hedged spaces, probably offended Kipling's sense of privacy (Wilson 1979: 178). But Wilson chides Kipling for his romantic conviction that he was entitled to set up a private fortress anywhere he chose, oblivious of the culture around him (Wilson 1979: 194). The irrational depression that overcame him at the house at Torquay (1896), although translated into personal terms, displaced onto a structure, and resolved in "The House Surgeon," was to pursue him throughout his life. Recognizable causes for depression, however, changed, and "'They'" (1904) is the result of the death of his "best-beloved" Josephine as well as the gradual breakdown of his sister Trix. The breakdown of his sister's mind took place during the years that he witnessed another more cosmic disintegration – that of conservative England. And the new political threat from the left compelled his retreat into a new home, Bateman's, in his much-loved countryside of Sussex.

Another kind of bridge building occurred in the late story that tried to deal with the abiding presence of his daughter after her death. "'They'" is both a fantasy of longing for his dead child Josephine (see Wilson 1979: 264) and a bridge between the ordinary or physical and the extraordinary or metaphysical, as well as a defense against the psychic, the metaphysical and the occult. It is about the narrator's accidental discovery, while motoring around the lush Sussex countryside, of a house full of children cared for by a blind woman. It is also a sensuous and elusive story made seductive by the call of the landscape and the children towards what one discovers to be death. The opening sentence prepares us for a magic geography filled with "miraculous brooks" and valleys "brim-full of liquid sunshine": "One view called me to another; one hill-top to its fellow half across the county, and since I could answer at no more trouble than the snapping forward of a lever, I let the county flow under my wheels" (*SSI* 93). Lost in the "confusing veils of the woods," he finds an exquisite Elizabethan manor surrounded by beautiful fountains and gardens filled with the sound of children's laughter and fleeting images of their faces behind windows, hedges, and bushes. Only on his third visit does he realize that the evasive "quick-footed wanderers" are in fact dead children whose spirits have been called into bodily being by the love of the blind woman. The recognition comes surprisingly, unexpectedly in the middle of a visit by a tenant to the blind woman. Suddenly he feels his

relaxed hand taken and turned softly between the soft hands of a child ... The little brushing kiss fell in the centre of my palm – as a gift on which the fingers were, once, expected to close: as the all-faithful, half reproachful signal of a waiting child not used to neglect even when grown-ups were busiest – a fragment of the mute code devised very long ago.
  Then I knew. (*SSI* 114)

The choices which now face the narrator are characteristic Kipling alternatives, either to return and engage himself with the super-natural and his rediscovered dead child, or return permanently to the land of the living. His decision to depart forever into the world of light and literal vision is "like the very parting of spirit and flesh," but the blind woman understands at once why for him it would be wrong to return. The reader does too. For the narrator, like Kipling, is one of the Sons of Martha who cannot afford to immerse himself perma-nently in the psychic world, who is terrified of tampering in the forbidden world of the occult because of his temperamental closeness to the unconscious. Kipling's biographers tell us not only of the richness of his dream life, but of the complexity of his psychic life, of his awareness of the psychic gifts both he and his sister Trix had "inherited" from the Celtic side of his family. (See Carrington 1986: 341–2; and Wilson 1979: 260–70.) Not only was his mother psychic, but his sister suffered a series of breakdowns that Kipling suspected were a consequence of tampering with her own buried powers. When pressured by his friends to contact mediums after the death of his son John in World War I, he answered with the poem "En-Dor."

> Oh the road to En-Dor is the Oldest road
> And the craziest road of all!
> Straight it runs to the Witch's abode,
> As it did in the days of Saul,
> And nothing has changed of the sorrow in store
> For such as go down on the road to En-Dor!   (*Verse* 264)

The autograph manuscript for "The Brushwood Boy" at the Morgan Library contains a significant section that Kipling censored. after the first paragraph where Cotter wonders why his dreams "fit into each other so":

He asked the Doctor that night at mess. "Oh that's easy enough," said the doctor who had five years service – "You've got two sides to your brain, you see, and they ought to work together but they don't always. One side gets a fraction of a second in front with a thought specially when you're half asleep and your reason, you see, isn't at work. Well the other half thinks the same thoughts on its own account and of course in dreams you've no sense of time and all the second half knows is that that thought has been thought before, years and years before, whereas its only a quarter of a fraction of a second old, really. You see? It's just as your brain works and of course that depends upon how you regulate your inside. A man in your condition oughtn't to dream." "Well I don't dream much but I'm awf'ly persistent in my dreams. Seem to pick 'em off just where I left off." "That's all nonsense, of course. It's the two halves of the brain not working together. They say that children dream more consistent dreams than grown people and when one comes to think of it, Cottar, you *are* a kid in most respects ... Very well I'll withdraw it (Cottar's hand was stretched to overturn the doctor's chair) – but it's only because you're so beastly strong. It's true just the same. You're a chap to be envied if you only knew it." (Pierpont Morgan: ms. 25–6)

The compulsion to return imaginatively to confirmation of internal division, to rework split structures into his fiction and then to censor the diagnoses of the division is Kipling's way of acknowledging the split in his personality that resulted from childhood abandonment and humiliation. Like the dream house in "'They,'" En-Dor and his own inner uncontrollable dream life were all part of Kipling's feared, multiple, and submerged private life which he claimed to marginalize and replace with the simpler life of work, action, and consciousness. But "'They'" also joins other nineteenth-century concerns with unseen dimensions of experience. Frederic Myers' essay "Multiplex Personality," which appeared in 1886 in the *Nineteenth Century*, discussed the brain as a vast factory whose looms weave time past and present into time future. Myers was among many early scientists of the unconscious who tried to explain the divided and paradoxical nature of the mind, of genius, and of the "subliminal personality" that might even be capable of communing with the dead (K. Miller 1985: 242). That Kipling also struggled with similar efforts to understand the psyche is particularly apparent in these and in other uncanny dream stories. In fact, Kipling's need to translate the nonverbal, ambiguous world of dreams into the coherence of language, part of his mechanism of mastery, is analogous to the scientist's desire for mastery over the unconscious and to the psychoanalyst's reduction of the visual dimension of dreams to linguistic phenomena.[2] Perhaps the awareness of multiple structures and sources that constituted the nature of colonial life became too threatening after he left India. Perhaps the reduction of the many to a few opposing structures seemed more manageable when once again he felt compelled to return to the land of cold, exacting English power. And perhaps that shift from the multiple to the few neatly opposed structures that he could then connect should be seen as Kipling's central turn and one that gave shape to his anxieties about the self and its empires.

CHAPTER 6

Kim: *empire of the beloved*

I

1897 was a year that frightened Kipling. It was of course Queen Victoria's Diamond Jubilee which Kipling refused to celebrate: "It's rather outside my beat and if I tried, I am afraid I should make a mess of it, but surely London is full of loyal poets who are all getting odes ready" (Birkenhead 1978: 176). Instead the year brought to climax a massive depression which he described as a "gathering blackness of mind and sorrow of the heart" (*SM* 129). Biographers follow Kipling's own lead in attributing his depression to the House at Torquay, to what he called "the Feng-Shui – the Spirit of the house itself" (*SM* 129). I prefer to see it as a multiply determined event provoked by the threatening collapse of many sustaining structures of empire, by turning points in what would be called, by at least one historian, the imperial sunset. (In his autobiography the paragraph describing his depression follows one in which he and his wife fall off a tandem bicycle.) The government of ever decreasing empires, it was becoming clear, depended on contradiction. As Max Beloff efficiently describes it, "The problem was thus to combine within a single system of government both an empire dedicated to the ideas of representative government and to a high measure of autonomy for its member nations, and an empire to which most responsible persons believed those principles to be inapplicable; either because they were unsuited to peoples of another and very different civilization or because they would, if introduced, lead to the complete severance of ties with the imperial metropolis" (p. 36). Victorian strategies in Africa, Arabia and the Persian gulf, furthermore, were the result of an ever more complex series of reactions in what the British saw as their central commitment to India (Beloff 1970: 37; Robinson, Gallagher and Denny).

145

1897 was also the year Kipling celebrated his election to the Atheneum with such friends as Cecil Rhodes and Alfred Milner – men who in different ways articulated the dreams and realities of Empire – Rhodes who dreamed of unlimited expansion into the stars if he could, and Milner of "limited expansion but unlimited tenacity" (Milner to Lord Goschen, June 22, 1890, quoted in Wrench 1958: 104). The decade had seen the emergence of the United States and imperial Germany as new naval and imperial powers, and an increase in hostilities between Britain and Russia for control over parts of the globe bordering on Russia – Persia, Afghanistan, North-West India, and China. England, complacently feigning ignorance of its dependence on such sustaining imperial structures, was a land whose inhabitants, Kipling felt, normally "never looked further than their annual seaside resorts" (*SM* 141). It was, however, as Kipling knew all too well, a land that paid the price for such resort tranquility by controlling far flung sea-routes which in turn relied on imperial networks (see Beloff 1970: 20ff. for more). The 1897 colonial conference recognized potential problems in lands as far flung as Australia, the Cape Colony, and Natal; the Boer resistance and parliamentary investigation into the Jameson raid had begun, and "into the midst of it all came the Great Queen's Diamond Jubilee, and a certain optimism that scared me" (*SM* 141). His immediate reaction to the facile celebration was to write "Recessional" as warning against a land "drunk with sight of power." James Morris captures the effect of such unexpected views from a writer like Kipling at this historical moment: "Like a slap in the face from an old roistering companion, Henry V turned princely, one morning that festive summer Kipling's poem *Recessional* appeared in *The Times*. It sounded a sombre, almost a frightened note, a warning against overconfidence, 'frantic boast and foolish word.' Its sacramental solemnity jarred, and seemed to imply that the Jubilee celebrations were all tinsel and conceit" (1968: 347).

After the Jubilee, Kipling and his family sailed to South Africa, a land whose color and light and manners reawakened the repressed nostalgia for India:

> The wayside magic, the threshold spells,
> Shall soon undo what the North has done –
> Because of the sights and sounds and the smells
> That ran with our youth in the eye of the sun.
> ("Song of the Wise Children," 1899, *Verse* 90)

There too Kipling developed his friendship with the man who lived out the fantasies grown men were expected to abandon – Cecil Rhodes – with whom he spoke the language of dreams. Rhodes would ask him questions as "disconcerting as those of a child. He said to me apropos of nothing in particular: 'What's your dream?' I answered that he was part of it" (*SM* 142). That conversation later found its way into a poem "The Fairies' Siege":

> I'd not give way for an Emperor,
> I'd hold my road for a King –
> To the Triple Crown I would not bow down –
> But this is a different thing.
> I'll not fight with the Powers of Air,
> Sentry, pass him through!
> Drawbridge let fall, 'tis the Lord of us all
> The Dreamer whose dreams come true! (Carrington 1986: 329)

But dreamers were no protection against other crises of imperialism and life.

The year (1898) that Kipling returned to work most intensely on *Kim* was also the year that saw new personal and political crises, the death of his closest uncle, Edward Burne-Jones, and the beginnings of his sister Trix's mental illness. 1898 is also generally recognized by historians as the turning point in Britain's imperial connections, the start of England's self-perception as "the weary Titan" (a phrase used by Chamberlain and subsequently by historians), the beginning of *ententes* with France and Russia against Germany, and the end of the Anglo-Japanese alliance. February 1898 also saw the destruction of the U.S. battleship Maine and the beginnings of the Spanish-American War and of Kipling's friendship with Theodore Roosevelt. Kipling's warning to the English had now expanded to include the Americans in the Philippines. Germany's entry into a new phase of open rivalry with Britain and the Czar's designs on British territory were ever the subject of Kipling's satires.

But *Kim* was the prize product of seven years: "In a gloomy, windy autumn Kim came back to me with insistence and I took it to be smoked over with my Father. Under our united tobaccos it grew like the Djinn released from the brass bottle ... I do not know what proportion of an iceberg is below water-line, but *Kim* as it finally appeared was about one-tenth of what the first lavish specification called for" (*SM* 134). "My Daemon," said Kipling, "was with me in the *Jungle Books*, *Kim*, and both Puck books ... One of the clauses in

our contract was that I should never follow up 'a success,' for by this
sin fell Napoleon and a few others" (*SM* 201–2).

Kim (published in 1901) is also the product of seven years
wandering through Africa, Australia, New Zealand, once again
India (1891), and the United States. It came after the *Jungle Books*,
after his marriage (1892), his children, and the death of Josephine
(1899). It captures both the fear of loss and the nostalgia for a lost
Indian past, a lost dream of possibility for an eternal childhood in an
imagined India, a fantasy of integration between the oppositional
roles of colonizer and colonized and of the master who rules and the
child who desires. It is also the result of a profound alienation from an
England in which he had not yet found what he was to call "a very-
own house" – that ultimate home which was to be Bateman's in
Sussex. Yet ironically *Kim* announces, even as it laments, Kipling's
choice of England over India.

At once a spy thriller, a picaresque adventure story, a maturation
story, and a quest romance, *Kim*'s complexity comes, in part, from the
curious stacking up of various genres: as spy thriller, it intermittently
pursues the problem of whether or not Kim and his lama will stop the
Russians; as picaresque adventure, it follows Kim's pursuits of "the
Great Game" along the Grand Trunk Road of life; as maturation
story it offers a variation on the familiar nineteenth-century theme of
the search for a father in its embodiment of a fragmented culture in
multiple father-figures; and as quest story, it involves two antithetical
searches – Kim's for the Red Bull on a Green Field, and the lama's
for the River of the Arrow. But even more importantly, its complexity
results from its efforts to negotiate the effects of the death of the
Father and to mediate the contrary but entangled demands of power
and love.

The major problems and contradictions in the novel are informed
and shaped by Kipling's divided sense of self, its multiple loyalties to
the power of empire during a time of intensified authority, and his
love for a lost India that blurred distinctions between the ruler and
the ruled. The inner quest, the search for an identity ("Who is Kim
– Kim – Kim?" *K* 185; also pp. 117, 143, 223, 282), suggests the
possibility of self-discovery and integration of his many selves, the
arrival at an identity mediated by the lama Kim learns to love. But
this search collides with his outer quest, the journey and the insistent
pursuit for definition in a search for a father (the Red Bull on a Green
Field) who will free him from some of the anxieties and problems

involved in such a search. Kim's love for the lama and his search for identity, in other words, are consistently mediated by ruling structures of power, and finally come under the control of the colonial system.

Kim and his world are introduced through images and events that appear to appropriate and subvert established imperial roles, and to suggest, through an oppositional discourse, possible alternatives to the system. But this is only an apparent subversion. Our first image in the opening sentence, for instance, is of an unnamed apparently native boy astride the gun Zam-Zammah in violation of city orders. Although this appears to introduce Kim as rebel, the order of the phrasing is significant: "He sat, in defiance of municipal orders, astride the gun Zam-Zammah on her brick platform opposite the old Ajaib-Gher – the Wonder House, as the natives called the Lahore Museum." Whereas the first part of the sentence suggests a rejection of authority, the second part complicates that impression by creating a new image of authority – of the boy in control of the gun. The sentence also allows two images to confront and collide against each other – the Gun and the Lahore Museum; and each is an emblem for a complex historical, cultural and political situation. The gun as the emblem of British authority ("Who hold Zam-Zammah, that 'fire-breathing dragon,' hold the Punjab," *K* 1), is geographically and symbolically opposed to the "Wonder-House" that is India. The curious, but historically necessary opposition between the two leads Kipling to reduce the threat of the first by perceiving it through childlike eyes to which it seems a quaint "fire-breathing dragon," and to reduce repeatedly the social and political complexity of India into the exquisite and timeless images displayed in a museum controlled by an English curator.

This opposition between the gun and the museum is repeated in other obvious oppositions between England and India, Kim and lama, and in a host of less obvious oppositions between hierarchy and chaos, aggression and passivity, masculine and feminine, and most significantly, in the sign of Kim's heritage and quest – the Red Bull on a Green Field. This emblem resonates tacitly through the novel, suggesting its political theme: the British redcoats charging through the fertile "green field" of India. (Or, perhaps ironically, the bull of the Irish High Kings in the green field of Ireland, another subjugated green place full of redcoats; the banner is from that of O'Hara's Irish regiment.) The political splitting repeats itself on other levels: the male aggression of the red bull opposed to the female fecundity of the green field, and Kim's split quest for the definition, not integration, of these qualities in his own personality – his manhood in the midst of the confusion of India's green fields. And it signifies the structure of the plot. The two men who prepare the way and make things ready for the red bull on a green field are not, as Kim thinks, the soldiers, but rather Kim and the lama, as well as the multiply paired fathers of the rest of the novel.

The simple story of Kim O'Rishti exists against the background of an absent dead father whose failure makes possible the Indianization of his son and risks the danger of boundary blurring between the colonizer and the colonized. The subsequent narrative of Kim's growing love for his chosen father figure, the unworldly lama, is contradicted by the story of the English Kim who discovers the absent father, desires (although this is never admitted in the text) to replace him, to fulfill the role in which his father failed, and thereby to attain the hierarchical position he merely mimes at the novel's opening – the paternal controller of all his Indian subjects, Muslims, Buddhists and Hindus alike. What appears to be a boy's adventure story is also a complex fantasy of idealized imperialism and colonialism, and the friendship between Kim and his lama is Kipling's fable of the ideal relationship between the Englishman (ever a boy at heart) and the Indian – eternally passive, unworldly, and childlike. As the creator of a colonial fable, Kipling confronts the necessary contradictions in colonial identity, but then resolves the contradictions by allowing Kim's love for the lama to blur the reality of his rejection of the lama's values. Private emotion transcends political splitting and, by such evasion, creates a Marxist's paradigm of bad faith and alienation. But Kim as orphaned Indianized hybrid is both produced and initially despised by the system; so that an alternative reading might also allow us to read the very existence of love for the lama as an alternative to the system's denial of such possibility.

Kipling sets up his patterns of opposition and contradiction in the opening chapter. After the initial image of the unknown child on the gun, the second paragraph identifies Kim by race and parentage. We are told he is English and therefore justified in kicking the Hindu boy off the trunnions, and that, though he is "burned black as any native" and consorts on terms of "perfect equality" with the small boys of the bazaar, "Kim was white." We learn that his father,

Kimball O'Hara, a sergeant of the Mavericks, an Irish regiment, fell to drinking and loafing after his wife died of cholera, and that he then fell into the company of a local half-caste woman who led him to opium and eventual death. As early as the second paragraph, we learn, along with Kim, something significant about the natives: they are to be controlled and kicked off trunnions, because if allowed control, their unrestrained ways can lead to the death of fathers. This half-caste woman vanishes from the book almost as soon as she is introduced. Kim apparently never thinks of her, and for her part, she apparently never wonders where he has gone and makes no attempt to contact him. She is the first of many women in the story, and an important part of Kim's initiation is splitting off women from men, internally as well as externally, assigning them rigid values, and building up defenses against them. Although the half-caste who raised him tells the missionaries she had been Kim's mother's sister, the narrator takes pains to counter the problem of miscegenation explicitly by reminding us that she is no kin, but an Other. And since we know that Kim's father was lured into drugs, desertion and death by a half-caste woman, we are alerted to her position in the hierarchy of natives set up and stereotyped early in the text.

The father's legacy to the boy (his "clearance-certificate," his signature, and his birth certificate) proves his identity as an Englishman and a Freemason. These details of parentage and of membership in a privileged race and club all justify and confirm the opening sentences of both the first and second paragraphs: the image of Kim as an emblem of British authority. They also undercut the opposing impression of Kim's defiant rejection of authority. The paragraphs also alternate, like the rest of the book, between confirming and denying Kim's essential whiteness, his identity as an Englishman, and his superiority over the natives, by juxtaposing those qualities against his native coloring, his native garb, and his inadequate command of English. The retention of English markers even within the acquired traits of nativism confirms the assumption that an Englishman's identity is unquestionable and supreme regardless of his appearance, language or disguise – a certainty undercut by Kim's later rejection of English structures of oppression. Kim is both the keeper of the gun and "Little Friend of all the World" – two roles that are incompatible, mutually exclusive, and capture exactly the inimical dilemma of empire. But the inadequacies and the charm of the book arise from the impossible fantasy that the

Englishman, if sufficiently deprived and Indianized in his formative years, can find a multitude of native parents who will cherish and indulge him as master, and to whom he can, in turn, play the twin roles of child and parent, "chela" and overlord, equal and "king-of-the-castle."

The absence of real parents is unaccompanied by grief or a sense of loss, and they are swiftly replaced by an abundance of bigger and better fathers. Unlike Pip, the creation of that other nineteenth-century novelist obsessed with problems of maturation and absent parents, who weeps over his first awareness of absence and aloneness, and whose anger at unloving, inadequate parental love is translated into social and fictional opposition to parental oppressors, Kipling's Kim compensates for his loss through finding and then controlling new fathers, and through aggressive triumph over all adversity. He makes rude remarks to native policemen who merely grin affectionately at the boy. We are told that Kim can afford rudeness and aggression against little Chota Lal and Abdulla the sweetmeat-seller's son because the policeman "knew Kim of old. So did the water carrier, sluicing water on the dry road from his goat-skinbag. So did Jawahir Singh, the museum carpenter, bent over new packing cases. So did everybody in sight except the peasants from the country, hurrying up to the Wonder House to view the things that men made in their own province and elsewhere. The museum was given up to Indian arts and manufactures, and anybody who sought wisdom could ask the curator to explain" (K 5). The first part of the quotation suggests that loss and victimization can be transcended through friendship with substitute parental figures; the second part of the quotation extends this hypothesis into a greater falsehood. That the hungry masses of Indian peasants have nothing more important to do than to "hurry" to the Museum of Art so that an English curator can explain to them Indian arts and crafts is an Orientalist fantasy that denies material reality and subjectivity to Indian peasants; furthermore, it appropriates Indian art into an autonomous reified commodity divorced from its identity with its cultural source. The logic so far suggests that loss of parents is compensated for by aggression and victimization which in turn is justified by denial, by defense, and by substitution. And the loss (though temporary) of one's own country, for the curator, can be compensated for by the appropriation of another's land and culture that can be reified into objects for the eye.

The lama's entrance onto the street scene comes against the background of what on one level is child's play for control of the Zam-Zammah, and what on another level is a competition among religions and races whose winner is decided in advance by Kim, who assumes that because "all Mussalmans fell off Zam-Zammah long ago!" (*K* 5) and "the Hindus fell off Zam-Zammah too" (*K* 5), he is the rightful successor and ruler. – *Justifies Imperialism*. [pg 4]

Against this background of barely veiled racial, religious and national competition, the lama appears at first to silence conflict and opposition by his rarity. But in fact he introduces new and ever more complex problems. Rather than representing the land, he is seen as a thing apart, as one who represents values that are unearthly and unworldly, who can be completely appreciated only by his English "chela" and by the English curator. Although his religion and his nationality set him apart from India, that difference does not signify the unified reality of such an entity called "India" and is exaggerated by readers who assume such a unified essence. The lama is a Tibetan Buddhist who has traveled south in search of a learned man who will help him find the sacred River of the Arrow (the river into which Lord Krishna cast his arrow), and incidentally to find a "chela." Appropriately, both his teacher, whom he calls a priest, and his "chela" turn out to be Englishmen. And the great Indian art treasures in the Art Museum are introduced in terms of their derivation and deviation from Western art:[1] *lama represents something other than 'other'.*

In the entrance hall stood the larger figures of the Greco-Buddhist sculptures done, savants know how long since, by forgotten workmen whose hands were feeling, and not unskilfully, for the mysteriously transmitted Grecian touch. (*K* 6)

The meeting between the lama and the curator becomes a meeting of two opposing worlds – East and West, the mind and the eye. And appropriately, the curator's gift to the lama is the gift of sight and space (spectacles, pencil and paper); the lama's gift (the ancient Chinese pen case) is of mind and time ("That is for a memory between thee and me – my pen case. It is something old – even as I am" [*K* 12]). The gift further suggests the Englishman's power to bestow upon the lama the gift of sight, a gift that buys him something much more rare than secondhand glasses, and the promise of an even greater gift, "a written picture of the Padma Samthora ... and of the Wheel of Life." The curator realizes that "they are few in the world who still have the secret of the conventional brush-pen Buddhist pictures which are, as it were, half written and half drawn" (*K* 12) and that he has the possessor of the secret before him.

What the curator has not yet possessed, Kim will. Sitting within hearing range, Kim with the insight and intuition of the born colonialist, recognizes that the lama is a new territory worth annexing and possessing:

> What he had overheard excited him wildly. This man was entirely new to all his experience, and he meant to investigate further: precisely as he would have investigated a new building or a strange festival in Lahore city. The lama was his trove, and he purposed to take possession. (*K* 12)

The new relationship between the lama and Kim picks up the oppositional configuration of all the other relationships so far in the story. Kim will be the aggressive and experienced possessor and protector of the lama, who "old, forlorn, and very empty" (*K* 12) expects care. The next father figure Kim seeks, finds, and controls in this chapter is Mahbub Ali, the Muslim Pathan horsetrader, whose violent and worldly attachments set up a further pattern of opposition to the unworldly, spiritual yearnings of the lama to be freed from attachment to the Wheel of Life.

The opening chapter has introduced us to dualities, not only in Kim's identity and loyalties, but in emblems associated with dual fathers. His absent father, a type of Jellaludin McIntosh (in "To Be Filed for Reference"), and the curator, modeled on Kipling's own father who was in fact the curator of the Lahore Museum, are split English fathers. The earthly Mahbub Ali and the spiritual lama are split Eastern fathers, a division to be repeated and parodied in other paired fathers in the novel. The chapter further introduces us to the opposing quests of Kim and the lama that amplify Kim's dual quests for alternate fathers. Each father suggests split and contradictory meanings (over)determined by specific social and political events, and each represents alternate ways of coping with imperial rule. Kim's father, on one level, may be read as a "failure" or a rebel who renounces adult responsibility by regressing into opium addiction, an Indian mistress and death; on another level, he is the one Kim chooses to pursue ("Perhaps they will make me king"[*K* 17]) because he is part of the ruling establishment and of the Irish regiment whose flag (the Red Bull on the Green Field) represents conquest and war against passive failures. The lama too has

conflicting functions: he is at once the childlike holy man whom Kim
will guide and father, but he is also Kim's ideal father who hopes to
teach him "other and better desires," whose great love for Kim
compels him to forgo not only his credo of nondesire and non-
attachment, but also his goal of freedom from the wheel of life.

The series of journeys that provide a three-part structure to the
novel allow Kim to negotiate his complex relationship to his own
identity and to the power of empire. In the first five chapters on the
train and on the road to Benares, he will defy yet serve its authority.
Although the lama's quest appears to give spiritual direction to the
journey, it is in fact energized and mediated by Kim's more worldly
Game and by the practical spy Mahbub Ali. The early meeting of
Kim and the lama, and Kim's open declaration of love and service to
him appears to provide an ideological frame to the novel: the wise,
passive and meditative lama who carries secrets of past wisdom can
offer an alternate path of life, a different logic of history and
spirituality to the active, rootless, English Kim. But in fact the lama's
otherworldly knowledge is undercut by Kim's worldly knowledge,
which in turn is reenforced by the narrator's stance and undercut by
Kim's irrational and socially unacceptable love for the lama.

Kipling's foregrounding of a street urchin through whose actions
and eyes he mediates the realities of imperial India and history makes
for a complex narrative strategy that is at once defensive and
oppositional. The split at the heart of Kipling's discourse is between
the official power of the colonizer and the unoffical desire of the
colonized, and his division reveals itself in the duality of Kim and in
Kipling's use of an authorial narrator who reflects the collective voice
of stereotyped club members in Simla – a voice that speaks in
opposition to the more personal and Indianized voice of Kim. Kim as
child happily sees history and war as a "Great Game" for which one
is prepared by playing little games. The rules of the Great Game
"permitted and even dictated the consideration of whole nations as
stepping stones, or as pawns ... for the riches and the rule over a third
country, which in turn became a mere stepping stone in the unending
process of power expansion and accumulation" (Arendt 1973: xviii).
Kim's role in the Game is as a minor spy. His understanding of the
Game is simply that it was "intrigue of some kind" (*K* 18) whose
worth lies in the occasional money and hot meals that Mahbub Ali
gives him as reward. The narrator tells us what Kim does not know,
"that Mahbub Ali ... was registered in one of the locked books of the

Indian Survey Department as C.25. IB." whose current job it is to leak information to British India about "five confederate Kings, who had no business to confederate" (*K* 21). The narrator's tone describing the intrigue is playful, confident and condescending in its assumption that the natives have "no business" to act, collude or conspire without the approval of the British.

The narrator also slips easily into the discourse of Orientalism and recalls the enigmatic and ironic voice of the narrators in the early Kipling stories. "All India," we are told, "is full of holy men stammering gospels in strange tongues; shaken and consumed in the fires of their own zeal; dreamers, babblers and visionaries: as it has been from the beginning and will continue to the end" (*K* 32). Kim, we are told, lies like an Oriental; and "All hours of the twenty-four are alike to Orientals" (*K* 26). The lama at first appears to embody different values in silence and inactivity, one recognized by the learned curator as a scholar and no "mere bead telling mendicant" (*K* 8). He is allowed speech, storytelling and subjectivity in the scene with the curator. But after he is "possessed" and taken over by Kim, we see him only in reaction to others. Only once are we privileged in the opening chapter to know what the lama actually sees and feels, and that is during the few minutes after he leaves the Art Museum: "The old man halted by Zam-Zammah and looked round till his eye fell on Kim. The inspiration of his pilgrimage had left him for awhile, and he felt old, forlorn, and very empty" (*K* 12). But from this point on, it is his practical inadequacies that are foregrounded. His tradition of begging in silence is rendered valueless by the nativized Kim: "Those who beg in silence starve in silence" (*K* 13). His habitual gesture is to bow his head so "that he might not see" (*K* 30); but Kim serves as his eyes. The games of the world set Kim's eyes aflame (*K* 20), as does the idea of possession. And the lure of possession and control is passed on to the reader and to the lama who is told to "Look" (*K* 31) at a painterly image of India: "Golden, rose, saffron, and pink, the morning mists smoked away across the flat green levels. All the rich Punjab lay out in the splendour of the keen sun" (*K* 31).

The journey empowers Kim into the role of efficient guide, seer and savior. Whereas new sights, sounds and experiences are an assault on the lama's sensibilities, Kim is charged and fired at each new encounter. The first part of their journey on the train exposes the lama's fears. He recoils from "the hollow echoing darkness, the glimmer of rails between the masonry platforms, and the maze of girders above. He stood in a gigantic stone hall paved, it seemed, with the sheeted dead" (*K* 26). And his first words, "This is the work of devils!" are countered by the Sikh artisan's assurance: "Do not be afraid ... Enter! This thing is the work of the government" (*K* 27). The lama's silence is opposed by the consistent chatter of the other members of the compartment. When Kim defends the lama's silence as "holy" because it "thinks upon matters hidden from thee," the soldier defines his own credo: "We of the Loodhiana Sikhs ... do not trouble our heads with doctrine. We fight" (*K* 28). Within this tiny compartment is cramped a microcosm of Indian types who represent not only India, but split male and female parental images (the wife and the courtesan, the husband and the ascetic) whose control Kim will evade while seeking and accepting their admiration and love. That he is different from the "Orientals" is certain, and the narrator regularly alerts us to the presence of Kim's white blood. Most significantly, the evidence of his white blood is seen in instant and spontaneous action which opposes him to most passive "Orientals", but particularly to the lama:

Somebody laughed at the little tattered figure ... Where a native would have lain down, Kim's white blood set him upon his feet. "Ay, War," he answered. (*K* 46)

The world of the train, like that of the road, consists of diverse people who are seen, heard and understood only by Kim and the narrator; it is therefore a world in which the lama plays a subordinate part. The people on the train repeat the oppositional structures set up by the dual quests of the novel for the Bull and the River: Kim and the lama, the husband and the ascetic, the soldier and the artist, the wife and the courtesan, the cultivator and the banker, the soldier and the priest. Ready to nurture and nourish Kim, this world, so the narrative has us believe, would happily ignore the lama were it not for Kim's mediation. Here, however, as in so many other instances, the narrator contradicts himself. On the one hand he would like to alert us to Kim's value as aggressive protector of the lama, who begs for his ticket and pleads for his food and curses the fields of farmers who will not allow them to pass through. On the other hand he wants to represent India as a static, stereotyped, maternal and nourishing land whose "gentle, tolerant folk" look reverently on each other's strangenesses. Here as elsewhere, the narrative voice appears trapped between seeing the world as hostile and as nurturing, between the values of activity and inactivity, the doers and the dreamers. And only a few pages later, when the lama wonders whether the road will be as kind to them as the hills had been to him before he met Kim – "All men are well-disposed throughout all the Hills," (*K* 71) – Kim responds instantly and drily "it is otherwise in Hind ... Their Gods are many-armed and malignant. Let them alone" (*K* 71). Even the old soldier undercuts the values of the lama. When the lama questions the value of the sword around his waist – "What profit to kill men?" the soldier replies: "Very little – as I know; but if evil men were not now and then slain it would not be a good world for weaponless dreamers. I do not speak without knowledge who have seen the land from Delhi south awash with blood" (*K* 52).

Kim, the lama and the narrator share a curious trait in their efforts to universalize the experience of Kim and the lama so that they come to represent, in a Didi and Gogo fashion, the reliance of the world of contemplation on the world of action, or some other dubious universal truth. The transcending catch-words begin with "all." Thus we know that "All India is full of holy men stammering gospels" (*K* 32), that "All earth would have picked thy bones within ten miles of Lahore city if I had not guarded thee" (*K* 61), that Kim walks in the "indescribable gait of the long-distance tramp all the world over" (*K* 61), that the new breed of English ruler born and bred in the land is more successful than the old: "The other, all new from Europe, suckled by white women and learning our tongues from books, are worse than the pestilence. They do harm to Kings" (*K* 76). This imperial tendency to unify, essentialize and transcendentalize is undercut, often within the text, as in scenes where Kim's personal and individualized voice resists expected Sahib-like behavior.

Kim's power, however, reveals itself in his celebratory consciousness, his magical delight in "seeing the world in real truth ... life as he would have it – bustling and shouting, the buckling of belts, and beating of bullocks and creaking of wheels, lighting of fires and cooking of food, and new sights at every turn of the approving eye" (*K* 73). When India is awake, Kim positions himself "in the middle of it, more awake and more excited than anyone" (*K* 73). S.P. Mohanty describes this as "a rhythmic explosion in the present moment" that embodies a "kind of agency, not simply passive contemplation ... a desire to pay attention, creatively discovering the world's 'real truth'" (*K* 23) but also notices that Kim's perceptions are privileged more than those of any Indian. Kim is empowered by a vision more useful than that of the lama because it attends to material rather than spiritual reality and therefore relies on his vigilance and ability to *see* what the lama cannot. This too becomes part of Kipling's strategy, which "contains" conflict by focusing on the visual and painterly images with which the narrator captures the adventure on the Grand Trunk Road. On that "broad, smiling river of life" (*K* 61) the opposing functions of Kim and the lama are captured by their frozen postures in which one turns inwards, the other outwards: "The lama, as usual, was deep in meditation, but Kim's bright eyes were open wide" (*K* 61) And the narrator, as intoxicated as Kim with the power of the gaze, ignores, marginalizes, and necessarily denigrates the mental experience of the lama. Splendid pages are devoted to describing the new castes, new people, new sounds, places, jokes, and images that strike Kim's eyes. By contrast, we are also explicitly told of what the lama does not see: "The lama never raised his eyes. He did not note the money lender ... Even the seller of Ganges-water he did not see ... He looked steadily at the ground, and strode as steadily hour after hour, his soul busied elsewhere" (*K* 62). But Kim sees what the narrator sees – "all India spread out to left and right" – and is in "the seventh heaven of joy" (*K* 63):

It was beautiful to behold the many-yoked grain and cotton wagons crawling over the country roads: one could hear their axles, complaining a mile away, coming nearer, till with shouts and yells and bad words they climbed up the steep incline and plunged on to the hard main road, carter reviling carter. It was equally beautiful to watch the people, little clumps of red and blue and pink and white and saffron, turning aside to go to their own villages, dispersing and growing small by twos and threes across the level plain. Kim felt these things though he could not give tongue to his feelings ... the sun was driving broad golden spokes through the lower branches of mango trees; the parakeets and doves were coming home in their hundreds; the chattering, gray-backed Seven Sisters, talking over the day's adventure, walked back and forth in twos and threes almost under the feet of the travellers. ... Swiftly the light gathered itself together, painted for an instant the faces and the cart-wheels and the bullocks' horns as red as blood. Then the night fell. (*K* 63–4)

By neutralizing the distance between the narrator and Kim, between first and third person narration, Kipling also collapses what had been oppositional in the stances of the ironic distanced narrator and the engaged and personal Kim. The narrative eye that sees light gathering around people, animals and objects is the painterly, impressionistic eye which must content itself with surface sensation and with seeing India from a loving distance as a series of unified friezes beyond the pale of conflict. So Kim's perspective, like those of the narrators and the master ethnographer he is soon to meet, relies on the mastery of the gaze divorced from thought and can, therefore, by focusing on the physical and immediate sense impression of the road, transcend any concern with its political geography.

If life on the road (with a little help from narrative and perspectival conflation) provokes strategies of simplified exclusion and transcendence, so does the portrayal of the lama. From seeming at first to be a spiritual figure promising the wisdom of meditative introspection, the lama progressively becomes a stick figure who mumbles such platitudes as "The land is good, all the country of the South is good – a great and terrible world" (*K* 67). From his early function as a father figure for the orphan Kim, the lama gradually reveals his practical inadequacies as his childlike dependence on Kim grows more explicit: "'O friend of all the World!' The lama had waked, and simply as a child bewildered in a strange bed, called for Kim" (*K* 70). And it is this familial and homosocial configuration that allows the reader to accept unquestioningly the overwhelming love that develops between the two:

"I have known many men in my so long life, and disciples not a few. But to none among men, if so be thou art woman-born, has my heart gone out as it has to thee – thoughtful, wise, and courteous, but something of a small imp."

"And I have never seen such a priest as thou." Kim considered the benevolent yellow face wrinkle by wrinkle. "It is less than three days since we took road together, and it is as though it were a hundred years." (*K* 70)

The lama is allowed this moment of humanity only after he has revealed his total dependence on Kim, not when he is being what he otherwise is – a silent, meditative lama whose desires for the "Search" are antithetical to Kim's for the "Game."

The oppositions of values grounded in fathers takes another turn in the second part of the novel where, in contrast to the new Western fathers who are ethnographers and men of power and knowledge, the lama's virtues and behavior increasingly appear gendered as feminine and consequently ineffectual. In contrast to the lama's (maternal) attachment, love, and delight in Kim for "thy joy at seeing these

feminine
ineffectual as in PZI.

things," and in contrast to the lama's unreserved love ("My heart went out to thee for thy charity and thy courtesy and the wisdom of thy little years" [*K* 92]), his new fathers, Father Victor and Father Bennett, initiate a regime of discipline, authority, and obedience: "You will be sent to a school." They meet Kim's protest against drill and routine – "I will not be a soldier" – with "You will be what you're told to be" (*K* 93). And so begins Kim's formal schooling in strategies of repression and discipline. The novel's perceptions of India change along with Kim's entry into the English world. The brilliant colors and forms on the Grand Trunk Road are suddenly negated as Kim, confronted by the bleak prospect of English school routines, thinks: "Sooner or later, if he chose, he could escape into great, gray, formless India, beyond tents and padres and colonels. Meantime... he would do his best to impress them. He too was a white man" (*K* 95). It is the white side of his self-divided head that has suddenly transformed the memory of "beautiful" India to "great gray, formless India" (*K* 95). Kim's "fettered soul" (*K* 100) will, in the second stage of his education, be subjected to the surveillance of white guards, priests and soldiers and their prisonlike lonely barracks and white tents.

II

The next five chapters (6–10), devoted to Kim's education and to his training in the art of surveying and spying, also introduce us to the function of ethnographic knowledge in perpetuating existing power relations in colonial India. From the ethnologist Colonel Creighton who has "bombarded" the Royal Society "for years with monographs on strange Asiatic cults and unknown customs" (*K* 174), and who now appears to control the Indian Secret Police, Kim learns that he is to enter the "Survey of India as a chain-man"(*K* 118), that he will someday be paid "for knowledge of what is behind those hills – for a picture of a river and a little news of what the people say in the villages there" (*K* 118). It is here too that Kim recognizes his loss of something nameless, a sense of self that was once autonomous, free, "Imaginary," associated with the streets where he had been raised by a nameless mother only to be found by a lama who takes over (and complicates) the role of mother by delivering Kim to the law of the ruling (and "Symbolic") Fathers. His entry into "the Gates of Learning" is also an entry into language and into an understanding of the rules of culture that he must master through language. As he works his way towards becoming his own prisoner and father, Kim must ironically learn the art of policing and surveillance that were responsible for his primary loss.

That knowledge, however, will not give him power. Whereas in his earlier life, before his fall into his heritage, he was "The friend of the Stars, who is the Friend of all the World," schooled in street knowledge and loved by all types of men and women, his newly acquired English education splits him as it were from himself and from his childhood desires: when he escapes from the English school, he "slips back" to dreaming and thinking in the vernacular (*K* 212), but in negotiating with the Great Game he must think "hard" in English (*K* 243). That division comes with some pride, but not without the pain, loneliness, and alienation he acknowledges to the lama: "I am all alone in this land," says Kim, "I know not where I go nor what shall befall me. My heart was in that letter I sent thee. Except for Mahbub Ali, and he is a Pathan, I have no friend save thee, Holy One. Do not altogether go away." (*K* 122). "'But whither shall I send my letters?' wailed Kim, clutching at the robe, all forgetful that he was a Sahib." The lama begs Kim not to weep, waits till he sees him go to the English school: "Dost thou love me? Then go, or my heart cracks... I will come again. Surely I will come again."... "'The Gates of Learning' shut with a clang" (*K* 123).

The imprisonment implied by the gates shutting on Kim gradually penetrates the fabric of the narrative and is assumed not only by the narrative voice but by Kim, who, ironically, struggles against it even as he is hypnotized by its power and charm. The most obvious change between the freedom of the early chapters and the incarceration of the next five is in the language, imagery and style. The impressionistic lyricism of Kim's perceptions on the road change to dry, factual, objective reporting of words and actions even as Kim splits the self that feels from the self that knows, the dreamer from the thinker. The reported, dramatic, and dialogue-ridden scenes of chapters 5 to 7 dominated by an authorial narrator who disassociates himself from Kim's perspective, for instance, contrasts tellingly with the following passage from chapter 4 in which the narrator seeing through Kim's loving eyes poeticizes the lama and his setting in images of color and light and nature:

It was a strange picture that Kim watched between drooped eyelids. The lama, very straight and erect, the deep folds of his yellow clothing slashed with black in the light of the *parao* fires precisely as a knotted tree trunk is slashed with the shadow of the long sun, addressed a tinsel and lacquered *ruth* which burned like a many-coloured jewel in the same uncertain light. The patterns of the gold-worked curtains ran up and down, melting and re-forming as the folds shook and quivered to the night wind; and when the talk grew more earnest the jewelled forefinger snapped out little sparks of light between the embroideries. Behind the cart was a wall of uncertain darkness speckled with little flames and alive with half-caught forms and faces and shadows. The voices of early evening had settled down to one soothing hum whose deepest note was the steady chumping of the bullocks above their chopped straw, and whose highest was the tinkle of a Bengali dancing-girl's *sitar*. (*K* 71)

Here we see the collapse of the authorial narrator and Kim who sees, feels and knows, but this almost omniscient knowledge, as D. A. Miller highlights in another context (1988: 25), is opposed to the power that rules in the political system of the novelistic world. And it is that power that intrudes between the narrator and Kim as Kim is delivered into the hands of the English. We have been used to seeing characters and places, as in the paragraph above, through Kim's loving eyes that substitute impressions for detail, because he and the narrator, while on the Grand Trunk Road, define themselves as one with and outside the races, religions, and factions that divide India. Consequently, they recurringly see all from a distance as a unified and harmonious picture. But once Kim enters the English Regiment's compound, the perspective changes, the narrator's perspective divides itself from Kim's, and the reader sees events through eyes other than Kim's. The narrative shift is part of a strategy to realign and alienate the reader's perspective and sympathies along with Kim's.

The scenes that precede and follow Kim's discovery by the Reverend Bennett are noticeably different for their curiously omniscient insights into the British point of view. For instance, after pages of Kim's characteristically Indianized perspective on Reverend Bennett ("The black dress, gold cross on the watch-chain, the hairless face, and the soft, black wideawake hat would have marked him as a holy man anywhere in all India" [*K* 82]), the stance shifts as the internal narrative perspective grows strangely external, anal-ogous or perhaps preparatory to Kim's own shifting position simultaneously inside and outside Indian culture. Thus, we are told that "the Reverend Arthur Bennett always left mess after that toast, and being rather tired by his march his movements were more abrupt than usual" (*K* 84), that "between himself and the Roman Catholic chaplain of the Irish contingent lay, as Bennett believed, an unbridgeable gulf, but it was noticeable that whenever the Church of England dealt with a human problem she was very likely to call in the Church of Rome. Bennett's official abhorrence of the Scarlet Woman and all her ways was only equalled by his private respect for Father Victor" (*K* 85). The narration shifts from being controlled by the "character" narrator, whose perceptions are first intermingled with Kim's, to the "reflector" narrator who absorbs and mimics the ingroup and ironic voice of English power (I am using Stanzel's distinctions and language), becoming thereby the collective voice of colonizing society. The opposition between those two kinds of narration is analogous to at least a part of Kim's growing internal divisions.

Colonial education and policing in this novel provide an occasional and inconsistent master voice at war with the other voices that resist and confirm its authority. Although Kim recurringly and eventually accepts the rules of the imperial masters, he spends most of his life avoiding their rules and surveillance, despising their ignorance ("They are only uncurried donkeys," *K* 88) and their prejudice ("He styled all natives 'niggers'; yet servants and sweepers called him abominable names to his face, and, misled by their deferential attitude, he never understood" *K* 106), their punishment and their abuse.

Accustomed as he is to street games of survival, Kim is equipped to shift allegiance from master to master as he continues playing the Great Game of colonial life. Just as the appeal of imperialism (according to Hannah Arendt) was to "those who had never been able to outgrow their boyhood ideals" to whom imperialism was "an accidental opportunity to escape a society in which a man had to forget his youth if he wanted to grow up" (*K* 211), so too the appeal of the Great Game to Kim is its repetition of the purposelessness, mystery, game playing, and secrecy of his childhood games in the bazaars. Yet Kim's profound and growing concern with his identity ("Who is Kim? He considered his own identity, a thing he had never done before, till his head swam" [*K* 108]), conflicts with his opposing delight in shedding identity, disguising himself, and entering the Great Game that, like his nightly boyish games, allows him the defense of anonymity, secrecy and autonomy. Again, Hannah Arendt's understanding of the imperial legend and the imperial character helps put Kim's actions into a wider context. The game of expansionism played by Rhodes and Cromer, for instance, was, she says,

the discovery of an expansion which was not driven by the specific appetite for a specific country but conceived as an endless process in which every country would serve only as stepping-stone for further expansion. In view of such a concept, the desire for glory can no longer be satisfied by the glorious triumph over a specific people for the sake of one's own people, nor can the scene of duty be fulfilled through the consciousness of specific services... once he has entered the maelstrom of an unending process of expansion, he will, as it were, cease to be what he was and obey the laws of the process, identify himself with anonymous forces that he is supposed to serve in order to keep the whole process in motion; he will think of himself as mere function, and eventually consider such functionality, such an incarnation of the dynamic trend, his highest possible achievement... These secret and anonymous agents of the force of expansion felt no obligation to man-made laws. The only "law" they obeyed was the "law" of expansion, and the only proof of their "lawfulness" was success. (Arendt 1973: 215)

The ideal of such a bureaucratic and lawless political body will always be, she continues to remind us, "the man behind the scenes who pulls the strings of history" (p.216). Colonel Creighton, the man behind the schemes in *Kim*, was a familiar figure in nineteenth-century colonial India, an ethnographer whose scientific aim was "that of salvaging cultural diversity, threatened with global Western-ization, especially during the age of colonization. The ethnographer would capture in writing the authenticity of changing cultures, so they could be entered into the record for the great comparative project of anthropology, which was to support the Western goal of social and economic progress" (Marcus and Fischer 1986: 24). Because of his scientific expertise, such a man was a prize recruit as spy, and to Kim he becomes a hero – "a man after his own heart – a tortuous and indirect person playing a hidden game" (*K* 117).

Kim's game is at each stage an ideologically charged preparation for the greater game he will enter at the end of the novel. But the political implications of the game are recurringly blurred and sentimentalized by the oppositional language of love.

"Dost *thou* give news for love, or dost thou sell it?" Kim asked.
"I sell and – I buy." Mahbub took a four-anna piece out of his belt and held it up.
"Eight!" said Kim, mechanically following the huckster instinct of the East.

Mahbub laughed, and put away the coin. "It is too easy to deal in that market, Friend of all the World. Tell me for love. Our lives lie in each other's hand." (*K* 134)

Love here and in scenes with the lama is used to counter and sacramentalize the insidiousness of the negotiation with power. Ironically too, the narrator's generalization about the "instinct of the East" is immediately contradicted by Mahbub's action in which he refuses to deal in such terms. What governs such an event in Kim's journey is an alienation from the real meaning of his implications in the power structure; it is (and I paraphrase Althusser) both a real and an imaginary relationship to the world, real because it reflects the actual systems of power controlling individual life and subjectivity, and imaginary because it resists and evades an understanding of how he and others are controlled and constructed by those systems of power and material reality. ("Ideology" as Althusser describes it is "not the system of the real relations which govern the existence of individuals, but the imaginary relation of those individuals to the real relations in which they live" [1971: 155].) Thus, Kim's real relationship to India will be that of spy, protector of British interests, colonialist, and imperialist. But his imaginary relationship to India will be as "The Friend of the Stars" and "The Friend of all the World" – a sort of one-man United Nations, both "chela" and overlord, servant and master. The many Eastern sayings that pepper the novel have the effect of smoothing over the contradictions in the text between reality and ideology, between the real, the imaginary, and the symbolic. Kim's childlike glee in participating in some mysterious game whose object is unclear to him (though clear to the reader), is contradicted by his awareness that the price he will pay for his complicity is the loss of his first self and the gain of full-time Sahibhood.

The journey towards "education" will also be a journey towards loss: this is made explicit in the contrast between the train to his school in Lucknow and his earlier joyful train ride in chapter 2 when Kim and his lama journeyed towards a different multicultural education. "This solitary passage was very different from that joyful down-journey in the third-class with the lama. 'Sahibs get little pleasure of travel,' he reflected. '*Hai mai*! I go from one place to another as it might be a kick-ball. It is my *Kismet*. No man can escape his *Kismet*. But I am to pray to Bibi Miriam, and I am a Sahib'... 'No; I am Kim...I am only Kim. Who is Kim?'" (*K* 117). In a suspended state of knowledge about himself and his fate, he sees himself only as "one insignificant person in all this roaring whirl of India, going southward to he knew not what fate" (*K* 117); but once informed by the colonel of his future as a "chain-man" then he sees himself firmly as a centered part of fate and history.

He loathes the fat and freckled drummer-boy "from the soles of his boots to his cap-ribbons" (*K* 99), and complains to Mahbub Ali that "the clothes are very heavy, but I am a Sahib and my heart is heavy too. They send me to a school and beat me. I do not like the air and water here" (*K* 102). Yet imperial values will be allowed to triumph by the end of this chapter. He despises the meals, the boys, the routine, and the loneliness of his new life: "The indifference of native crowds he was used to; but the strong loneliness among white men preyed on him" (*K* 103). He is beaten without reason (*K* 106), dressed in clothes that "crippled body and mind alike" (*K* 106), and spends "days of torment" in "echoing white rooms" (*K* 106). His fantasies of freedom, however, are subverted not only by the English but by the lama who ironically becomes an instrument of imperial authority, and by Mahbub Ali who argues for his return to the regiments: "Be patient. Once a Sahib, always a Sahib" (*K* 107). But the change in his attitude towards the English happens the moment he recognizes Colonel Creighton's mastery of the native language and custom, his godlike combination of power and knowledge (cf. Said 1987: 31ff): "Kim was contented. No man could be a fool who knew the language so intimately, who moved so gently and silently, and whose eyes were so different from the dull fat eyes of other Sahibs" (*K* 118).

Under the invisible tutelage of the ethnographer and the spy, Kim accepts the discontents that accompany the journey from nature to imperial culture as he learns "that one is a Sahib, and that some day, when examinations are passed, one will command natives. Kim made a note of this, for he began to understand where examinations led" (*K* 125). Because "The jackal that lives in the wilds of Mazendaran can only be caught by the hounds of Mazendaran" (*K* 129), Kim knows that he as a native-born Sahib is also the born spy destined to control the jackals.

But even as he willingly submits to colonial training, Kim yearns for escape into what is now obviously an imaginary India uncontaminated by the politics of English constraints; it is this aspect of Kipling's narrative that provides its energizing and oppositional dimension. Though diligent as a student, "Kim yearned for the caress of soft mud squishing up between the toes, as his mouth watered for mutton stewed with butter and cabbages, for rice speckled with strong-scented cardamoms, for the saffron-tinted rice, garlic and onions, and the forbidden greasy sweetmeats of the bazaars. They would feed him raw beef on a platter at the barrack school" (*K* 125). This contradiction in Kim parallels the ideological contradiction in the representation of India. In some scenes natives swear to their reliance on the benevolence of colonial government, and the lama would, it seems, perish without Kim's care. Yet, in other scenes the reverse seems true; the lama in fact pays for Kim's education, gets along splendidly without Kim, and India itself appears to be a land of generous plenty that can take care of itself and of Kim. These contradictions do not negate each other. I draw attention to them to counter Said's point (in his introduction to *Kim*) that Kipling's India is a land without conflict (p. 23). Although political conflict may literally be absent in his novel, the discourse of desire for the lama and for an India unconnected to the English opposes and resists the colonial ideology that excludes such a liaison, and by so doing exposes unresolvable dilemmas in the colonial system.

What is striking, for instance, in this section is the rhythmic alternation of opposing desires, of the discrepancy between Kim's love for freedom and his capitulation to authority, between the impression created by imagery, declaration, and action, and the ideological choice Kim makes at its end. Once freed of English constraint, we are told "In all India that night was no human being so joyful as Kim" (*K* 127), that Kim's journey once he is on the road again is "all pure delight" (*K* 145), that the scene and the surroundings lift "Kim's heart to song within him" (*K* 145), and that opposed to this life-giving involvement ("breath of his little nostrils" [*K* 13]) was the sterile memory of "neat white cots of St Xavier's" which gave him "joy as keen as the repetition of the multiplication-table in English" (*K* 137). Yet, this period in Kim's life will see him choose English order over native chaos and sacrifice desire for power. The hated multiplication tables in English will be what redeems Kim at the end of his final test for the service.

That final test (chapters 9–10) will take place under the tutelage of one Lurgan Sahib (a sinister version of Policeman Strickland) and of Colonel Creighton, whose knowledge of detail, trickery, and native culture makes them masters in both worlds. If as Jameson suggests, the imagery of the eye provides "a privileged language for the description of epistemological disorders" (1972: 206), then it is both appropriate and ironic that the final testing of Kim should be a test of his control over precisely the sense of sight he (like the narrator) has so easily relied on in the past. Told by Lurgan that the jar he has just seen smashed before his eyes will return to wholeness, Kim finds himself at first beginning to submit to the illusion:

there was one large piece of the jar where there had been three ... Yet the jar – how slowly the thoughts came! – the jar had been smashed before his eyes ... "Look! It is coming into shape," said Lurgan Sahib. So far Kim had been thinking in Hindi, but a tremor came on him, and with an effort like that of a swimmer before sharks, who hurls himself half out of the water, his mind leaped up from a darkness that was swallowing it and took refuge in – the multiplication tables in English! (*K* 154)

Kim's and the narrator's "Orientalism" divides Hindi from English, magic from mathematics, and subsequently creates binary oppositions between the dangerous, dark, shark-filled world of India that threatens to swallow Kim, and the white, cold, controlled world of the Sahib that saves. The entire novel, is, in a way, a series of attempts to play one system of values against another and to see the results: what would happen if you denied the world of practical reason, action, the eye and the multiplication tables? You would have a lama who refuses to "look." What would happen if you denied the dark, chaotic, delightful and magical world of India? You would have a world of cold, white Sahibs whose eyes policed natives and denied them the world that Kim was privileged to see when away from their control.

Like so many other scenes, this episode of Kim's training dramatizes a paradigmatic colonial situation: the demonstration of power through knowledge and subsequent triumph of the colonizer over his deepest anxiety – loss of self in India. Beneath the surface drama of this scene lie layers of fantasy, at least one of which disturbs and questions the apparent triumph of the rational mind. The master colonialist, Lurgan, is himself a composite of unacknowledged contradictions, coldly calculating on one level, but on another, vulnerable to the hysteria of his young Hindu assistant with whom he reenacts a sinister and homoerotic drama. He appears at first to undermine his own function in the text. But read within the theoretical problems raised by colonial discourse (and articulated most recently by Said and (Bhabha) he reproduces an (ambivalent) strategy that creates a space that is both a site of learning and discovery and a site of dreams, of fear, and of desire. His workshop is a curious combination of a toyshop, a magic and jewelry shop, a schoolroom, and a deviantly triangulated family home. The outwardly triumphant scene of mastery, education, and testing conceals a disturbing and homosocial inner family drama: "Ah! He is jealous, so jealous. I wonder if he will try to poison me again in my breakfast, and make me cook it twice" (*K* 155). So too the triumph of Kim's education which will qualify him to survey, measure, and spy for the English, will also lead him to split the chosen father he loves into educator and child, to turn him into an unconscious object of Orientalist discourse where the lama can be placed into oppositional positions and ultimately betrayed.

III

The last part of the book, chapters 11–15, Kim's double journey for which we have been prepared from the start, carries forward the plot of the Great Game and brings to an ending the plot of the lama's search for the River of the Arrow. But the ending also returns us to the problem of Kim's origins and identity. Kim is born again after his illness, but he is reborn to a cry that returns from the past: "I am Kim. I am Kim. And what is Kim?" (*K* 282). He returns to life "powerless" upon the breast of the Sahiba who breathes life into him (*K* 283). Kim's fall into the Law of the Father, into the Symbolic order of colonial civilization, circles around the problem of unconscious desire by appropriating desire into the field of power, by refusing to admit to his lama that he is a Sahib and not merely his "chela" ("Why plague me with this talk, Holy One? ... It vexes me. I am *not* a Sahib. I am thy *chela*" [*K* 270]); and, finally, by giving the lama the last word in the story.

The completion of Kim's education is marked by his preparation of a report with a map of a "wild," "walled," "mysterious city... where the wells are four hundred feet deep, and lined throughout with camel bone" (*K* 170). The geography of the landscape to be mastered recalls other hidden and mysterious cities in Kipling's early short stories that trapped ("The Strange Ride of Morrowbie Jukes") or threatened English protagonists ("In the House of Suddhoo," "The City of Dreadful Night," "Beyond the Pale"). The difference is that here there is less fear of the unknown because it is now only a space to be colonized and mapped into knowledge. For his "graduation," upon completing this report, he is rewarded with two symbolic gifts – a costume and a gun. It is Mahbub Ali who presents him with this "dress of honour," a gold embroidered Pathan garment and a mother of pearl, nickel-plated, self-extracting .450 revolver that completes the splendor and takes "Kim's delighted breath away" (*K* 171). Once again, we are reminded of the opening scene and the announced opposition between the museum and the gun with its implications of control and knowledge over the native. And here again, native India can be contained (or tricked) by an English boy in Pathan disguise so long as he has the gun.

During the final and crucial journey to the north, Kim is accompanied again by split fathers who represent past desire and future order – the lama and Hurree Babu. These antithetical figures cluster around polarities established early in the novel by the English father with his emblem of the Red Bull on a Green Field and the Eastern father with his spiritual search. The political and the spiritual father fit the antithetical expectations of the Symbolic and the Imaginary. The lama as the Imaginary parent belongs to an earlier stage of development that precedes later consciousness of political categories and social power. The relationships with Symbolic fathers, however, are determined, as Lacan would have us understand, by a social organization so abstract and intangible that it is known only through such symbolic terms as the Game, or the Great Game, or the flag of the Red Bull on a Green Field. It also involves a mode of human interaction that, determined by isolation, uniformity and "statistical anonymity," is serial rather than unified by a group: "Seriality is a vast optical illusion, a kind of collective hallucination projected out of individual solitude onto an imaginary being thought of as 'public opinion' or simply 'they'" (Jameson 1971: 248). In such serial situations, individuals act only to intensify their serial helplessness, causing what they most fear against themselves. Thus Kim, though he is most afraid of being alone and isolated from his life in the native bazaars, commits actions that progressively alienate him from the group of natives with whom he has enjoyed an easy camaraderie.

That the last three chapters conflate not only the Search and the Game, but the Imaginary and the Symbolic, Indian dream and English reality, is part of the oppositional strategy of the text in which

colonial order appropriates native desire. (My language owes
something to Michel de Certeau's "On the Oppositional Practices of
Everyday Life.") The figurative conflation is prepared for at the
opening of chapter 13: "Who goes to the Hills goes to his mother."
The basic configuration of landscape involves an ascent into the hills
followed by a descent onto the plains and into the river. The hills –
overdetermined as feminine and spiritual "home" and as masculine,
political testing ground – seem, at first, to provide a way out of the
world of work into an idealized space where the lama and Kim can
meditate on the problems of entrapment in the wheel of life, "the
more so since, as the lama said, they were freed from its visible
temptations" (K 232). Kim's love for the lama and his declared
devotion to his cause seems unconsciously to denounce the ideology
that negates the lama's value. On the other hand, the hills are a place
of business for Kim, the workplace of spies from both the British and
Russian secret services who aim to turn the garden into a map, to
structure, to colonize, and to contain the Indian within European
structures. Yet, although the two meanings of the hills appear to
contradict each other, in effect, the first tends to idealize and
legitimize the second. The spiritual geography of the hills lends its
luster to the political geography of imperialist intent.

Kim's oscillation between the Sahibs and the lama, the school and
the road is a movement between the need for mechanical anonymity
and competition and the opposing need for dependence and bonds of
kinship with all the responsibility those bonds entail. The life of a
Sahib in school, or out of it, is inevitably a life of cold competition
whose final reward will be Kim's function as a cog in the imperial
machine. His life on the road with the lama, on the contrary, is a
carnival that inverts and democratizes the imperial hierarchy of
class, creed, color and race. By begging for the lama and serving as his
eyes, he supports him, fathers him, and becomes his guide. So
intensely does Kim need that sense of bonding, dependence, and
indispensable service that he is willing to lie for its privilege. Thus he
tells the lama that he is a scribe and that he is "all free" (K 191),
which of course he is not; he is as clearly bound to the "serial"
hierarchy of Sahibs Creighton and Lurgan and the British Secret
Service as is the lama to his wheel. And finally he pretends he has
returned in order to pursue their original search when in fact he has
returned to use the lama as a cover for his mission to the northern
hills. The lama's subsequent words to Kim prepare us for the

boundary confusion between the spiritual search and the English Game: "Thou wast sent for an aid. That aid removed, my Search came to naught. Therefore we go out again together, and our Search is sure" (*K* 193). Their searches are of course contrary. The lama, used to aloneness and autonomy, wishes freedom from his remaining fraction of attachment to life and illusion, whereas Kim's search is for the opposite; what he wants is ever more binding attachments to fathers, Sahibs, and secret services. Kim creates the illusion of a free spirit who yearns for a lifetime supply of the same, but his actions contradict that impression. Still, Kim's attachments far outweigh his autonomy. Even his deception of the lama seems forgivable because of his repeated declarations of love: "Kim, who had loved him without reason, now loved him for fifty good reasons" (*K* 213). Love, then, serves both as an oppositional discourse opening a possibility of an alternate method of negotiation with the Other and also as an excuse to transcend personal betrayals.

Because Kim is made to seem unaware of his oscillation between dependence and autonomy, his meditations on his actions frequently seem forced and arbitrary. Neither he nor his creator appears entirely in control of motivations which seem to be energized by a variety of wish-fulfilling impulses. That perhaps accounts too for the frequent changes in narrative voice from the certain, omniscient, and distant narrator, to the insecure and involved subjective narrator. Such changes in voice create a characteristic indecisiveness and glide in the Kipling voice, a kind of evasiveness that raises issues and problems it does not intend to resolve. Kim's characteristic moments of introspection, for instance, are curiously depersonalized by shifts in voice and perspective:

"Well is the Game called great! I was four days a scullion at Quetta, waiting on the wife of the man whose book I stole. And that was part of the Great Game! From the South – God knows how far – came up the Mahratta, playing the Great Game in fear of his life. Now I shall go far and far into the North playing the Great Game. Truly, it runs like a shuttle throughout all Hind. And my share and my joy" – he smiled to the darkness – "I owe to the lama here. Also to Mahbub Ali – also to Creighton Sahib, but chiefly to the Holy One. He is right – a great and a wonderful world – and I am Kim – Kim – Kim – alone – one person – in the middle of it all." (*K* 224)

As with his other freely associated meditations, this sequence of thoughts runs not in English, but in Hindustanee. Yet the leaps and shifts are characteristic of his deflective narrative strategy. Even

though this is presumably fragmented thought, its sequential logic is
self-contradictory. After Kim lists his adventures and his function in
the Game, and after the lengthy list of fathers to whom he owes his
joy, the reader is hard put to believe Kim's subsequent declaration of
aloneness. Kipling never allows Kim to be alone. Yet the cry
reproduces the opposition submerged at the beginning that the
narrative of Kim's quest intends to, but never does, resolve.

But because the recognition of aloneness appears so unexpectedly
at unusual spaces in the text, it deserves more attention. The
opposition between aloneness and belonging, like the other oppositions between the values of Kim and the values of the lama, create
social and ideological contradictions that structure not only the
entire text, but the everyday life of the colonial. Kim's illusion and
excuse for being, the justification for his mode of activity, is that he
had appropriated the power that accompanies his familial bonding
to Mahbub Ali, to the Sahiba, to the lama, and indeed to half of
India (*K* 283). If that is true, then his lament belongs to a grief and
loss outside this plot, a grief without a specific object, one perhaps
repressed and denied by the author that returns to haunt the
narrative repeatedly with no change regardless of the situation or
context. But the opposing movement in the text, Kim's identity as a
Sahib, generates a contradiction: he cannot be a Sahib and friend,
child, and son to Indians simultaneously; and that unacknowledged
contradiction with its embedded loss is associated, through metonymy, to the recurring cry of Kim "all alone." The figural
construction of the "great and wonderful" India of which Kim can
be an ecstatic part belongs to the Imaginary mode of understanding,
an ahistoric time when Kim's life could safely ignore social and
political hierarchies. And because such a time never existed, it is
necessarily a creation of Kipling's childhood Indian imagination.
"Kim-all-alone," however, is a consequence of his "fall" into what
Lacan calls "The-name-of-the-Father," the discovery of his colonial
identity which awakens him to a sense of his function in a larger
abstract machine and which is a creation of Kipling's adult Symbolic
and consequently, alienated imagination (see Jameson 1977). The
submerged problem of Kim's aloneness ("In all India is no one so
alone as I! If I die today, who shall bring the news – and to whom?"
[*K* 185]) is confronted in the last two chapters not on a social but on
the individual and personal level in terms of the lama's self-sacrificial
love for his "chela." Thus, although the question of Kim's aloneness

is raised on the Symbolic level of the text, its resolution will be found on the wish-fulfilling (or Imaginary) level of action. The combined forces of the lama and the hills ("Who goes to the hills goes to his mother" [*K* 230]) provides Kim with pre-Oedipal paternal and maternal forces on which to project his yearnings to belong to a primal family – the last consolation before he must truly part from the lama and enter as an alienated adult into the bitter heritage of his dead father – the British Secret Service.

The journey to the hills, like the rest of the book, operates on twin symbolic levels. It is both a fantasy of regression and a fantasy of realized ideology. Whereas on the first level, the lama is triumphant as lone discoverer of his river within and as lover of the "chela" for whom he renounces freedom from the wheel, on the second level, the lama is a museum piece, a nonviolent, nonactive absurdity in a world of guns, Russian spies and violence. If on the private and Imaginary level, the lama gains strength, youth, and prestige, on the Symbolic and social level he is finally advised to recognize his own helplessness in a world where only the strong survive, and, further, to accept his need for the likes of Sahibs like Kim to ensure his continued saintliness. But on both levels, the ending transfigures the events that lead up to the conclusion.[2]

The descent from the hills into Shamlegh takes Kim to a further stage of his fantasy of omnipotence: here he will meet the legendary Lisbeth, from the story after her name in *Plain Tales from the Hills*. In the earlier story, Lisbeth is seduced and abandoned by her English lover whom she has nursed to life. Here, Kim will be favorably compared to the earlier Sahib because he will evade her past role as the sexually submissive "Oriental" female by recasting and confirming his more enduring friendship with her present and newly empowered identity. The woman of Shamlegh and the woman from Kulu help to conclude the series of women that appear marginally in the text. If it is through her sexuality that she has been allowed power in the past, Kim will deny her that power, yet will accept and invite her friendship. Lisbeth's past relationship with Sahibs has been bitter. Sexually exploited and abandoned, she suggests the larger betrayal of the Indians by their colonizers (McClure 1981: 75–6). Kim will refuse her sexual invitation, not only to show his moral superiority over callous Sahibs, but also to prove that he has passed a crucial test of colonial manhood – the denial of sexuality. Though country born, he will not be a Jellaludin McIntosh or a Kimball

O'Hara, prey to native women, sex, and drugs. Rather he will transcend such weaknesses and in so doing become a type of super colonialist, simultaneously of the people and yet above them. The woman from Kulu, the widow, beyond sexuality, is the mother who gives Kim and the lama relief in the form of food and shelter when they most need it. Her division of women into two types echoes Kipling's fears in other Indian stories: "I have seen something of this world ... and there are but two sorts of women in it – those who take the strength out of a man and those who put it back. Once I was that one, and now I am this" (*K* 276). There are in fact no women in this book who "take the strength out of a man"; even the courtesan we met earlier in the train is "a kindly nun" who gives charity to the lama. And the women in the brothel who help disguise Kim all treat him as a son. Just as there are no sexual women in the book, there are also no nationalists, or natives who would prefer to be freed from imperialist control. The desexualizing and disembodying effect in Kim's attitudes towards his own sexuality is a sort of colonization of the self and of one's own desires. And the rigid definition and circumscribing of the roles of women as supporters or destroyers of men colonizes, controls, and marginalizes their function in the larger culture. So too the splitting of natives into such oppositions as the active and the contemplative prepares us for the privileging of the first over the second category, which will, in effect, be colonized and turned into a museum piece in order to be preserved.

Kim is about a child's discovery and recovery of identity and agency built upon a series of losses within an India he is about to lose, a child whose primary identification is with a lama whose parentage he must also lose if he is to enter the colonial order. By alienating him from his first (Indian) objects of desire, Kim's search for the Red Bull on a Green Field dooms him to endless disappointment, aloneness and alienation. His collaboration with the lama's search, however, blurs and transfigures the limits of Kim's search for origins, his identity, and his end. Although Kim has been transformed from a youthful, reckless, happy adventurer into a cog in the imperialist wheel, the ending blesses and sacramentalizes this change by investing it with the displaced glow of the lama's transformation.

But the scene of closure appears to transcend the issues of identity and origins raised at each stage of Kim's initiation to the colonial order he inherits from his father. The last words of the novel belong not to Kim but to the lama. And it is this final evasion that gives me the greatest problems as a reader: part of the concluding irony is that the powers earlier allotted to the lama – the powers of contemplation, meditation, vision, repose and nonaction – are subverted at the end of the novel by the plot, by the ideology, and by the lama's final act. By choosing freely to return from Nirvana for the sake of Kim, the lama commits an action that is at once human, loving, sacrificial and also supportive of official ideology. By choosing love for the Sahib Kim over freedom from the Wheel of Life, the lama is appropriated into the values of action associated with such warriors as Mahbub and the colonial Sahibs. But of course, the lama also commits an act of self-sacrifice characteristic of the Boddhisatva – the holy figure who postpones his own entry into Nirvana to help others find the way; so here Kipling conflates two previously antithetical ideologies (the Christian/Western and the Buddhist) in valorizing the world of action, will and choice over the renunciation and austerity that dominated traditional Hindu thought. Kim, however, has obfuscated: is he deluding the lama into thinking that as his "chela," he too is ready to be delivered from the Wheel of Life? That he enters such a bargain in the name of love is part of the problematic emotional field in which Kim operates all through his fictional life. Split by irreconcilable loyalties and loves and doomed to progressive alienation from the objects of his desire, Kim will eventually have to deny the lama, to whom the author gives the last, ironic, and materially false words in the novel: "'Son of my Soul, I have wrenched my soul back from the Threshold of Freedom to free thee from all sin – as I am free, and sinless. Just is the Wheel! Certain is our deliverance. Come!' He crossed his hands on his lap and smiled, as a man may who has won Salvation for himself and his beloved" (*K* 289).

A luminous freeze-frame on which to end a novel, the scene leaves Kim and the reader hanging in mid-air, as all that has been solid (in terms of constructing an idealized community in which Kim is a small part of a larger Indian whole) melts into the air of visionary illusion and prayer. Yet, this end is also a beginning, or rather a colonial fantasy that suggests an impossible origin for a new colonialist, one with a split sense of the constitution of self, who disavows difference from the native, yet knows otherwise.

IV

Epilogue

A novel that ends in the glow of such ironic certainty suggests not
only the deeply divided ambivalence of colonial discourse but also the
contextual radiance of turn-of-the-century arrogance and self-doubt.
Certainly, 1897-1901 were watershed years whose glorified celebrations of jubilees, as fragile as crystal, were constructed on the abyss
of contradiction between rhetoric and reality, fantasy and defense.
But more immediately, at the heart of Kim's ambivalence is a
profound moment of personal and historical anguish – to be a Sahib
he must allow the "two sides" of his head to evolve and internalize
the contradictions of what Bhabha calls the "colonial moment." One
side accepts (along with power and knowledge) the myth of Kim as
beloved child of India and the other articulates difference, separation, and division from the fantasy of connection with India. It is
the moment, too, of Kim's entry into the Symbolic and into history
as a subject, as a knowledgeable agent whose actions will turn him
towards surveillance and power. The age of empire too, as so many
historians, most recently and eloquently Eric Hobsbawm, have
observed, is marked by a curious self-destructiveness, "victim of the
very contradictions inherent in its advance" (Hobsbawm 1989: 10).
The energy and ambition of those dreamers of empire sprang from
the pressures and strains of an impossibly confined life in a threatened
island desperate for the release and exploitation of colonization.

   J. A. Hobson, Lenin, Cecil Rhodes and Kipling all knew the same
story – that control of information and the "policing" of daily life
were essential to power (Giddens 1981: 169ff), that far from being a
moral agency, the imperial state (like the capitalist state) relies on
exploitation to protect the interests of a dominant class, and that it
therefore violates the interests of the majority in both England and its
empires. They merely orchestrated it differently: Hobson focused on
the economic roots of imperialism and on the desire of financial
capitalists to develop, at public expense, foreign markets for surplus
goods and capital; Lenin's famous definition of imperialism as the
monopoly stage of capitalism implied an insidious scenario where
private cartels dominate world markets; Rhodes energized his
campaigns, companies, and colonies with megalomaniacal dreams of
a global political and economic empire controlled by Britain as the
road to salvation. Kipling, less idealistic than Rhodes, more aware of

the fragility of individuals and the societies they construct, wished to deny the economic basis of imperial dreams by constructing synthetic world orders, the day's work of bridge building and self-sacrifice as justification for colonization. The cost of such defense was the splitting of the self and its empire into the private or Imaginary, and the public or the Symbolic. Kipling's moral and familial universalism depended on the existence of the Other and yet marginalized and eventually negated its significance. His dream of empire would turn the world into a friendly jungle to protect Mowgli and his animal friends. The problem in the dream, of course, is that for the jungle to turn friendly, it must first be conquered; and that too is what Sandison would call the crisis of empire where the "subject" or "principal is at once aggressive and embattled in a foreign and menacing world which he nevertheless seeks to appropriate" (1967: 62).

Such contradictions are still part of the dreams of empire, alive today in the rhetoric and actions of world powers: ethnic idealization now serves, as George Kennan once wrote of Marxist idealism, as "the fig leaf" covering the violence of national practice. After the second World War, the centers of imperial control shifted mainly to North America where the imperial system, no longer directly responsible to the colony, is now controlled by multinational corporations and "world managers."[3] The principal resources of the world are voraciously exploited by invisible international corporations whose demands for oil, bananas, and other raw materials dictate the contradictory policies of the United States whose languages of "democracy" support counter-democratic forces in countries from the Middle East to South and Central America.

The poet of empire is also the Indian child whose fear of the abyss is turned into poetry, whose fundamental relationship to the outside world, mediated through language, presents a program of survival to the outside world of readers. That personal program (like the program of imperialism itself) must rest on deep ambivalence towards its obscure object of desire. And if Kipling has anything to say to us today, it is a way to see the contradictions and the costs of such programs of survival. The cost in his novels, stories and poems – however defensive and facetious the armor – is horrendous because it dehumanizes, alienates, and destroys the dream jungle home of Kipling's underground, Indian, childhood self. The face that haunts him, blind and weeping, that can never wipe its eyes, the anguished image of inexpressible private loss, is also an image of the source for empire, and by extension, of the self denied, abused, and victimized by the rigorous deeds of Englishmen in quest of dreams of empire. And the blindness is produced and inflicted by a culture that must be blind to its own ideological contradictions. As in his well-known, oft anthologized and misread poem "If," where the narrator assumes a social system built on nightmare contradictions, the ambivalence of Kipling's stories also lies in their paradoxical reaction against and affirmation of power and imperialism.

This book has drawn attention to the forms that contained the anxiety of one particular writer of empire, Rudyard Kipling. But in the process it has also suggested that the history of empire and of personalities produced by empire repeats itself, and that Kipling constructs a pathology of selves which illuminates the pathology of empire. Understanding Kipling's stories requires us to reread their representations of self in terms of the culture of empire, and then again, of representations of empire in terms of the self. The continual lesson of Kipling (and other colonial writers) is that our own views of otherness and Others are also grounded in psychohistory, that the anxieties of empire *are* the anxieties of family. Our creation of new world orders, our ways of synthesizing and ordering ourselves and others are an extension of the psychopathology of everyday life, and also a defense and antidote to the anxieties of division. The anxiety of imperial systems is still intact, its appetite displaced on to the "free" market. The dates and subjects may have changed, but the racist heritage, the compulsion to unify, centralize, and master society, nature, and world economies, the voracious rapacity that veils itself in multinational garbs, the confusion between public disguise and inner reality (as in American presidential performance or in Peronist theatrics, or wars of "liberation"), and the greater questions of economic inequalities between fenced world and unfenced jungle, between the first and third world, have not changed. The third world is still judged in terms of its adoption of first world political, cultural, and economic values, Kim must learn the multiplication tables in English, and the Bander-Log (the Monkey-People in the *Jungle Books*) – Indian, Irish, Arab, Central or Native American – must learn to respect and adopt the rule of power, law, and government represented by neo-imperialism's consistently insidious forms of surveillance and control.

Notes

1 *The Quarterly Review*, April 1829, p. 342; quoted in Bodelson 1968: 13.
2 Studies of Kipling's early fiction have undergone considerable revision in the last fifty years. Outside of Irving Howe's valuable *Portable Kipling* (1982) and the four influential biographies by Charles Carrington (1955), Philip Mason (1975), Angus Wilson (1977), and Lord Birkenhead (1978), Edmund Wilson's important essay, "The Kipling that Nobody Read" (1942), in *Kipling's Mind and Art*, ed. Andrew Rutherford (Stanford University Press, 1964) was the first of several works to draw attention to Kipling's dark psychological complexity. It jarred readers into the possibility of another approach to texts they had written off as the product of a "barbaric" age from whose real politics they wished to disassociate themselves. Elliot L. Gilbert drew attention to the peculiarities of such reader responses in *The Good Kipling: Studies in the Short Story* (Oberlin: Ohio University Press, 1970). C. S. Lewis' shrewd essay, "Kipling's World," (1948) in *Kipling and the Critics*, ed. Elliot L. Gilbert (New York University Press, 1965) damned with faint praise the excesses in Kipling's art ("all unrelieved vitamins"), named him as our first poet of work, yet caught a glimpse of the paradox of "unwearied knowingness" against a background of nothingness. J. M. S. Tompkins' *The Art of Rudyard Kipling* (London: Methuen, 1959), a thoughtful study of his work, focused on its "permanent human and moral themes" rather than "its political relations" (p. xi), thus establishing critical precedent for splitting Kipling the "artist" from Kipling the "imperialist," and for reading his work in terms of a development from the simple to the complex. Her assumption, not disputed by many other critics, is that Kipling's art gathers "depth" as it develops. So Harold Orel's introduction to his collection of *Critical Essays* safely concludes: "I know of no modern critic who would contradict her [Tompkins'] final judgment: 'The worst faults, as the strongest evidences of original genius, are in the first half of his work,'" *Critical Essays on Rudyard Kipling* (Boston: G. K. Hall & Co., 1989), p. 14.

The argument of my book opposes these readings. In spite of my admiration for their contribution to Kipling scholarship, I do not concur with the assumption that chronology means development or that Kipling's investigations grow deeper with time. Rather, I think the importance of the early tales and Indian stories rests precisely in their complex articulation of colonial discourse in all of its ambivalence.

The complexity of critical assessment of Kipling continued in the sixties with Randall Jarrell's statement that Kipling was "a great genius; and a great neurotic; and a great professional, one of the most skillful writers who have ever existed" ("Introduction" to *The Best Short Stories of Rudyard Kipling*, reprinted in Gilbert, 1965). Andrew Rutherford's collection of splendid essays by, among others, Alan Sandison, George Shepperson and Mark Kinkead-Weekes, opened up spaces for a diversity of critical approaches to Kipling's art, (Rutherford ed., *Kipling's Mind and Art: Selected Critical Essays* [Stanford University Press, 1964]). Louis Cornell's *Kipling in India* (London: Macmillan, 1966) is a seminal study of his Indian tales; yet, although he focuses on some of the stories I use, our methods and conclusions are radically different: Cornell believes his earliest stories were "a false start," that "it was through newspaper sketches, not grotesque tales, that the main course of his development was to lie" (p. 108). Other than McClure's work, not much else of substance or length has been written on Kipling's early tales. The most recent collection of essays, edited by Phillip Mallett, *Kipling Considered* (New York: St. Martin's Press, 1989) has only one essay on Kipling's Indian stories. John McClure's *Kipling and Conrad: The Colonial Fiction* (Cambridge: Harvard University Press, 1981) is particularly useful in foregrounding the differences in the unconscious political agendas in Kipling's fiction of the 1880s and 1890s.

2 SOMETHING OF HIMSELF

1 The term is from Albert Stone's *Autobiographical Occasions and Original Acts: Versions of American Identity from Henry Adams to Nate Shaw* (Philadelphia: University of Pennsylvania Press, 1982). Because autobiography involves certain structures and patterns of inclusion and omission that are also the shaping principles of fiction, it is itself a form of fiction. And because most fiction serves as the field in which the writer displays conflicting aspects of his own values and psychology, most fiction is a form of poetic autobiography (Spengemann 1980: 132). The most valuable study of the evolution of "forms" of autobiography is William C. Spengemann's *The Forms of Autobiography: Episodes in the History of a Literary Genre* (New Haven: Yale University Press, 1980). See also Paul John Eakin, *Fictions in Autobiography: Studies in the Art of Self-Invention* (Princeton University Press, 1980) and Avrom Fleishman, *Figures of Autobiography: the Language of Self-Writing in Victorian and Modern England* (Berkeley: University of California Press, 1983). Theories of autobiography have also discussed the dialectics of self and persona and the varied efforts of the autobiographer to resolve conflicts between

public and private selves. Kipling's frame provides him with a characteristic form of resolution – a formal and emotional distance between himself and the personal and historical events recalled. See also: Louis Renza, "The Veto of the Imagination: A Theory of Autobiography," *New Literary History*, IX (Autumn 1977): 1–26; William Howarth, "Some Principles of Autobiography," in James Olney's *Autobiography: Essays Theoretical and Critical* (Princeton University Press, 1980), pp. 84–114.

3 THE PROBLEM OF OTHERNESS: A HUNDRED SORROWS

1 Patrick Brantlinger's sharp reading of literary representations of the 1857 Mutiny draws attention to a variety of interpretations from Disraeli to Marx to G. O. Trevelyan's scandalous epic *Cawnpore* (London: Macmillan, 1865). Disraeli read the revolt as the result of "reformist" policy which destroyed native authority, native property and native religion. Marx focused on greedy land policy and abusive practices of tax collectors. Trevelyan, however, like many other popular sensationalists, attributed the causes of unrest to Indian (Hindu and Muslim) depravity, superstition and madness (*ibid.*, p.203). In so doing, he chose to represent the central drama of the event by focusing on a single spot – the well at Cawnpore – whose depths reflect colonial fears of latent Indian evil. The geography of the well, of course, recalls other hearts of nativist darkness evoked most memorably by Kipling in the Gau-Mukh (*Letters of Marque*), Haggard in the Caves of Kor (*She*) and Forster in the Marabar Caves (*A Passage to India*).

2 The problem of desire in Kipling connects with other concerns in colonial discourse about childhood and femininity, and in Kipling's particular interest in the child. Ashis Nandy has drawn attention to colonial devaluation of femininity, androgyny, childishness and child-likeness, and any form of old age and physical infirmity. He identifies two Kiplings: "the hero loyal to Western civilization and the Indianized Westerner who hated the West within him ... the hero who interfaced cultures and the anti-hero who despised cultural hybrids and bemoaned the unclear sense of self in him," *The Intimate Enemy: Loss and Recovery of Self under Colonialism* (Oxford University Press, 1983), p. 68. Kipling, Nandy suggests, lived and died fighting his happier "softer" self (*ibid.*, p. 70). Desire, for Kipling, as in philosophy and psychology, was seen ambivalently as a lack, a yearning for what is absent. The term, of course, as Elizabeth Grosz most recently reminds us, has had a long history of alternate associations. For Plato, desire was for the good and the beautiful; for Freud, desire is motivated by the loss of the unattainable mother; for Spinoza desire is the process of energetic endeavor to achieve and to make. Grosz draws attention to the sexual coding of desire that becomes negative when (as in Plato and Freud) it implies lack and femininity and that becomes positive when (as in

Spinoza and Nietzsche) it is conceptualized as male and generative. Kipling's colonizers must repress negative desire in order to rule by reason; the natives, however, are allowed access to feminine desire which inevitably weakens, maims or kills them.

3 For a fine reading of anthropological knowledge in Burton, Kipling and Carroll, see Daniel Bivona, *Desire and Contradiction: Imperial Visions and Domestic Debates in Victorian Literature* (Manchester University Press, 1990).

4 THE WORST MUCKERS

1 For other readings of "The Man Who Would Be King," see Manfred Draudt, who argues (unconvincingly) for a Laingian reading of Peachey's madness, in "Reality or Delusion? Narrative Technique and Meaning in Kipling's 'The Man Who Would Be King,'" *English Studies* 69 (1984): 316–26. See also Thomas Shippey and Michael Short who attempt a linguistic reading of multiple frames as ironic commentary on events and as a method of raising doubt about the reliability of both Carnehan and the "I" narrator in "Framing and Distancing in Kipling's 'The Man Who Would Be King,'" *The Journal of Narrative Technique*, 2 (1972): 58–87; and Jeffrey Meyers (*Fiction and the Colonial Experience.* Ipswich: The Boydell Press, 1973) and Benita Parry (*Delusions and Discoveries: Studies on India in the British Imagination 1880–1930.* Berkeley: University of California Press, 1972), who emphasize the moral failures of the adventurers as caricatures of colonialists but ignore the rhetorical complexities of Kipling's discourse. The finest reading of the story, to which all subsequent readings of Kipling's ironic use of the Bible are indebted, is Paul Fussell's "Irony, Freemasonry and Humane Ethics in Kipling's 'The Man Who Would Be King,'" *ELH* 25 (1958): 216–33.

2 Fussell suggests that in this history of two reprehensible vagabonds Kipling might have intentionally parodied the 1723 book by James Anderson on *The Constitution of the Free-Masons* that chronicles the almost divine early history of Freemasonry beginning with Noah, Moses and Solomon.

3 In an 1885 letter to his aunt Edith Macdonald, Kipling wrote: "Further I have really embarked to the tune of 237 foolscap pages on my novel – Mother Maturin – an Anglo-Indian episode. Like Topsy 'it growed' while I wrote and I find myself now committed to a two volume business at least. Its not one bit nice or proper but it carries a grim sort of a moral with it and tries to deal with the unutterable horrors of lower class Eurasian and native life as they exist outside reports and reports and reports. I haven't got the Pater's verdict on what I've done. He comes up in a couple of Days and will then sit in judgement. Trixie says its awfully horrid; Mother says its nasty but powerful and I know it to be in large measure true." (C. Carrington, *Rudyard Kipling: His Life and Work* [London: Macmillan, 1986] p. 103).

5 THE BRIDGE BUILDERS

1 Ann Parry's insightful essay on "Imperialism in 'The Bridge-Builders':
Metaphor or Reality?" *Kipling Journal* (March-June 1986): 12–22;
9–15, was the first to draw attention to the importance of Peroo as
evidence of a "vision" of the future of India as native. She reads the
bridge as "part of the infrastructure for Imperial control...The
relationship of the bridge to India, it seems, is like the relationship of
original sin to man: the bridge becomes an ineradicable part of the
nature of India, determining her fate" (*ibid.*, p. 17).

2 See Martin Jay, "In the Empire of the Gaze: Foucault and the
Denigration of Vision in Twentieth-century French Thought" (in Hoy
175–204); his discussion of Foucault's sinister reading of "ocular-
centrism" and "the gaze" as alienating and objectifying models of
knowledge in Western thought could remind us of nineteenth-century
"Orientalist" judgments of Eastern art and of Kipling's use of the
Museum and of the power of sight over other senses in *Kim*. The external
gaze becomes internalized with the entry of Policeman Day into the
nightly dreams of the Brushwood Boy, and becomes part of everyday
family life as we see his mother enter his bedroom and reveal his most
intimate secret to the father. Read in terms of resistance to daytime
surveillance, the dream is one of several means to escape the empire of
the gaze controlled by Policeman Day who comes to take the children
back from the City of Sleep. The song in the story laments the waking of
the children from the comfort of sleep into the cold gaze of day:

> Look – we may look – at the Merciful Town,
> But we may not enter in!
> Outcasts all, from her guarded wall
> Back to our watch we creep:
> We – pity us! oh, pity us! –
> We wakeful; oh, pity us! –
> We that go back with Policeman Day –
> Back from the City of Sleep!

See also Mark Kinkead-Weekes' important and provocative essay
"Vision in Kipling's Novels" in *Kipling's Mind and Art*, ed. Andrew
Rutherford (Stanford University Press, 1964), for a reading of sight and
perception in *The Light that Failed* and in *Kim*.

6 *KIM*: EMPIRE OF THE BELOVED

1 Jonah Raskin, *The Mythology of Imperialism* (New York: Random House,
1971), p. 117ff. Raskin mentions the politics of British ideas of Indian art
articulated by such critics as John Ruskin, who, by using Greek art as the
measure of "natural" and rational perfection, implied the corollary
absence of "natural form," order and system in Indian painting and
sculpture. More recently, Partha Mitter, *Much Maligned Monsters: History*

of European Reactions to Indian Art (Oxford: Clarendon Press, 1977) and Keya Ganguly, "Colonial Discourse and the History of Indian Art: A Re-Visionist Reading," in *Journal of Communication Inquiry* 12 (1988): 39–52, have drawn attention to the reproduction of colonial ideology in the discourses of Indian Art History, and to the infantilizing of native art and by extension of natives as part of a dominant imperial agenda.

2 "Ends are ends only when they are not negative but frankly transfigure the events in which they were immanent." Frank Kermode, *The Sense of an Ending* (London: Oxford University Press, 1966, p. 175).

3 See Barnet and Muller's *Global Reach* (New York: Simon and Schuster, 1974) that discusses the capitalist strategies of interdependency between multinational executives or "world managers" and native elites.

Bibliography

PRIMARY SOURCES: KIPLING

Fletcher, C.R.L., and Rudyard Kipling. *A History of England*. Oxford: Clarendon Press, 1911.

Kipling, Rudyard. *The Day's Work*. Ed. Thomas Pinney. Oxford University Press, 1987.

The Jungle Book. Ed. W.W. Robson. Oxford University Press, 1987.

The Second Jungle Book. Ed. W.W. Robson. Oxford University Press, 1987.

Kim. Ed. Alan Sandison. Oxford University Press, 1987.

Life's Handicap. Ed. A.O.J. Cockshut. Oxford University Press, 1987.

The Man Who Would Be King and Other Stories. Ed. Louis L. Cornell. Oxford University Press, 1987.

Plain Tales from the Hills. Ed. Andrew Rutherford. Oxford University Press, 1987.

Stalky & Co. Ed. Isabel Quigly. Oxford University Press, 1987.

Actions and Reactions. New York: Doubleday, 1909.

Soldiers Three; The Story of the Gadbys; In Black and White. New York: Doubleday, 1914.

Many Inventions. New York: Appleton and Co, 1899.

From Sea to Sea; Letters of Marque. Garden City, New York: Doubleday, Doran, 1932.

From Sea to Sea; American Notes; City of Dreadful Night. Garden City, New York: Doubleday, Doran, 1932.

Something of Myself. Garden City, New York: Doubleday, Doran, 1937.

Rudyard Kipling's Verse: Definitive Edition. New York: Doubleday, 1940.

Short Stories: vol. 1: A Sahibs' War and Other Stories. Ed. Andrew Rutherford. New York: Penguin, 1971.

Short Stories: vol. 2: Friendly Brook and Other Stories. Ed. Andrew Rutherford. New York: Penguin, 1971.

The Kipling Papers, Sussex University, England.

Kipling manuscripts, Pierpont Morgan Library. New York.

SECONDARY SOURCES

Althusser, Louis. *Lenin and Philosophy and Other Essays*. Trans. Ben Brewster. London: New Left Books, 1971.

Annan, Noel. "Kipling's Place in the History of Ideas," in *Kipling's Mind and Art*. Ed. Andrew Rutherford. Stanford University Press, 1964, 97–125.
Arendt, Hannah. *The Origins of Totalitarianism*. New York, Harcourt, 1973.
Asad, Talal, ed. *Anthropology and the Colonial Encounter*. New York: Humanities, 1973.
Aziz, K. K. *British and Muslim India*. London: Heinemann, 1963.
Bakhtin, M. M. *The Dialogic Imagination*. Trans. Caryl Emerson and Michael Holquist. University of Texas Press, 1981.
  Problems of Dostoevsky's Poetics. Trans. R. W. Rotsel. Ann Arbor: Ardis, 1973.
Barnet, Richard and Ronald Muller. *Global Reach*. New York: Simon and Schuster, 1974.
Barthes, Roland. *Mythologies*. London: Jonathan Cape, 1972.
Beloff, Max. *Imperial Sunset: Britain's Liberal Empire, 1897–1921*. New York: Knopf, 1970.
Bhabha, Homi K. "Of Mimicry and Man: The Ambivalence of Colonial Discourse," *October* 28 (1984): 125–33.
  "Sly Civility," *October* 34 (1985): 71–80.
  "Signs Taken for Wonders: Questions of Ambivalence and Authority under a Tree Outside Delhi, May 1817," *Critical Inquiry*, 12 (1985): 144–65.
  "The Other Question: Difference, Discrimination and the Discourse of Colonialism," in *Literature, Politics & Theory: Papers from the Essex Conference 1976–1984*. Ed. Francis Barker, *et al*. London: Methuen, 1986, 148–72.
Birkenhead, Lord. *Rudyard Kipling*. London: Weidenfeld and Nicholson, 1978.
Bivona, Daniel. *Desire and Contradiction: Imperial Visions and Domestic Debates in Victorian Literature*. Manchester University Press, 1990.
Bloom, Harold. *Rudyard Kipling: Modern Critical Views*. New York: Chelsea House, 1987.
Bodelsen, C. A. *Aspects of Kipling's Art*. Manchester University Press, 1964.
  Studies in Mid-Victorian Imperialism. New York: Howard Fertig, 1968.
Bourdieu, Pierre. "Delegation and Political Fetishism." *Thesis Eleven*, no. 10/11 (1984–5): 56–70.
Brantlinger, Patrick. *Rule of Darkness: British Literature and Imperialism, 1830–1914*. Ithaca: Cornell University Press, 1988.
Bristow, Joseph. *Empire Boys: Adventure in A Man's World*. London: Harper Collins, 1991.
Brooks, Peter. *Reading for the Plot: Design and Intention in Narrative*. New York: Alfred A. Knopf, 1984.
Carrington, Charles. *Rudyard Kipling: His Life and Work*. London: Macmillan, 1986.
Cornell, Louis L. *Kipling in India*. London: Macmillan, 1966.
De Certeau, Michel. "On the Oppositional Practices of Everyday Life," *Social Text* 3 (1980): 3–43.

Deleuze, Gilles and Felix Guattari. *Kafka: Towards a Minor Literature*. Trans. Dana Polan. Minneapolis: University of Minnesota Press. 1986.

A Thousand Plateaus. Trans. Brian Massumi. Minneapolis: University of Minnesota Press, 1987.

Draudt, Manfred. "Reality or Delusion? Narrative Technique and Meaning in Kipling's 'The Man Who Would Be King,'" *English Studies*, 69 (1984): 316–26.

Eagleton, Terry. *Criticism and Ideology*. London: New Left Books, 1976.

Eakin, Paul John. *Fictions in Autobiography: Studies in the Art of Self-Invention*. Princeton University Press, 1980.

Edwardes, M. *British India*: 1772–1947. London: Sidgwick, 1967.

Bound to Exile: The Victorians in India. New York: Praeger, 1969.

Fanon, Franz. *The Wretched of the Earth*. New York: Grove, 1967.

Black Skin, White Masks. New York: Grove, 1967.

Fleishman, Avrom. *Figures of Autobiography: The Language of Self-Writing in Victorian and Modern England*. Berkeley: University of California Press, 1983.

Foucault, Michel. *Discipline and Punish*. Trans. A. Sheridan. New York: Pantheon, 1977.

Freud, Sigmund. *The Standard Edition of the Complete Psychological Works of Sigmund Freud*. Trans. James Strachey. Vol. 23. London: Hogarth Press, 1964.

Frye, Northrop. *Anatomy of Criticism: Four Essays*. Princeton University Press, 1957.

Fussell, Paul Jr. "Irony, Freemasonry and Humane Ethics in Kipling's 'The Man Who Would Be King,'" *ELH* 25 (1958): 216–33.

Ganguly, Keya. "Colonial Discourse and the History of Indian Art: A Re-Visionist Reading." *Journal of Communication Inquiry*, 12 (1988): 39–52.

Giddens, Anthony. *A Contemporary Critique of Historical Materialism: Vol 1: Power, Property and The State*. Berkeley: University of California Press, 1981.

Gilbert, Elliot L. ed. *Kipling and the Critics*. New York University Press, 1965.

The Good Kipling: Studies in the Short Story. Oberlin: Ohio University Press, 1970.

Gramsci, Antonio. *Selections from the Prison Notebooks*. Trans. Quintin Hoare and Geoffrey N. Smith. New York: International Publishers, 1971.

Green, Martin. *Dreams of Adventure, Deeds of Empire*. New York: Basic Books, 1979.

The English Novel in the Twentieth Century: The Doom of Empire. London: Routledge, 1984.

Grosz, Elizabeth. "Bodies, Desire and Representation," *Artlink* 8/1 (1988): 34–9.

Hobsbawm, Eric. *The Age of Empire*: 1875–1914. New York: Vintage, 1989.

Hobson, John A. *Imperialism: A Study*. London: Allen and Unwin, 1902.

Howard, Jean E. "The New Historicism in Renaissance Studies," *English Literary Renaissance* (Winter 1986): 13–43.

Howarth, William. "Some Principles of Autobiography," in James Olney, ed. *Autobiography: Essays Theoretical and Critical.* Princeton University Press, 1980, 84–114.

Howe, Irving. "Introduction," *The Portable Kipling.* New York: Penguin, 1982.

Hoy, David Couzens, ed. *Foucault: A Critical Reader.* New York: Basil Blackwell, 1986.

Hutchins, Francis G. *The Illusion of Permanence: British Imperialism in India.* Princeton University Press, 1967.

Islam, Shamsul. *Kipling's "Law."* London: Macmillan, 1975.

Jameson, Fredric. *The Political Unconscious.* Ithaca: Cornell University Press, 1981.

Marxism and Form. Princeton University Press, 1971.

The Prison-House of Language. Princeton University Press, 1972.

"Imaginary and Symbolic in Lacan: Marxism, Psychoanalytic Criticism, and the Problem of the Subject," *Yale French Studies* (1977): 338–95.

JanMohamed, Abdul R. *Manichean Aesthetics: The Politics of Literature in Colonial Africa.* Amherst: University of Massachusetts Press, 1983.

"The Economy of Manichean Allegory: The Function of Racial Difference in Colonialist Literature." in "*Race*," *Writing, and Difference.* Ed. Henry Louis Gates. University of Chicago Press, 1986, 78–106.

Jarrell, Randall. "On Preparing to Read Kipling," in *Kipling and the Critics.* Ed. Elliot L. Gilbert. New York University Press, 1965, 135–49.

Kafka, Franz. *Selected Stories.* New York: Modern Library, 1952.

Keesing, Felix M. "Applied Anthropology in Colonial Administration," *The Science of Man in the World Crisis.* Ed. Ralph Linton. New York: Columbia University Press, 1945, 373–98.

Kemp, Sandra. *Kipling's Hidden Narratives.* Oxford: Basil Blackwell, 1988.

Kermode, Frank. *The Sense of an Ending.* London: Oxford University Press, 1966.

Kiernan, V. G. *The Lords of Human Kind: Black Man, Yellow Man, and White Man in an Age of Empire.* Boston: Little, Brown, 1969.

Kincaid, Dennis. *British Social Life in India 1608–1937.* London: Routledge, 1973.

Kinkead-Weekes, Mark. "Vision in Kipling's Novels," in *Kipling's Mind and Art.* Ed. Andrew Rutherford. Stanford University Press, 1964.

Koebner, Richard, and Helmut D. Schmidt. *Imperialism: The Story and Significance of a Political Word, 1840–1960.* Cambridge University Press, 1964.

Kristeva, Julia. "On the Melancholic Imaginary," in *Discourse in Psychoanalysis and Literature.* Ed. Shlomith Rimmon-Kenan. New York: Methuen, 1987.

Lefebvre, Henri. *Everyday Life in the Modern World.* Trans. Sacha Rabinovitch. New York: Harper and Row, 1971.

Lenin, V. I. *Imperialism: The Highest Stage of Capitalism.* New York: International Publishers, 1939.

Lewis, C. S. "Kipling's World," *Kipling and the Critics*, ed. Elliot L. Gilbert. New York University Press, 1965, 99–117.

Lyotard, Jean-Francois, "The Tensor," *Oxford Literary Review*, 7: i-ii (1985): 25–40.

McClure, John. *Kipling and Conrad: The Colonial Fiction*. Cambridge: Harvard University Press, 1981.

Macherey, Pierre. *A Theory of Literary Production*. Trans. G. Wall. London: Routledge, 1978.

Majumdar, R. C. *The History and Culture of the Indian People: British Paramountcy and Indian Renaissance. Part II.* Bombay: Bharatiya Vidya Bhavan, 1965.

Mallett, Phillip, ed. *Kipling Considered*. New York: St. Martin's Press, 1989.

Mannoni, O. *Prospero and Caliban: The Psychology of Colonization*. New York: Praeger, 1964.

Marcus, George E. and Michael M. J. Fisher. *Anthropology as Cultural Critique*. University of Chicago Press, 1986.

Martin, Jr., Briton. *New India 1885: British Official Policy and the Emergence of the Indian National Congress*. Berkeley: University of California Press, 1969.

Mason, Philip. *Kipling: The Glass, The Shadow and The Fire*. New York: Harper and Row, 1975.

Mehrotra, S. R. *India and the Commonwealth 1885–1929*. London: Allen and Unwin, 1965.

Memmi, Albert. *The Colonizer and the Colonized*. Trans. Howard Greenfield. Boston: Beacon. 1985.

Meyers, Jeffrey. *Fiction and the Colonial Experience*. Ipswich: The Boydell Press, 1973.

Miller, D. A. *The Novel and the Police*. Berkeley: University of California Press, 1988.

Miller, Karl. *Doubles: Studies in Literary History*. Oxford University Press, 1985.

Mitter, Partha. *Much Maligned Monsters: History of European Reactions to Indian Art*. Oxford: Clarendon Press, 1977.

Mohanty, S. P. "Kipling's Children and the Colour Line," *Race & Class*, 31 (1989): 21–40.

Moore-Gilbert, B. J. *Kipling and "Orientalism."* London: Croom Helm, 1986.

Moorhouse, Geoffrey. *India Britannica*. New York: Harper and Row, 1983.

Morris, James. *Pax Britannica: The Climax of an Empire*. Middlesex: Penguin, 1968.

Nandy, Ashis. *The Intimate Enemy: Loss and Recovery of Self under Colonialism*. Oxford University Press, 1983.

Olney, James. *Metaphors of Self: The Meaning of Autobiography*. Princeton University Press, 1972.

ed. *Autobiography: Essays Theoretical and Critical*. Princeton University Press, 1980.

Orel, Harold, ed. *Critical Essays on Rudyard Kipling*. Boston: G. K. Hall and Co., 1989.

Page, Norman. *A Kipling Companion*. New York: Macmillan, 1984.

Parry, Ann. "Imperialism in 'The Bridge-Builders': Metaphor or Reality?" *Kipling Journal* (March – June 1986): 12–22; 9–15.

Parry, Benita. *Delusions and Discoveries: Studies on India in the British Imagination 1880–1930*. Berkeley: University of California Press, 1972.

"Problems in Current Theories of Colonial Discourse." *Oxford Literary Review*, 9 (1987): 27–58.

Pinney, Thomas, ed. *Kipling's India: Uncollected Sketches 1884–88*. London: Macmillan, 1986.

ed. *Something of Myself and Other Autobiographical Writings*. Cambridge University Press, 1990.

Plessner, Helmuth. *Laughing and Crying: A Study in the Limits of Human Behavior*. Trans. James S. Churchill and Marjorie Grene. Evanston: Northwestern University Press, 1970.

Poole, Adrian. "Kipling's Upper Case," in *Kipling Considered*. Ed. Phillip Mallett. New York: St. Martin's Press, 1989.

Quigley, Isabel. "Introduction," to *Stalky & Co*. Oxford University Press, 1987.

Raskin, Jonah. *The Mythology of Imperialism*. New York: Random House, 1971.

Renza, Louis. "The Veto of the Imagination: A Theory of Autobiography," *New Literary History*, IX (Autumn 1977): 1–26.

Ricoeur, Paul. *Freud and Philosophy*, Trans. Denis Savage. New Haven: Yale University Press, 1970.

Robinson, Ronald, and John Gallagher, with Alice Denny. *Africa and the Victorians: The Climax of Imperialism in the Dark Continent*. New York: St. Martin's Press, 1961.

Rosenthal, Michael. *The Character Factory: Baden-Powell's Boy Scouts and the Imperatives of Empire*. New York: Pantheon, 1984.

Rutherford, Andrew, ed. *Kipling's Mind and Art: Selected Critical Essays*. Stanford University Press, 1964,

Said, Edward. *Orientalism*. New York: Vintage, 1979.

"Introduction." Rudyard Kipling, *Kim*. New York: Penguin, 1987.

Sales, Roger. *English Literature in History 1780–1830*. New York: St. Martin's Press, 1983.

Sandison, Alan. *The Wheel of Empire*. New York: St. Martin's Press, 1967.

Schumpteter, Joseph. *The Sociology of Imperialism*. New York: Meridian Books, 1955.

Sennet, Richard. *The Fall of Public Man: On the Social Psychology of Capitalism*. New York: Random House, 1978.

Shahane, Vasant A. *Rudyard Kipling: Activist and Artist*. Carbondale: Southern Illinois University Press, 1973.

Shippey, Thomas A. and Michael Short, "Framing and Distancing in Kipling's 'The Man Who Would Be King,'" *The Journal of Narrative Technique*, 2 (1972): 58–87.

Spence, Donald. "Narrative Recursion," in *Discourse in Psychoanalysis and Literature*. Ed. Shlomith Rimmon-Kenan. New York: Methuen, 1987.

Spengemann, William C. *The Forms of Autobiography: Episodes in the History of a Literary Genre.* New Haven: Yale University Press, 1980.

Spurr, David. "Colonialist Journalism: Stanley to Didion," *Raritan*, V (1985): 35–50.

Stallybrass, Peter, and Allon White. *The Politics and Poetics of Transgression.* Ithaca: Cornell University Press, 1986.

Stanzel, F. K. *A Theory of Narrative.* Trans. Charlotte Goedsche. New York: Cambridge University Press, 1986,

Stewart, Susan. *On Longing.* Baltimore: Johns Hopkins University Press, 1985.

Stone, Albert. *Autobiographical Occasions and Original Acts: Versions of American Identity from Henry Adams to Nate Shaw.* Philadelphia: University of Pennsylvania Press, 1982.

Street, Brian V. *The Savage in Literature.* London: Routledge and Kegan Paul, 1975.

Sullivan, Zohreh T. "Race, Gender and Imperial Ideology in the Nineteenth Century," *Nineteenth-Century Contexts*, 13 (1989): 19–33.

Thornton, A. P. *The Imperial Idea and its Enemies: A Study in British Power.* London: Macmillan, 1963.

Tompkins, J. M. S. *The Art of Rudyard Kipling.* London: Methuen, 1959.

Varley, Henry Leland. "Imperialism and Kipling," *Journal of the History of Ideas*, 14 (1953): 124–5.

Veeser, H. Aram, ed. *The New Historicism.* New York: Routledge, 1989.

Vishwanathan, Gauri. "The Beginnings of English Literary Study in British India," *Oxford Literary Review.* 9 (1987): 2–26.

Volosinov, V. N. *Marxism and the Philosophy of Language.* New York: Seminar Press, 1973.

Weber, Samuel. *Return to Freud: Jacques Lacan's Dislocation of Psychoanalysis.* Trans. Michael Levine. Cambridge University Press, 1991.

Wedderburn, W. *Allan Octavian Hume.* London: T. Fisher Unwin, 1913.

White, Hayden. *Tropics of Discourse.* Baltimore: Johns Hopkins University Press, 1978.

Williams, Raymond. *Culture and Society, 1780–1950.* London: Chatto and Windus, 1958.

Wilson, Angus. *The Strange Ride of Rudyard Kipling: His Life and Work.* New York: Penguin, 1979.

Wilson, Edmund. *The Wound and the Bow.* New York: Farrar, Straus and Giroux, 1978.
   "The Kipling that Nobody Read." in *Kipling's Mind and Art.* Ed. Andrew Rutherford. Stanford University Press, 1964.

Wrench, J. E. *Alfred, Lord Milner.* London: Eyre and Spottiswoode, 1958.

Wright, Elizabeth. *Psychoanalytic Criticism: Theory in Practice.* London: Methuen, 1984.

Wurgaft, Lewis D. *The Imperial Imagination.* Middletown: Wesleyan University Press, 1983.

Young, Robert. *White Mythologies: Writing History and the West.* London: Routledge, 1990.

Index

47
12
———
94
470
564

39